STELLA DALLAS

Books by Fannie Hurst

STELLA DALLAS

OLIVE HIGGINS PROUTY

PERENNIAL LIBRARY

HARPER & ROW, PUBLISHERS, NEW YORK
GRAND RAPIDS, PHILADELPHIA, ST. LOUIS, SAN FRANCISCO
LONDON, SINGAPORE, SYDNEY, TOKYO, TORONTO

F🐎Y
PRODUCTIONS

First PERENNIAL LIBRARY edition published 1990.

Designer: Kim Llewellyn

LIBRARY OF CONGRESS CATALOG CARD NUMBER 89-45706

ISBN 0-06-096449-9

90 91 92 93 94 MPC 10 9 8 7 6 5 4 3 2 1

STELLA DALLAS

1

Laurel was thirteen years old. Her hair was the color of ripe horse-chestnuts, and had the same gloss. She wore it in a long smooth bang in front, which reached nearly to her eyebrows, and in long smooth curls behind, which reached nearly to her waist. Laurel's mother always placed one of the curls over each shoulder after she had made them perfect by much brushing and smoothing over a dexterous forefinger. Laurel always, with a quiet, almost imperceptible, little motion of her head, placed them behind as soon as her mother turned away.

Laurel's clothes were consistent with the extreme bang and the long curls. There was never anything casual or careless about her costumes. When she appeared for breakfast in the big hotel dining-room dressed in one of her violet ginghams, smocked in seal-brown, with seal-brown stockings, and seal-brown shoes, and a seal-brown hat, she was like an Elsie DeWolfe room in the perfection of her color scheme.

She always changed for luncheon, as did her mother and most of the other smartly dressed women in the hotel, and again for dinner; and always the shoes and stockings, ribbons, hats, sweaters, and what-not harmonized with her various linens, pastel-shaded Japanese crêpes, organdies, or hand-embroidered serges for cool days.

"That Dallas woman must spend about all her time over that child's clothes," Laurel had one day overheard from behind the high back of one of the hotel-piazza rocking-chairs.

Laurel was sitting by an open window in an empty cardroom just behind the chairs. Laurel liked to sit and listen to what the women talked about on the other side of that high cane wall of chair-backs. Sometimes, however, she heard things that made her grave, contemplative eyes still graver and still more contemplative. There had been scorn in the voice which had referred to her mother.

"I wonder," she thought, "if we didn't dress quite so well, people mightn't be nicer."

She waited for more enlightening remarks from behind the chair-backs, but none were forthcoming, so she rose, sauntered out of the cardroom, wandered down a long deserted corridor, and drifted into the hotel foyer.

She was tall for thirteen, with long slim legs, long slim arms, and a long slim body. "Nice eyes, kiddie, but you'd make mighty poor eating," one of the habitués of the poolroom had said to Laurel one day, as she stood staring at the clicking balls on the bright green felt, and he had pinched one of Laurel's pipestem arms—bare from the elbow down, and brown now to her finger-tips.

Laurel did have nice eyes. They were gray eyes, set well apart. They had long, well-defined brows—level, almost parallel to the straight bang above which nearly touched them. There was in Laurel's eyes a look of wistful inquiry, an almost spiritual expression sometimes. They were more than nice eyes. They were beautiful eyes. In contemplating them, one forgot her freckles. For Laurel had freckles. In spite of lemon-juice every night—in spite of various concoctions, which so far had not disturbed the fine texture of her dark smooth skin, still she had freckles. But beneath the freckles there was a glow, like the glow beneath the flecked tan of a russet apple. This, and the freckles, and the spiritual something in her eyes gave her a sort of woodsy charm, which no amount of garnishing could conceal. She was seldom seen on the floor of the hotel ballroom dancing with the other children. Usually she could be found standing somewhere by herself, quiet and composed; or sitting in a chair with a book. Yet there was something about Laurel, standing or sitting, or walking slowly down the long length of the dining-room behind her mother to their table in a far corner, that recalled certain pictures of young girls dancing in the woods—Isadora Duncan pupils, perhaps—slim, sleek, sylvan creatures in Greek draperies.

Laurel leaned up against one of the pillars in the hotel foyer and gazed about her. The place was wrapped in its usual mid-afternoon lifelessness—a few idle bellboys on the bench at the foot of the broad staircase; a couple of idle elevators; a solitary clerk behind the brass grill over the mahogany desk; dozens upon dozens of empty armchairs; in one of them an old man, with a King Orange nose, sound asleep; in a far corner four women playing silent bridge.

As Laurel gazed at the women, her eyes took on their peculiar contemplative expression. She knew who they were. Three of the players were prominent social leaders in the hotel-world; and the fourth, the poor, pinched-looking, unattractive little creature in black, was Mrs. Tom Lawrence, who had arrived two days ago. Laurel had learned all about Mrs. Tom Lawrence from behind the chair-backs. As she stared, her eyes narrowed. "They're being nice to Mrs. Lawrence," she thought, "and Mrs. Lawrence is divorced, while mother is only 'separated.'"

She slid into the deep-seated lap of an enormous leather armchair near by. Through the big front doors she could catch a glimpse of a group of girls about her own age, seated on the piazza railing, swinging their legs, and eating candy. One of the girls was the daughter of the pretty Mrs. Cameron, now playing bridge in the far corner. Laurel did not join the girls. She didn't give mothers at a summer hotel a second opportunity to call, "Come, dear, I think you'd better come in now," to their children when she became one of a group; nor the children themselves to link arms and move away from her.

This year she had scarcely given them a first opportunity. Somehow things had been worse this year than ever before, and right from the start, too.

She looked up at the loud-ticking clock. It was only quarter after four. Her mother had told her that she must amuse herself this afternoon. She always had to do that, whenever her mother was going to be busy in the bedroom they shared, "washing out a few things." There wasn't room for two, when there was laundering going on.

Laurel sighed, rose from the big chair and wandered over to the glass-covered case of candies; stared at them for a minute or two; turned away; listlessly observed a rack of picture postcards. Finally she meandered down a long corridor past a series of cardrooms to a little pink parlor at the end. From behind a cushion on a sofa, she drew forth a book, and tucking it under her arm returned to the big chair. She curled herself up in it, child-fashion, and opened the book well towards the middle. She began to read.

The old man woke up and left his chair. The game of bridge came to an end. The four players disappeared. The group of girls on the railing outside drifted apart. But Laurel didn't once glance up. She hardly moved for a whole hour and a half except to turn the pages of the book. The hotel had suddenly ceased to exist for Laurel Dallas. Her heart was bleeding for David Copperfield.

Laurel never read "David Copperfield" when her mother was with her. To-day the book, as usual, would be returned to its hiding-place behind the cushion in the little parlor when she had finished with it. Laurel never carried it with her upstairs for her mother to catch a glimpse of, and make remarks upon. Of course her mother had had to know that she had tucked it, with several other books, into a corner of the bottom of her trunk when they had last packed. But there was no need in flaunting it before her mother's eyes. On the fly-leaf of Laurel's "David Copperfield" was written: "To Laurel, from her father," with Christmas and a date below. There had been a whole boxful of them.

"Books!" her mother had said with an exclamation of disappointment when they had been received the preceding December, "a whole pile of old-fashioned books!"

Laurel knew her mother preferred something more modern, when it came to printed matter—informing literature that kept one up-to-date as to what was going on in the world of clothes, and fashion, and society; photo-play magazines, with some theater-talk in them, and a few snappy short stories. The table in the bedroom which Laurel shared

Her mother preferred
something more
modern, when it came
to printed matter.

with her mother was always littered with a dog-eared collection of such periodicals.

Laurel took the elevator up to that bedroom now. It was after six o'clock, and by this time, she calculated, the ironing-sheet and forbidden electric-iron would be safely tucked out of sight in the bottom of her mother's trunk.

3

It wasn't an attractive bedroom. It was tucked way up under the eaves, had slanting walls, and a single curtainless window. Its furniture was much too big for it—made it look sick and shrunken, like a child in cast-off clothes many sizes too large. The iron bed, white enamel once but nicked and battered now, extended halfway across the window-pane; and there was a perfectly tremendous stuffed armchair in the room, discarded from some parlor below evidently, a shabby affair which, shut up in this little coop, was like some big ugly animal crammed into a circus cage—a rhinoceros Laurel decided, for it was the same dingy color, and its back and arms were worn bare and napless.

The walls of the room were covered with unpleasant reminders of former occupants—long brown streaks made by the striking of sulphur matches, oil-stains, ink-spots, splotches where flies and mosquitoes had met bloody deaths, and bruises here and there exuding dry plaster. Behind the commode the faded, jaundiced-colored paper bore the whitish, pocked appearance of a face once swept by smallpox; and where the bed was shoved close against the wall the paper was rubbed shiny and amber-colored. Laurel thought it was the worst "cheapest room" that she and her mother had ever occupied for a whole season.

Laurel was experienced in cheapest rooms. They were all more or less alike. That is, there was always something chronic and incurable the matter with them. They were either up very high beneath the eaves, possibly a floor above where the elevator ran, or down very low beside a noisy service-room, or groaning elevator-shaft. Some of them had queer smells. Some developed queer smells. Most of them were furnished with discards, and all of them were equipped with the everlasting commode, bowl-and-pitcher, and unlovely slop-basin.

Laurel used to dread her first glimpse of the latest "cheapest room" her mother had engaged, trailing with a sinking heart after the scornful bellboy who guided them along endless halls and corridors, farther and farther away from the luxury of the office downstairs, to the door of the undesirable little apartment, flinging it open, it seemed to Laurel, with a gesture of disgust. But Laurel's mother told her she ought to be thankful that such things as "cheapest rooms" existed. "It is only by occupying the cheapest room in the house, that you and I can go to nice hotels, where nice people go," Mrs. Dallas explained to her daughter.

The hotels which Mrs. Dallas patronized were always elaborate affairs with expensive, porte-cochèred entrances, big impressive foyers lit by enormous inverted alabaster bowls, and dining-rooms of ballroom dimensions filled with round tables, and mahogany chairs, and during the crowded dinner hour, an army of waiters with huge oval trays rushing about like darting water-bugs.

To Laurel there was something magic in the fact that it was possible under the same roof to eat and sleep in such different surroundings. She used to pretend that, like Cinderella, a wand was waved over her, too, when she emerged from the shabbiness of some "cheapest rooms" and approached the splendor of some ground-floors with their bright lights, bright music, long stretches of soft carpet springy as moss, with women trailing over it on their way to the dining-room for dinner— pretty, rich-looking women with bare necks, and shoulders powdered as white as gardenias.

But their necks and shoulders weren't any barer nor any whiter than Laurel's mother's, nor their cheeks any rosier, nor were they any prettier! Laurel thought that her mother was the very prettiest lady that she had ever seen in any hotel!

One morning in late August Laurel woke up very early in the slant-ceilinged bedroom under the eaves. She knew it was early, not because the traveling-clock in its worn leather case on the bureau across the room told her so (the clock was turned so she couldn't see its face), but because it was so still, and because she always woke early on the morning of the day set for her yearly visit to her father.

She wished she knew how early it was. A summer hotel, even the service wing, slept so late. The sun could tell Laurel nothing. The sun rose from out the ocean, and of course the "cheapest room" hadn't a glimpse of the ocean.

Laurel didn't dare risk getting up and looking at the clock, for, not for anything, would she have disturbed her mother asleep beside her. Her mother had probably been up until nearly morning to finish her packing. No. She would simply have to wait for the alarm-clocks in the servants' quarters across the alley-way. They usually began to go off about six to six-thirty. In the meanwhile she must lie very quietly and not joggle the bed. Cautiously she folded her hands beneath her head, and proceeded to content herself as best she could, gazing about with slow-moving, wide-awake eyes.

There, opposite her, hanging from the electric-light fixture on the wall, was her traveling-suit carefully arranged upon a stretcher. It was the first real suit with separate coat and skirt that Laurel had ever had! Would her father like it, she wondered? Would he like the close little black velvet hat that went with it, with the bunch of red berries on the side? Her mother had copied the hat from a thirty-dollar model, which she had priced in a shop in Boston. It made her look very grown up. Would her father like to have her look grown up?

Beside the suit stood Laurel's trunk. It was a wardrobe trunk—a beautiful trunk, Laurel thought. Brand-new. It was all ready to be closed. Her dresses, freshly pressed and hanging in order, simply had to be pushed back into the empty space behind. The little drawers beside the dresses were already shut snug and tight. The drawers were filled, Laurel well knew, with various-colored ribbons, bows, and sashes, to match the dresses; shoes and stockings; and piles of soft white under-clothes in perfect repair. Her mother had been busy for a fortnight with white thread and darning-cotton. For a missing button or a tiny hole used to disturb Laurel's father years ago.

The beautiful trunk, and its beautiful contents, clashed with its present surroundings. Laurel was aware of it. It flashed over her, with a little stab of joy, that to-morrow morning when she woke up and glanced across the room at her trunk, it would be harmonizing with mahogany and plate-glass and a soft velvet carpet, and a glimpse through an open door of tiles and shining white porcelain. Too bad, oh, too bad, it flashed over her, with another stab that wasn't joy, that to-morrow morning her mother couldn't be waking up with her and glancing across at the trunk. Her mother did love grand rooms so! Her mother did love New York so! To-morrow when Laurel woke up there would be the rumble of New York outside her window hundreds of feet below.

Very carefully Laurel turned her head upon her folded hands and looked at her mother. She wasn't pretty in the early morning in a battered old iron bed, of course. No lady can be pretty with her mouth hanging open, and her hair all mussy and tousled. Laurel's mother's hair looked like straw, now—dry and dead. But when she did it up and put the magic net on it, it seemed to come alive. It was the same with the early-morning ashen look of her skin. It disappeared completely, along with the shadows, and queer greenish hollow places, and tiny wrinkles, when she was ready to step out of the mean little room. It was wonderful what Laurel's mother could do with a little powder and a little rouge, and a bit of chamois skin. It seemed to Laurel there was real magic there—no pretence, as in her Cinderella game.

She turned away from her mother. It wasn't fair to look at a picture till it was finished.

5

It was fully half an hour later when Laurel gazing at the ceiling became aware that her mother was no longer breathing out loud. She knew even without looking that her mother's blue eyes were wide open. She could feel them staring at her!

She turned her head towards her. Her mother was indeed staring at her!

"Hello," said Laurel, smiling tenderly.

"Hello," said her mother, still staring.

"What's the matter? What are you thinking of?" softly Laurel inquired.

"I was thinking what a burning *shame* you haven't naturally curly hair!" her mother exclaimed. "It makes me about sick to think of you down there for a whole month, with your hair hanging down as straight as a stick."

"Oh, it looks all right."

"I wish now I had had you have a Permanent. Some children are having it, and I don't believe for a minute that it would do good strong hair like yours a mite of harm, the way it's done way down at the ends for long curls, so I'm told. One reason I can keep your hair long like some of the most distinguished children, instead of bobbing it off like an errand girl's in a department store, is because I'm always Johnny-on-the-spot with the curling rags. There's nothing worse than long, straight, Indian hair these days. Oh, I *do* wish I had had the Permanent, but I simply couldn't afford it and your new trunk, too. It would be pleasant if your father gave you a few things you *need* once in a while. For goodness' sakes," she broke off, "if your father asks you when you're down there this time, what books you want for Christmas, tell him you can get books for nothing from the Public Library, but there's no public institution where you can get fur coats for nothing, or a wrist-watch, and all the girls you know—or *ought* to know—have fur coats now, and wrist-watches of their own."

"I'll tell him," Laurel said. "Shan't we get up pretty soon?"

"Terribly anxious to get started, aren't you?"

"Oh, no, I'm not anxious a bit," Laurel denied, and she stuck her hands back again under her head as proof; "I'm in no hurry. But it's only three hours to train-time, and I thought——"

"Never mind. That's all right. I don't blame you, kiddie," her mother said, and her eyes suddenly filled with tears. "Funny," she remarked, with her eyes still upon Laurel, "how I can't seem to remember what you look like once you get away." She sniffed. "I'm going to just about *die* without you, Lollie!" she exclaimed.

"I know it," said Laurel calmly, staring up at the ceiling, but with not a sign of tears herself.

Her mother sniffed again. "And to think," she said, "I didn't want you once. I didn't want you a bit before you were born." Then with a sudden determination she threw back the bedclothes. "Come," she ejaculated, "let's *do* get up!" and she swung her feet around onto the bare floor.

6

She was a fat, shapeless little ball of a woman in her nightgown. A plain unattractive nightgown it was, made of a crinkly material that didn't require ironing, with a soiled blue ribbon straggling halfway round the neck. She pulled on a cheap cotton-crêpe kimono over the nightgown. The kimono had been lavender once, but it had faded to somewhat the same ashen color as her face now. She slipped her feet into some bedroom slippers very much out of repair.

She was the sort of woman whose exterior was never slack or hasty. She was never guilty of substituting a pin for a stitch where it *showed,* but her negligées and night-clothes were always in a state of neglect and shabbiness. Even Laurel had begun to observe that. The first time Laurel had exclaimed, shocked, "Why, mother, there's the same hole in the toe of your stocking that was there yesterday!" Mrs. Dallas had smiled. How like her father it was! Stephen had had the same foolish blind dislike for a hole, or a rip, or a missing button, which nobody was ever going to see.

Wrapped round in her unlovely draperies, Mrs. Dallas now scuffed across the little room to the cheap oak bureau.

"Darn this thing!" she murmured, as she fumbled with the back-boneless mirror, which always needed a wad of paper or a hairbrush stuck in its side, to hold it in position. "My! what a sight I am!" she exclaimed, when finally the contrary thing consented to give her back her reflection. "I certainly am some beauty at seven o'clock in the morning," she laughed, and she put both her hands to her head, pushing down the stiff towlike material, sticking out in a wild ungainly fashion about her face. Then, raising her chin, and frowning a little, she stroked her throat once or twice, where there hung, flabby and inert this morning, an unmistakable double chin.

It was a fitful sort of double chin. Showed much more at times than at others. Seemed to have periods of being sulky and stubborn. Mrs. Dallas was always in a state of indecision as to whether the thing showed less with a low, loose collar, or a high, tight one. This indecision was felt only in connection with daytime costumes, however, for at night in evening-dress she had long ago concluded that the lower the gown the less noticeable the superfluous chin. Once you got below the Dutch neck-line, Mrs. Dallas's skin was as white and firm as a young girl's. She had always had beautiful neck and shoulders, and they didn't grow old and sallow along with her face.

Mrs. Dallas believed that if a woman was clever, and made enough of that feature of hers which chanced to have remained young, whether it was hair, or figure, or complexion, or neck-and-shoulders, defects and blemishes would become less obvious. Unfortunate, of course, that convention deemed that *her* "young" feature could be exhibited only at night. Still, she told herself, she should be thankful that such inventions as powder and paint existed, corsets, and curling-irons, electric massages, and electric needles. For she had a horror of growing old and unattractive—a horror connected with the memories of her own mother.

She could recall that twenty years ago her mother had been gray and shapeless, her face covered with light brown moth-spots, wrinkles, and long hairs here and there—a spiritless creature, who wore loose, mouse-colored wrappers and flat men's shoes. Stella Dallas (Stella Martin she was then) was ashamed to have her young men friends catch a glimpse of her mother when they came to call in the red cottage house in Cataract Village outside the city of Milhampton. Laurel should never be ashamed of *her* mother like that, before *her* young-men friends, Mrs. Dallas decided, not if a little thought and effort could prevent it. Besides, there was another reason for keeping up a young appearance.

Not for eight years had she laid eyes upon her husband, nor he upon her, as far as she knew. It hardly seemed possible, for she had been to New York often, and the hotels where she and Laurel summered were very likely places for automobile parties to spend a day and night. Stephen might walk right into the office or dining-room or parlor any day where she chanced to be seated. If he should, he simply mustn't find her too changed. He mustn't find an old woman in place of the unquestionable belle she had been in their set the fall his business took him to New York.

The elaborate process of her mother's dressing had great interest for Laurel. Sometimes she would watch it from the bed, and other times from a chair near by, sitting, bare-necked and bare-armed in her underclothes with the comb and brush in her hand, waiting for her mother to unroll the eight tight wads around her head, and make them into long loose curls.

She had a long while to wait, for it took her mother a long while to dress. Laurel would pop into *her* clothes in no time, her slim pipe-stem arms and legs simply flashing into the right places, and her quick fingers buttoning and fastening with lightning speed. Laurel worked like a machine, when she dressed. Her mother worked like an artist, whose effects are accomplished by many fine and careful strokes, and many stops, standing away frequently from her work to observe it with a critical and often a dissatisfied eye.

She would not be ready to apply her skill to Laurel until she was complete herself, except for just the finishing touch of her dress. When she would be ready for Laurel, the flabby fleshiness under the nightgown would have become all beautiful firm curves inside the flower-brocaded pink corsets; and the shapeless mop of tow would have become all beautiful firm curves too, like the hair on the wax busts in the show-windows of fashionable hair-dressing shops. Her eyes would have become ever so blue, and ever so large beneath transforming eyebrows that arched. The centers of her cheeks would be pink, and her lips red, and her neck and shoulders, bare of course without her dress, would be milky white, with lovely little lavender veins showing faintly here and there, like the guiding lines Laurel used sometimes when she wrote a letter, showing faintly through thick white note-paper.

When Laurel moved over before the mirror and stood in front of her mother for her hair to be done, and caught the reflection of her own freckled face and sunburned neck and arms, bony and hard, and her dark hair with the forbidding bang, it seemed to her that the pink and whiteness above her was like an angel's in comparison.

"When shall you begin to put rouge and powder on *me*, mother?" one day Laurel had asked.

"Not until nice girls your age begin to put it on," her mother replied briefly, with the practicalness that guided all her decisions in regard to Laurel as to what was proper or improper, appropriate or inappropriate.

It was because Mrs. Dallas adhered to models so scrupulously that Laurel's clothes were never cheap or flashy in appearance. Mrs. Dallas was like certain dressmakers, who know how to impart elegance and refinement to the clothes they make for others, while their own costumes are often extreme and unpleasantly conspicuous. Mrs. Dallas wore a good deal of imitation jewelry herself—large imitation pearls around her neck, large imitation pearls in her ears. But Laurel never wore jewelry at all, except a string of tiny gold beads.

The little Holland girl never wore jewelry at all, except a string of tiny gold beads. The little Holland girl was one of Mrs. Dallas's models. In Milhampton the Henry Hollands were one of "the four hundred"— one of the first ten of "the four hundred," in Mrs. Dallas's opinion. Laurel did not attend the same dancing-class which Stephanie Holland attended, but Mrs. Dallas often attended it, looking down from her balcony seat (to occupy which no ticket of admission was required) onto the polished floor below, studying, scrutinizing, and recording in as thorough and business-like a way as a dressmaker at a fashion-show in New York.

When Mrs. Dallas and Laurel sat down at their table in the big hotel dining-room an hour later, Laurel was all ready for her long journey to New York, and Mrs. Dallas all ready for her shorter one to Boston, where at the appointed meeting-place in the South Station she was to pass Laurel over as usual to the spectacled Miss Simpson.

The hotel guests seated near Laurel and her mother observed their traveling clothes. One of them later, in the hotel lobby, approached Laurel as she sat, half-hidden in a high-backed armchair, waiting for her mother. Her neat black-enameled suitcase stood beside her, and her silver-handled umbrella lay across her knees.

"Are you and your mammar leaving us to-day?" asked the lady.

"*I* am," Laurel replied.

"But not your mammar?"

Laurel wished she wouldn't say "mammar."

"No. Mother isn't."

"Oh, so that's it! You're going alone! And where are you going?"

"To New York."

"To New York! How nice! To visit, I suppose?"

Laurel nodded.

"Let's see. I believe I've heard your pappar lives in New York," remarked the lady. Any reference to her father always put Laurel on the defensive. "Doesn't your pappar live there?" the lady persisted.

"I call him father," said Laurel, flushing.

"You funny child! Well, doesn't your father live in New York?"

"My father has business in New York which takes him there frequently," Laurel replied as she had heard her mother reply dozens of times before.

"Oh, I see! And you're going to New York to visit your father. Is that it?" purred the lady.

There were sharp claws behind that purr, Laurel knew. Also she knew that it was not customary for little girls to visit their fathers alone. So now she replied, "No, I'm going to visit a hotel."

"But you'll see your father, of course?"

It appeared quite legitimate, Laurel had long ago discovered, for grown-up people to ask questions of a child which they'd never think of asking each other. Therefore, she decided, it was legitimate for children to remain silent when they chose. Of course she wasn't a *little* child who might refuse to speak and not mean to be rude, but if people *would* keep on asking questions as if she were only six, she would keep on being silent. She was silent now. She closed her lips firmly, and from beneath her long bang stared blankly across the lobby. The lady repeated her question.

"You'll see your father, won't you?"

Laurel continued her blank stare. Her eyes took on a vacant, far-away expression, as if she had suddenly fallen to day-dreaming, and was thousands of miles away from the hotel lobby and the lady. In reality she was keenly conscious of the moment and the place, and was keenly suffering, too. Laurel didn't like being rude. She would like to answer every question ever asked her. Only she couldn't always. People nudged, and smiled, and raised their eyebrows sometimes.

"Well," said the lady, less sweetly now, "I'm sure your mother will miss you, whomever you're going to see, for she doesn't seem to have made many intimate friends in the hotel."

How unkind! How cruel! It swept over Laurel that she would like to make up a face at this woman—this hateful, ugly woman. (She *was* ugly. She had a complexion like dough. Beside her mother's rose-petal cheeks, hers were like toadstools. Beside her mother's bright hair, hers was like dull pewter.) Laurel glowered at the lady's retreating back. She had perfectly enormous hips!

"What was Mrs. Lamson saying, kiddie?" asked Laurel's mother a moment later bustling up to her.

"Nothing much."

"Being nice?"

"Oh, yes," said Laurel brightly. Her mother was terribly anxious for people to be "nice," and Laurel almost as anxious that she should believe them so. "She thought my new hat was ever so pretty," she prevaricated smoothly.

"I bet she didn't guess how little it cost," shrugged Mrs. Dallas.

"Well, I didn't tell her," said Laurel.

When Laurel kissed her mother good-bye on the platform at the station, there wasn't a tear in her eyes, although her mother's pretty cheeks were all smeared with them underneath the concealing big-meshed white veil. The arms she put around her mother's neck didn't cling nor clutch, like the arms that held *her* so tightly, and her kiss was cool and brief. But in her throat there was a big lump, and about her mouth there was a drawn, set look that meant she was clenching her teeth together hard, as she stood by the car window, and waved and waved to the lovely pink-and-white figure left behind in the smoke.

CHAPTER TWO

1

Laurel could always pick out her father in the waiting group behind the gate at the end of the long granolithic walk outside the train in New York, twenty or thirty seconds before he saw her. This was because her eyes were so keen and sharp, while her father was a little near-sighted; and because, too, there was a change in Laurel from year to year, while her father always looked the same.

Laurel and her father were always a little formal and constrained with each other at first. Laurel never could adjust herself quickly to the fact that this distinguished-looking gentleman, with the close-shaven cheeks, little black mustache, and keen gray eyes, was her own father, whom, if he lived at home as other girls' fathers did, she would be familiar enough with to climb over, and tug and pull at, perhaps. It took a little while for him, too, she imagined, to believe that she—freckled, long-banged, and black—was his.

She seemed perfectly calm and quiet when she put her hand in his, and he leaned and kissed her, but really her heart was beating fearfully.

Inside the taxicab on the way to the hotel, where Laurel and Miss Simpson were to stay, Laurel would sit beside Miss Simpson, and her father would occupy the seat opposite them. Most of the conversation, as they rumbled along, would be between Miss Simpson and her father—about the recent journey, the weather in Boston, the weather here, unimportant subjects, with long lapses of silence between; and upon arriving at the hotel, Laurel's father would leave them at the elevator-door, and go away quickly as if he were glad to escape.

Upstairs in the luxurious three-roomed apartment which he had engaged for Laurel, there would be all sorts of surprises—dolls and elaborate toys, when Laurel was younger; candy and flowers, and a dear little fitted work-basket this time, and a pile of brand-new books, lying on the table beside the silk-shaded reading-lamp.

Laurel's father lived in bachelor's apartments not far away from the hotel. It was easy for him to come in every morning and have breakfast alone with Laurel close beside one of the high windows in the private apartment, while Miss Simpson went downstairs to the dining-room. A waiter in black, who treated Laurel as if she were a princess, and her father as if he were a king, would roll in a table with a snowy cloth on it and shining china, with all sorts of delicious smells creeping out from beneath inverted silver bowls.

It would be usually at this first breakfast alone together that the real reunion between Laurel and her father would begin. This time, however, when her father left Laurel at the elevator-door, he had said he would return at seven-thirty, and they would go to dinner somewhere together, if Miss Simpson would pardon his stealing his little girl away the very first night. So on this visit Laurel's and her father's first real words of greeting took place inside the dusky interior of the taxicab that bore them to the restaurant which he had selected. It was the first time in a whole year that they had been alone together.

They sat in silence for a moment or two, after the door had slammed upon them. Then, "Well, here we are," said Laurel's father.

"Yes," murmured Laurel.

"How are you, Laurel?" he asked.

"All right."

"What sort of a year has it been?"

"All right."

Just the shortest, most conventional of questions—just the shortest, most non-committal of answers, but full of significance to them both; full of the promise of the dawning of the old sweet intimacy which never failed to steal over Laurel and her father, once they got rid of preliminaries, and to possess them like sunshine on a cloudless day, once it breaks through the mists and fogs of early morning.

Laurel's father sat away as far as possible from her and surveyed her from top to toe. The close little toque with the red berries gave her a mature look that was unfamiliar. He sighed.

"You're growing up, Lollie," he said gently.

Whenever Laurel's father called her Lollie, it always brought the vision of her mother sharply before her eyes. Her mother and father were the only two people in the world who had ever called her the silly little baby-name of Lollie—"Lolliepops" once it had been. She shoved the vision away as soon as possible. It hurt somehow. Her mother would have so loved the lights outside the taxicab window, and the taxicab too. She and her mother seldom afforded a taxicab.

"It's my new hat that makes me look grown up," said Laurel with never a reference to the creator of it. Laurel never mentioned her mother to her father. Some fine instinct within her kept her lips as sealed as his. "Don't you like it?" she inquired, a little wistfully, for her father was still gazing at her with a sort of abstracted look which she didn't comprehend.

"What? The hat? Oh, yes. I like the hat very much," he assured her. "It's very nice, and your suit too. I like your suit, Laurel. Only you're growing up, and I don't know that I like that. I don't suppose I shall dare kiss you many years longer in the station before people," he laughed. "Young ladies don't like being kissed in public, I'm told."

Laurel laughed, too—a nervous, pleased little laugh, and moved a little nearer.

"I've finished all the reading," she confided to him proudly.

"You don't mean all of it!"

"Yes, every book you put on the list," she announced, eyes shining.

"Good work, Laurel."

"Oh, it wasn't work. I love to read."

"Do you really?"

"I didn't used to so much. It just seemed to come this year—liking it so, I mean." She turned her face towards him. "When you read a book you like a lot," she went on, "do you try to stop between sentences and look around and think it over, like eating a piece of candy just as slowly as you can, so it will last longer?"

"It used to be like that," he smiled, and he reached over and put his hand over Laurel's. "I'm glad you like to read, Laurel," he said, "for I like to, too. I've hoped you'd like to read when you grew up."

Laurel looked down at her father's hand, and then quickly out of the window, as if not to frighten it away.

"Isn't it funny how many things there are that *you* like that *I* like too?" she said softly. "I was counting them up coming down on the train."

"Are there? Tell me. What?"

"Well—there's books, and woods, and camping, and dogs, and horses, and fall better than spring, and dark meat better than light, and roast beef better than chicken, and salad better than dessert, and—and—"

"Yes, go on," her father encouraged.

"Well, picture galleries, and Madame Butterfly, and that Mrs. Morrison, and—"

"That Mrs. Morrison!" her father interrupted.

"Yes. Don't you remember last year one afternoon at tea?"

"I supposed you'd forgotten all about Mrs. Morrison."

"I haven't," said Laurel.

"You saw her for only about a half an hour."

"I know it. But you know what you said before-hand?"

"What did I say?"

"Why, for me to notice her, and listen to her nice voice, for she was somebody you'd like me to grow up to be like."

"Did I say that?"

Laurel nodded.

"And you did really like her?"

"Oh, yes! She was ever so nice to me! She gave me a little silver pencil out of her bag."

"And she has invited you to spend a few days with her during this visit of yours, at her summer home on Long Island."

Laurel was silent a moment.

"Will you be there?" she inquired.

"I'm sorry. I can't. I've got to be away. That is why she has invited you, so you won't be lonely here in New York. I must be in Chicago for a few days next week on business. I don't like missing even a day of your visit, but it's necessary."

"I wouldn't mind just staying at the hotel with Miss Simpson."

"Why, I thought you said you liked Mrs. Morrison."

"I do—only—I'm used to hotels. I'm not lonely in them. I don't believe I should like visiting. Has Mrs. Morrison any children?"

"Oh, yes. Several. You'll have a splendid time."

"I think I'd rather stay at the hotel," said Laurel.

"Well, we'll see. Don't have to decide to-night. It's only for a few days anyhow. We're going to have our two weeks together in the woods just the same."

2

Stephen Dallas always tried to arrange his affairs so as to be able to take Laurel off alone with him for two weeks somewhere. The month she spent with him was usually August or September, and he usually took her into the woods.

Stephen had an idea that the farther away from people and conventionalities he could get Laurel, the more susceptible she would be to him, and to his suggestions. However, it seemed sometimes absurd even to hope to be much of a factor in forming the child's tastes and inclinations. He had only thirty short days with her each year, and he knew that during the long lapses between her visits, the influence she lived under was not conducive to the growth of the kind of seeds he planted.

When Laurel was a little girl, seven or eight years old, often Stephen would ask her what form of amusement she would prefer for an afternoon, and almost invariably she replied, when they were in New York, "Oh, the merry-go-round, or the monkeys at the Zoo." He didn't always give her the merry-go-round, nor the monkeys either. He was forever being torn between his inclination to indulge her slightest whim or wish, and thereby win her approval, and a desire to remould those whims and wishes.

When Laurel was ten years old, Stephen began taking her to picture galleries, in an attempt to instill in her some appreciation of beauty in art. Children like colored pictures, he argued. Why not give them good ones? He used to take her to hear good music too. Some of the symphonies, he told her, were just fairy tales told by violins, harps, French horns, and tambourines. Before a concert he took great pains to explain to Laurel the story which the various instruments were going to tell her. She would listen to his explanation fast enough, but more likely than not would fall asleep during the symphony itself.

When she was eleven years old, Stephen arranged to have Laurel visit him during the winter season, and took her for the first time to grand opera; also he took her, that same year, to several Shakesperean plays; to a beautifully staged classic for children; to a lovely fairy-like performance of dancing; all the while trying to place before her beauty in whatever form. When they were in the woods together, following a trail, helping the guides to make camp, cutting balsam boughs, gathering firewood, sitting for long hours in a boat on some lovely lake, listening for bird-calls, watching for a deer to steal down to the water's edge to drink, it was beauty in its natural form, then, that Stephen Dallas was placing before Laurel. He himself bought the clothes that Laurel wore on these trips of theirs into the woods. He took the keenest delight in selecting the rough little flannel shirts, the khaki trousers, and stout boots, visiting sporting-shop after sporting-shop before he was satisfied.

"I never saw so devoted a father as you, Stephen Dallas," one of his women friends said to him one day, during one of Laurel's visits. He had been refusing all his invitations.

Stephen Dallas had smiled and shrugged in reply. Most men, he told himself, weren't obliged to cram a year's fatherhood into one short month. They could spread it along. And most fathers, or many anyhow, in guiding their children were not obliged to exert their strength against another pair of oars, constantly pulling in another direction.

When Laurel came to visit her father for the first time he used every device and scheme he could think of to make her want to come again. It was always a little like that. Surprising, he said to himself, that he was so anxious for her to want to come again. He would think it more normal, wrapped up as he was in his business, and dead as was all desire in connection with the mistaken marriage he had made during the early years of his career in Milhampton, if he had wished to forget and bury everything related to it. Let other people forget and bury it

23

too. If Laurel had been a boy who would grow up to bear his name, he might understand his hopes and ambitions for the child. But a girl—a solemn-eyed, long-banged little girl! He was only forty. His life was full of demands, of interests of the keenest sort, of friends, too, the best in the world. Yet the pleasure that he felt at any expression of affection from Laurel could make his eyes grow misty. And lately—last year, and the year before—a choking wave of pride would sweep over him now and then, as he observed her, or listened to some of her quiet comments.

To hear her exclaim that she loved reading—the sort of reading he had prescribed for her—had obliged him to swallow once or twice before trusting himself to speak. And picture galleries! He had thought her utterly bored by them. She was a polite little creature. She had never said she didn't like them, but after the first half-hour or so in a gallery, she usually made inquiry as to how much longer they were going to stay.

"I didn't know you liked picture galleries, Laurel," he said to her later, seated at a little table beside a trickling fountain with goldfish and twinkling lights—blue and pink and yellow—shining in its depths, and tinkling Hawaiian music sounding from somewhere in the distance. "You never said you did."

"I didn't know it until lately," said Laurel. "It came to me all in a flash. You know how liking things does come in a flash sometimes."

"No. Tell me."

He was fearfully afraid she wouldn't. She was like the gray-tailed squirrels in the park in some ways, at times ready to be friendly and intimate, and at other times shy of him, and as timid as a chipmunk.

"Well, the first time I knew I liked the woods,"—Ah! one of her trustful moods—"wasn't when I was up there *in* them, but right in a city street, looking into an art-store window at a picture of a trail just like lots of trails we've tramped. It flashed over me right there on the crowded city sidewalk, 'I just love the woods!' And last winter our teacher took our class at school to an art gallery one afternoon, and when I got the first queer smell, and heard the first echo-y sounds that go with art galleries, it came over me what fun *we'd* had picking out

24

our favorite pictures in art galleries here in New York, and going afterwards to get hot chocolate somewhere, and all of a sudden it flashed over me, 'Why, I just love art galleries!' "

"And 'Madame Butterfly'?"

"Yes, the same way," she told him. "I thought I'd forgotten all about it, except the fat woman who sat in front of us, and how she hadn't gotten the powder on even, on the back of her neck; but one day last summer the orchestra at the hotel where mother—where *we*— were staying, played a piece that I knew I'd heard before, and I peeked over the violinist's shoulder, and found out what it was. And all of a sudden I saw that lovely Japanese lady in the beautiful white satin kimono on her porch with the pink sky beyond, singing about her baby. The orchestra played it lots of times after that. I asked them to, and it's my favorite piece of music now."

Laurel's father looked away from her. Some of his seeds, then, had taken root and were growing. Even among thorns! He must plant and plant and plant, then, while it was still the planting season.

3

Later that same night, in Laurel's room at the hotel, Stephen sat down beside her by the reading-lamp, and glanced through the pile of books he had selected for her. "Idylls of the King" was one of the books.

"What do you say we save this one to read out loud in the woods?" he inquired.

Laurel, sunk in a soft deep armchair, the fitted work-basket in her lap, the box of candy open on the table near by, didn't hear him apparently.

"Are there any 'cheapest rooms' in this hotel?" she asked, gazing speculatively at the old-rose draperies at the high windows, and at the expanse of lace beyond.

"Don't you like these rooms, Laurel?"

"Oh, yes! Yes! Only—"

The crystal clock on the mahogany mantel had just struck ten-thirty.

The Wednesday night "movies" at the summer hotel would be finishing about now. Laurel's mother, all dressed up in her pretty clothes, would be going upstairs to the horrid little bedroom, very soon, alone.

"Only what?" her father asked.

"Oh, nothing. I've been wondering what it would look like beside this one—that's all."

That wasn't all. Her father felt sure it wasn't all. But many of her thoughts he was unable to follow to their source. A faint suspicion disturbed him. Surely the allowance he sent to Laurel's mother was sufficient. He could vouch that as long as a sure three hundred and fifty dollars was coming to Stella every month, she would live well wherever she was. She delighted in living well.

"Why should you be thinking about cheap rooms?" he asked.

"No reason," Laurel replied shortly.

She was not going to tell him anyhow. That was clear. Useless to coax her.

Before he left her for the night, he said to her, "I really think you'd like it at Mrs. Morrison's, Laurel."

"Do you want me to go?"

"Well, I want you to know Mrs. Morrison," he replied. "I feel that when you are with me I must give you the best of everything I can, Laurel, and when Mrs. Morrison invited you to stay with her I was very happy to give you five whole days of life in her home."

"If it's just for me, then, I think I'd rather stay here, if you don't mind."

Stephen looked down at a book on the table and opened it. He was standing up all ready to go.

"I don't mind," he said, gazing at the printed page, but not seeing it, "only," he went on, "I should feel sorry, I suppose, if you didn't like some little present I'd picked out for you which I thought very nice. And so, too, I suppose I shall feel a little disappointed if you don't wish to go to Mrs. Morrison's." He closed the book. "But of course I don't really mind. You're the one to be pleased."

He did mind. He minded awfully. He always minded when his voice was low and serious, like that.

"I'll go," said Laurel.

"Oh, you don't have to, my dear."

"I'd *like* to go," she assured him brightly, which was true. Laurel would like to do anything to please her father.

CHAPTER THREE

1

Laurel was to go to Mrs. Morrison's the following Monday. She dreaded the visit. She was suspicious of women, and especially suspicious of mothers. One of the reasons Laurel always looked forward with such joy to the month with her father was that there never were any slights—never any fear of any slights. His presence seemed to prevent the possibility of slights. Everybody to whom he introduced her in his fine proud manner as "my daughter Laurel," treated her with the same kindness—almost deference—with which they treated him. Mrs. Morrison had been kindness itself to her a year ago, at tea in the hotel, but her father had been there then. Ladies had a way of being kind when men were about, Laurel had discovered. It was being left alone with Mrs. Morrison that she dreaded.

Besides, Laurel knew very little about the etiquette of private homes. She was familiar with the ways and customs of a hotel. Knew the proper manner to assume towards waiters, and porters, and clerks; knew, too, the proper fee to pay bellboys and chambermaids, if she asked them to do anything for her, which she seldom did, for dimes and quaters were never freely squandered by Laurel and her mother on ice-water or extra blankets for cool nights. But she was uncertain about the proper manner to assume towards servants in a private home. In the winter-time she and her mother lived in an apartment hotel. How many servants were there usually, anyhow, and what did you call them, and what fee did you give them? And when, and how, and for what? Or didn't you give them a fee at all? And just how, she wondered, should you dress in a private home? Did a girl of thirteen change three times a day, for instance, and put on an organdie for dinner? And who did her hair? Miss Simpson, it appeared, was not to accompany Laurel to Mrs. Morrison's. Miss Simpson wasn't very good at hair. She never even attempted curls. But she could get snarls out, and brush, and divide fairly well, under direction. Laurel was helpless without somebody.

Laurel mentioned none of her perplexities to her father. If she did he might wonder why it was she knew so little about homes. It might reflect upon her mother. For at the private school she attended in the winter-time, she often heard intimate friends talking about spending nights with each other. Laurel had no such intimate friends at the school. That she hadn't was one of the many galling failures of Mrs. Dallas's ambitions for her daughter. Laurel was not unaware of it. No. Her father should know nothing of her ignorance.

On many topics Laurel was as frank and open with her father as any artless child. But she had her reservations. She had great expanses of thought and experience she never let him glimpse at. She never mentioned her mother's name to him. She made as little reference as possible even to her life with her mother. By the time she was thirteen this silence had become like a wall between Laurel and her father. Stephen was aware of it. It loomed high and blank between them, and shut much of Laurel away from him. But it also shut much of Stella, too.

Once the mention of Stella's name, even as ''mother'' on Laurel's lips, had hurt Stephen. The years had cured him of the hurt, but still he thought it wiser to let the barrier remain. For one reason—it was kinder to Stella. Laurel's silence made it easier for him never to criticize Stella and, therefore, appear to influence the child against her mother. There were many things to criticize, and if they were brought to his attention in detail, he would be sure to wish to alter them. This he could not do without interference with Stella. Interference with Stella would open up new issues, and lead to unpleasant complications. And after all Laurel was Stella's child. Stella had been necessary to Laurel. He could never have been a nurse to a little girl of six. Had he been determined to control Laurel's bringing-up, then he ought to have been willing to have endured Stella. He had made his decision. He had never regretted it.

He took Laurel down to Mrs. Morrison's in his automobile. She talked very little as the car sped over the smooth roads, through pretty settlement after pretty settlement. When finally Stephen announced, "The next town's ours," Laurel murmured miserably, "You'll surely be back for me Saturday, won't you?"

Stephen laughed. "Surely," he said. "Why, you'd think I was putting you in an institution." And a little later he sang out cheerfully, "Here we are at the prison-gates!" and turned the car in between two cement posts, partly ivy-covered, and up a short curving drive.

The house was cement, and partly ivy-covered, too, like the posts. It was set low, seemed to cling to the ground, and the close-cropped lawn ran right up to long French windows on either side of the front door.

The French windows were open, and from out of one of them stepped Mrs. Morrison. She waved her hand at Stephen and Laurel, and called out in a high pretty voice, "Hello!" then walked rapidly towards the approaching car to meet it.

Laurel noticed that she was dressed in an ordinary white skirt and outing waist, and wore tennis shoes. She was at the door of the car when it stopped, and, before Laurel's father had a chance to open it, she had stretched out her arm in front of him—ignoring him completely—grasped one of Laurel's hands, and was saying in the lovely voice Laurel remembered, "Hello, Laurel." She said "Laurel," not "Laurrul"—like most people. Her voice was like a bell. "I'm *ever* so glad to see you. I've been waiting and waiting for you. Get out, dear. Let her out, Stephen." She hadn't paid any attention to Stephen till then. "Your trunk has come," she said, still addressing Laurel, still ignoring her father—or almost, for she flung him only the briefest little "Hello," as he stepped out of the automobile beside her—"and for the last hour I've been thinking you yourself were coming every time I heard a horn blowing outside our drive."

As Laurel stepped off the running-board, Mrs. Morrison put her arm around her and kissed her lightly on the cheek. Afterwards she left her arm there in a casual sort of way as if she forgot to remove it.

"Let's come into the house *this* way," she suggested, and gently drew Laurel across the lawn towards the French windows. "I've tea and cakes all ready," she said in a low tone, as if it was a confidence not meant for Stephen's ears. "And cinnamon toast." She gave Laurel's shoulders the tiniest little bit of squeeze.

Arm in arm with Mrs. Morrison, Laurel stepped across the low threshold of the French window into a big, generous, library-sort of room, with a grand piano at one end, and books all around the dark walls.

It was as easy as that, getting into the house, and all of the way down Laurel had been making herself miserable wondering just how it would be accomplished—whether there would be a butler as in most movies, to answer the bell, or a maid; and if the butler or the maid took your suitcase, like bellboys in hotels, or if you just held onto it yourself. Laurel's father had told her that he must run directly back to New York, after leaving her at Mrs. Morrison's, to catch his train. She had supposed that he had meant he couldn't even see her across the threshold. But no. He followed her into the big room, carrying her suitcase himself, and showed no sign of hurrying away.

There was an Irish setter in the room, lying down by a big chair as Laurel entered it with Mrs. Morrison.

"This is Laurel, Michael," called out Mrs. Morrison to the dog. "Come and tell her how glad we are to see her."

The dog got up, stretched, and wagged his tail languidly, then, with a sudden brightening of expression, a sudden tightening of muscles he barked twice, and shoved past Mrs. Morrison and Laurel towards Stephen, making joyous little whining sounds as he fell to lavishing damp dog-kisses on the hand that held Laurel's suitcase.

"There's no doubt about how glad he is to see your father, is there?" laughed Mrs. Morrison. "Michael adores your father, Laurel, as we all do around here," she added carelessly. "Come, we'll run upstairs, and wash our hands. Give me the suitcase, Stephen."

"Laurel will take the suitcase," said Stephen. "It's not heavy."

"Yes, I'll take it," said Laurel.

"All right. Come along. And, oh, Stephen," Mrs. Morrison called back over her shoulder, in that sort of singing voice of hers, "just light the hot water, will you please?"

There was a tea-table, with a white cloth near one of the windows, with shining silver on it, and shining tea-cups and a plate or two of snowy sandwiches and a basket of frosted cakes. "We'll be down in a minute."

2

Upstairs, inside the most exquisite little bathroom Laurel had ever stepped foot in—creamy tiles clear to the ceiling, creamy floor, creamy fittings, not a scrap of nickel in sight—everything all smooth shining porcelain, like the inside of a beautiful china cup, Laurel thought— Mrs. Morrison said, "Here's the washcloth, and here's the soap, and here's the towel. Use them, and then come into *this* room. It's mine. I'm going to have you in with me. And take off your things. Put them on the bed next to the wall—your bed—then come downstairs. And don't be long. I'll hurry down ahead and get your father started on his tea. He's got to go right back to town." And she left Laurel.

Very carefully Laurel followed her directions, gazing wonderingly about her as she did so, examining various details with investigating nose and fingertips; sniffing the soap; ever so cautiously opening the door of the medicine chest; touching with a gentle forefinger the silk window-hangings in the bedroom; touching with the same gentle fore-finger its ivory-colored walls; the shade on the lamp on the table between the beds. It was made of real filet! So, too, were the curious little pillows like that on the beds. (Laurel had never seen tiny pillows like that on grown-up beds.) So, too, was the bureau-scarf, and the tidy on the back of the big winged-chair by the window. All real filet! And just the simplest little piece of filet cost six-fifty in the neckwear department!

Standing in the center of the bedroom, Laurel drew in a deep breath, and gazed about her. What a lovely bedroom it was! Yellowish—like pale sunshine. She decided that it was lovelier even than her present luxurious apartment at the hotel. It was lovelier than any apartment in any hotel she had ever caught a glimpse of through half-open doors, on her way to and from elevators.

After she had taken off her hat and coat and laid them on the bed next to the wall as directed *(her* bed, she would be sleeping in it tonight!) she opened the door, and went out into the upper hall. She stole noiselessly down the broad staircase—there was a tall, slender, light-mahogany grandfather's clock on the landing, and a high window with pink-and-white petunias making it bright in a window-box outside—and noiselessly approached the door of the big room where she had left her father.

There were others in the room now besides her father and Mrs. Morrison. She could tell from the voices. She stopped when she reached the threshold. Nobody saw her, nobody heard her, and she had a moment to gaze unobserved at the scene before her.

It was like a scene at the "movies," with all those books, and the piano, and the comfortable chairs, and the big portrait hanging over the fireplace, and the pretty lady behind the steaming tea-kettle, and the dog, and the boys (there were three boys in the room. One of them, the littlest one, was seated in her father's lap)—only it was real! There were real bindings on the books, real reading in them, there was real tea in the tea-pot. The people were real, and their feelings for each other were real, too. She, standing on the outside, was the only unreal thing in this home scene.

She looked at her father. Suddenly the room faded, disappeared, and a close-up of his face dawned on the screen before her, as it were. Why, her father was gazing at the lady behind the tea-kettle, as if—as if—! Laurel had seen too many close-ups of faces not to recognize that look! She drew in her breath sharply. It flashed over Laurel that perhaps this man wasn't really her father after all! She stirred, moved a foot.

Mrs. Morrison glanced over her shoulder.

"Oh! come here, Laurel," she exclaimed at sight of her, and stretched out her arm, and kept it stretched out until Laurel had stepped within its circle.

"This is Laurel, boys," she said briefly. Then, still holding Laurel, not giving her even a chance to go through the agony of a series of curtsies, she went on, "These are your new friends, Laurel. Cornelius, over there by the piano, is the oldest. 'Con' we call him for short. And Dane comes next. 'Great Dane' they call him at school. But *I* call him *little* Dane. And the little boy in your father's lap is Frederick. 'Rick' is his nickname. He's the baby—five years old now. We haven't any little girl for you, Laurel," she sighed. How lucky! No girls! Boys weren't half as cruel.

"And now," Mrs. Morrison broke off, "I wonder would you pass this cup of tea I'm making to your father? And, Con dear, will you pass the sandwiches? Get down, Rickie, and run and get your rabbit and bring it in and show it to Laurel. And, Dane, take Michael out. Michael," she explained to Laurel, "is not fond of Mercedes's society, Mercedes being the rabbit," she smiled.

They were all busy in no time—all but Mrs. Morrison and Stephen, each rushing about on some errand or other. There wasn't a chance for pause or embarrassment. The same rare insight and understanding which made Helen Morrison's dinner-parties such a success was quite as reliable with children, or with servants, or with the factory girls at the settlement-house in which she was interested. Not only did everybody with whom Helen Morrison worked and played get on beautifully with *her,* but under her gentle management they got on beautifully with one another, too. And yet she seemed to make no effort at adjusting herself to the various ages, groups, and classes with which she came in contact. That was why she was so successful with Laurel. It was her apparent unawareness that she was saying or doing the diplomatic thing that broke through the barrier of silence and reserve which Laurel hid behind whenever she met strangers.

The women whom Laurel met when visiting her father never by any chance, even indirectly, referred to her mother. It would have been a "break" if they had. Laurel knew that. But Mrs. Morrison made such a break. Mrs. Morrison referred to her mother, and the very first night, too, scarcely an hour after her father had said good-bye.

They were upstairs together, unpacking. No chambermaid, no lady's-maid assisted at the task. In fact Laurel had begun to wonder if any servants existed in this household. Mrs. Morrison alone helped her, carefully hanging dress after dress in a closet near by, and exclaiming over each one, how pretty she thought it was. What a lovely color! Like jonquils one; like violets another; like a meadow spotted with tiny daisies, a certain English print.

It was when she was hanging up the last dress in the closet that she remarked, ever so naturally, "I think your mother has beautiful taste, Laurel."

Laurel looked up quickly. She had replied so far by only necessary yes-thank-yous and no-thank-yous to Mrs. Morrison, and if-you-pleases—that sort of thing, but now she exclaimed, "My mother has the most beautiful taste in the world!"

She didn't know she was going to say just that, nor that her words were going to rush out in such an unfamiliar fashion. She blushed.

But Mrs. Morrison didn't seem to think her reply odd. She didn't even look at her. She said:

"I've always wanted a little girl. It's such fun to dress them. I can see your mother has had great fun getting all your pretty things to match and blend."

Later when Laurel asked her which dress she should put on for dinner, Mrs. Morrison replied, "Why, I don't know, I'm sure. Which dress do you think your mother would have you put on?"

She kept on referring to her mother casually like that right along. "Perhaps," thought Laurel, "she doesn't know there's any reason not to." And yet, being a friend of her father's, how could she help but know that her mother and father didn't live together like other people. Perhaps she didn't know *why* they didn't live together, just as Laurel herself didn't know why. Whatever the explanation, Mrs. Morrison's frank and open recognition of her mother as a human being, and a human being, too, not unlike her lovely self, warmed Laurel, thawed out her mistrust and fear.

"My mother has the most beautiful taste in the world!"

Before twenty-four hours had passed Laurel was worshiping Mrs. Morrison with that admiring kind of worship that a young girl, not quite a child, and yet not quite a woman, often feels for some stranger who stops and smiles.

CHAPTER FOUR

1

She didn't talk very much at first. She was too engrossed observing unfamiliar surroundings and watching Mrs. Morrison. It was as interesting as reading a new book almost. The ways and habits of a private home were very curious. For instance, you were introduced to the servants. A maid in spick-and-span gray-and-white did appear finally. "Hannah," Mrs. Morrison said to her familiarly, "this is our guest, Miss Laurel. Laurel, Hannah is the one to ask if there's anything you want. She is a fairy. You've only to make a wish out loud before her, and it comes true."

And the ways and habits of a lady in a private home were curious, too—at least Mrs. Morrison's were curious. Marveling, Laurel observed the lightning speed with which she dressed. It seemed to Laurel that she was a fairy, too, for she had only to wish herself ready for dinner, or breakfast, or lunch, and she *was* ready inside of ten minutes.

It was fascinating to watch her do her hair. She would take out four or five hairpins from it, shake her head till the hair fell soft to her shoulders, brush the shining mass hastily a minute, twist it up, and stick the four or five hairpins back again, hardly looking into the mirror at all.

Laurel had thought Mrs. Morrison lovely to look at the first time she saw her a year ago, at the hotel, but ladies were often lovely to look at when they were dressed up. The amazing thing about Mrs. Morrison was that she was lovely to look at always, even in the early morning, even before she got up! She wasn't young. At least Laurel didn't think she was young. She was old enough to be Con's mother, and Con was older than Laurel. There were besides just a few gray hairs. You didn't see them till she let her hair down.

She had beautiful hair—dark, almost black. At night beneath the strong light of the silk-shaded lamp by the piano, it was like the breast of a dark-feathered pigeon in the sunshine—iridescent. She had long slender fingers—very white, and long slender arms, and a long slender neck. The line of her neck in profile had just the same curve from her throat to the tip of her chin (which was usually lifted) as the lady's in the moon. And she did her hair low, just like the lady in the moon, and it fluffed the same way, too, about her brow and ears, for she wore no net. She was like moonlight in lots of ways, Laurel concluded. Almost no color at all in her cheeks. And the dress she wore the first evening was pale yellow. And she didn't wear a single ornament to brighten it up.

Occupying the same room with Mrs. Morrison, it took much less time than otherwise for Laurel's shyness to wear away. Perhaps Mrs. Morrison was aware with what amazing rapidity the homely processes of dressing build up an intimacy. But, whether or not her motive was to win her way into Laurel's confidence the more quickly, or simply to take every precaution in guarding the child against homesickness, twice the number of hours spent in the drawing-room or garden would not have been sufficient to establish the degree of familiarity which made it possible for Laurel to put into words many of her questions and wonderings before she had been three days a guest of Mrs. Morrison.

"Have you a Permanent?" she asked bluntly the third morning as she sat gazing at Mrs. Morrison, seated before the altar-like dressing-table with nothing on it but two candlesticks and an old silver box, and four or five tortoise-shell hairpins.

"Yes," Mrs. Morrison replied, smiling, "but not the kind you mean. I was born with mine."

Still gazing, Laurel inquired a moment later, "Don't you ever use rouge, or an eyebrow pencil?"

"No."

"Why not?"

"Oh, I don't know. Why do you ask, Laurel?"

"No reason. I was only wondering." Then after a pause Laurel added, "I think you'd be lovely with pink cheeks."

"I would be nicer, wouldn't I?" she agreed, and she stuck in the last hairpin, got up, gathered together a few soft muslin things from a drawer near by (she put on clean clothes every morning: her laundry bill must be terrific), and, wrapped round in a lemon-colored china-silk kimono, passed into one of the little twin bathrooms adjoining, and closed the door.

Laurel heard the click of enamel handles being turned, the violent gush of a stream of water in the marble shower-bath, and a second or two later, or so it seemed, Mrs. Morrison reappeared, as fresh as a pond-lily in her crisp lingerie.

Laurel inquired of her, "If you think you'd be nicer with pink cheeks, then why don't you make them pink?"

"Oh, it takes such a lot of time!" laughed Mrs. Morrison. "And then, besides," she added, "I would always be getting them spoiled. I like to be outdoors so much, digging in the garden, riding horseback, romping with the boys in all sorts of weather. If I did use rouge, Laurel," she went on more seriously, "and an eyebrow pencil, as you suggested, I should want to do it exquisitely, like an artist, so that no one's sense of beauty could possibly be offended."

"Offended?"

"Yes. To some people paint and powder on the human face is distasteful."

"Is it?"

"Like paint and powder on the petals of a flower, I suppose."

"Oh!"

There was a long pause. Laurel broke it at last.

"Is that why you haven't a string of pearls?"

"Is *what* why, Laurel?"

"Because pearls on your neck would be to some people like pearls on flowers?"

"Oh, no," Helen Morrison replied, managing not even to smile. "I haven't a string of pearls because they're so expensive."

"Imitation pearls aren't very expensive."

"Oh, imitation!"

Laurel considered. Her mother had often told her that her pearls and imitation diamond bar-pin would pass for the genuine articles anywhere. "They look just like the real ones," she told Mrs. Morrison. "Oh, no, Laurel, not to a person who knows pearls. They lack inner beauty, just as a wax figure lacks soul. To the really discerning they're as lifeless and unbeautiful as that." Then, with a sudden happy inspiration, as she thought, Helen Morrison added, "Your mother has trimmed several of your pretty dresses with narrow filet lace, but there isn't an inch of imitation filet."

No, of course not, because imitation filet "never fooled anybody," Laurel's mother had often told her. In fact, she had said, and only a short fortnight ago, that there wasn't anything a woman could make more show with, at present, than a lot of splashy real lace, or anything that could kill her socially as surely as the imitation stuff.

Laurel wondered if to the really discerning her mother's imitation pearls were like imitation filet.

2

The next day Laurel asked Mrs. Morrison if she had ever seen her mother. Her mother's name by then was mentioned with perfect ease between them.

"No, I never have, Laurel," said Mrs. Morrison. "Tell me about her." They were walking in the garden. "Is she like you?"

"Oh, no," said Laurel. "She's not the least like me. She hasn't a single freckle. And her hair is yellow. She was born with it yellow, like you with your Permanent." Which was true. Mrs. Dallas had not tampered with the color of her hair as yet. "Her eyes," Laurel went on, "are blue—the color of that little blue pitcher you said was Delft, that you used one morning at breakfast. And her skin is like the cream in it."

"She must be lovely."

"Oh, she is, she is," flashed Laurel.

"Haven't you her picture?"

"No. Not here." After a pause Laurel added gravely, "I never bring her picture to New York when I come to see my father."

It was the first reference she had made to the relation that existed between her mother and father. But Mrs. Morrison made as casual a reply to it, as if it had been a frequent topic of conversation between them.

"Of course you don't. I didn't think for a minute. Naturally it's kinder not to."

Oh, how easy it was to talk to Mrs. Morrison! Questions Laurel had long wanted to know the answers to crowded to her lips. "Why are my mother and father different from other mothers and fathers? Why don't they live together? Why aren't people nice to my mother? And why are they nice to my father?" But she didn't allow one of them to escape. Not yet. Nor did Mrs. Morrison allow a question to escape either. They simply walked on in silence till they came to a turn in the garden path where some late pansies were blooming.

"Let's pick some," said Mrs. Morrison.

"Let's," said Laurel, and they leaned down together over the low-growing flowers.

Laurel's heart was beating fast. She could feel it. Between herself and this lovely lady the gossamer-like bond of sympathy, as delicate at first as a thread of a spider's web, had become now as strong as the silk cable pearls are strung on. It would bear actual spoken words about her father's and mother's separation!

"Is there anything in the world softer than the petal of a pansy!" remarked Mrs. Morrison, pressing one of the flowers against her lips, and gently drawing it across them.

Laurel laid a flower against *her* lips, too, and, closing her eyes, likewise tested its texture.

"The end of a horse's nose is as soft," she said contemplatively, "and," she went on, eyes still closed, "the back of a little tiny baby's head, where they'll let you kiss it."

Mrs. Morrison broke into a laugh.

"Dear delightful Laurel! That's so! That's so!" And suddenly she took hold of one of Laurel's hands and drew the back of that, too, across her lips, and kissed it.

That playful little kiss of Helen Morrison's on the back of Laurel's hand made Laurel's world whirl round her giddily for a moment. No one had ever kissed her on the hand before! It was a caress entirely different from an ordinary kiss upon the lips. She felt exalted, like a young knight in armor before his lady. She wished she dared kneel on the ground and kiss the hem of Mrs. Morrison's dress!

3

Laurel wondered a great deal about Mrs. Morrison's husband, and finally one day concluded to inquire about him.

"Is your husband away on business?" she began politely.

"Why, no. Didn't you know? Didn't your father tell you?"

Laurel shook her head. "No, father has told me nothing."

"He is not living, Laurel," gently Mrs. Morrison announced.

"Oh," said Laurel. "Of course," she went on, "I knew he wasn't *really* away on business, because of the drawers in the chiffonier being perfectly empty, and the closet beside yours, too, where you hung my things. But I didn't see any pictures of him around, so I thought perhaps you were separated."

"The portrait in the big gold frame in the living-room is a picture of him, Laurel, and that's a copy of it, in the silver frame on my dressing-table."

"Is *he* your husband?" exclaimed Laurel.

She had studied the portrait. The man in the portrait looked like a grandfather! He had long drooping mustaches, almost white, and the sockets of his eyes hung down like the eyes of a hunting-hound, Laurel had seen in the Maine woods once.

"Yes. Why?"

"He looks too old for *you!*"

"Does he? Well, he *was* older, but, oh, ever so kind, and the father of my dear boys, and," she added after a pause, "the father of my little girl, too."

"Your little girl?"

"Yes, Laurel, my only little girl. She died, before she was old enough to walk without holding tight onto one of my fingers."

"What was her name?"

"Carol."

"How old would she be?"

"About as old as you, I think."

"Did she have light hair, or dark?"

"Dark."

"Curly?"

"No, straight. Oh, how we did try to make it curl," laughed Mrs. Morrison.

"But I guess she didn't have freckles," said Laurel.

"Not *then*. But I think she would have had, when she grew up. She liked the sun, and out-of-doors. I'd have loved to have had her have *ever* so freckly a nose!"

"Do you *like* freckles?" Laurel exclaimed, wide-eyed, and amazed.

As easily as that, they wandered into the holy of holies of Helen Morrison's heart, and wandered out again.

4

When Mrs. Morrison had helped Laurel unpack her trunk on the first afternoon, she had been doubtful as to how her athletic young sons would get along with the little spick-and-span, bandbox girl she rather guessed Laurel to be. There were no stout boots, nor rough clothes of any sort among Laurel's things. There was a bathing-suit, but it was an elaborate fragile affair made of black satin, trimmed with orange. Excellent for exhibition on the beach, but it didn't look very appropriate for use in a certain deep black swimming-hole which the boys had discovered between two barnacled rocks. However, she needn't have worried.

The first night after dinner Con had inquired of Laurel, "Do you ride?"

It seemed there was a stable back of the house.

"I ride *some*."

"Can you swim?" Dane had asked.

"I swim a *little*."

To Mrs. Morrison's amazement, to the boys' amazement, too—and to their admiration besides—Laurel's "some" and "little" proved a great deal.

Next morning dressed in an old knickerbocker suit of Dane's (Laurel had never needed her riding-clothes in New York before), after she had ridden four or five times around the paddock back of the stable, she had called out, "Does he jump?" and the next time around she had taken one of the hurdles with perfect ease and familiarity.

It was the same with swimming. It didn't matter if her suit was satin, the swimming-hole didn't daunt her. She could dive better than Con! Laurel had taken swimming-lessons ever since she could remember. She had taken riding-lessons since she was eight. She had taken lessons in every sport which her mother considered fashionable and in which instructions could be bought.

"The funny thing is," said Con to Laurel the second day, "you don't play tennis."

But in games which required partners, Laurel had not had much experience. Solitaire sports were her specialty. However, she was pretty good at golf, she told Con. There had usually been a professional at the links connected with the summer hotels which her mother patronized.

"We'll try it," said Con, "and I'll teach you tennis."

He wouldn't acknowledge that he liked Laurel. None of the boys went as far as that. "But she isn't silly, and she isn't afraid of things!" he told his mother.

"They get along together beautifully, Stephen," said Helen Morrison to Laurel's father the night he came to take Laurel away.

It was after dinner. They were sitting in the garden terrace just outside the big room, where the portrait hung. Through the open windows, uncurtained towards the terrace, they could see Laurel seated with the

45

two older of the boys at a table, busy over some sort of game with cards, with Michael stretched out comfortably at their feet.

"I've enjoyed every moment of her," Helen went on, gazing fondly at the group inside the room. "Only," and there was a sudden change in her voice, "it's brought home to me afresh what I've missed—all these years. Oh, we've had such fun together!" she broke off gaily. "Girls' sort of fun," she laughed; "doing each other's hair, for instance—trying on each other's hats—that sort of thing. Boys—men, couldn't understand. And her questions! Don't you love little girls' blunt questions? Darling things, I think, like awkward little colts and calves—oh, Laurel's a dear child, Stephen. I've kept pretending she was mine," she exclaimed lightly.

"Oh, Helen! if she only were!"

There wasn't a trace of lightness in Stephen's exclamation.

"I couldn't have equipped her any better for the present-day activities of a young girl's life than her own mother has done, Stephen," said Helen. "There doesn't appear to be a muscle or a bone in her body that has been neglected."

"I'm thinking about her soul," Stephen remarked.

"It hasn't lost any of its beauty yet, Stephen." Helen assured him, "She's as unspoiled a little girl as I know—so pleased (so genuinely pleased, too—you can tell by the shine in her eyes) at the least kindness or attention. And the combination in her of sophistication and innocence is a source of constant surprise to me—a source of constant joy, too. Oh, you needn't be afraid. So far the undesirable influences haven't hurt Laurel a bit."

"But she's getting older, Helen. Her youth and innocence cannot protect her always."

"Oh, I know, I know," agreed Helen; "I've thought of that, too. It's a pity. I'm so sorry, Stephen. Let her stay with me often—whenever you can. See them in there—all so happy. Don't take her to a hotel when she comes for the visits. Bring her to me here, or to the town house, if we've moved in."

Driving back to New York that night over the almost deserted road (it was late. "Very late for thirteen," Mrs. Morrison had laughed, as she had tucked Laurel into a warm coat of her own), Laurel sat beside her father like a little stone image for the first ten minutes.

There was something exciting about the beautiful coat that wrapped her round so close. It was a little as if Mrs. Morrison herself held her, wrapped her round in her kindness. Every once in a while Laurel would rub her cheek against the soft fur of the high collar. It felt like Mrs. Morrison's hair the day after it had been washed, and she had let Laurel brush it, and twist it up, and stick the hairpins in. It *smelled* like it, too—fresh, clean like a flower-garden after rain. Laurel drew in great deep breaths of the soft brown sable. "It's Mrs. Morrison," she pretended with all the sentimentality of thirteen.

Gazing up into the sky from out of the fur collar, Laurel could see the full round moon above her. "She's following me to New York," she made-believe. "She's going to follow me wherever I go, always and always, and I can look up at her and see her whenever the moon is full, and tell her how lovely I think she is, and try to be like her. I shan't care so much if people *are* horrid after this."

"Well, Laurel," interrupted Stephen, "how did you get along?"

"All right."

"Was it very terrible?"

"Not very."

"How did you like the boys?"

"All right."

"And how did you like Mrs. Morrison?"

Gazing up at the moon, Laurel replied fervently, "I think Mrs. Morrison is the loveliest lady I ever knew."

"Do you?" her father exclaimed; "oh, do you, Lollie, dear?"

Lollie! Suddenly Laurel stiffened inside the long coat. Lollie!

"I mean," she added, with the exaltation all gone out of her voice, "I mean next to—next to—" it had to be. She couldn't avoid the word—"next to my mother."

All the rest of the way back to the hotel Laurel didn't once glance up at the moon. How could she—oh, how could she have become a part of the picture on the screen, while her mother was still in the audience, out there, in the dark, looking on.

CHAPTER FIVE

1

After Mrs. Dallas had said good-bye to Laurel, she retraced her steps
along the narrow platform beside the train, and immediately sought
refuge in the ladies' public dressing-room in the station. Standing in
front of the long horizontal mirror with the row of wash-basins beneath,
she removed her hat and veil, and leaning forward drew one of the
basins full of steaming water. With her bare hands she bathed her
smarting eyes and smeared cheeks. The hot water was as soothing as
hot soup to a sore throat. She dried her face and hands on a piece of
crêpe paper from a roll near by. Afterwards, opening a little red leather
case which she always carried with her, she laid it before her on the
washstand, first blowing into it, once or twice, to remove a little of the
loose pink powder that had shaken out of its container, and was as thick
as dust in a carpet-sweeper.

Briskly, in a business-like fashion, Mrs. Dallas proceeded to remedy
the damage wrought by her tears, working dexterously with various
little sticks and tubes, without any attempt at concealment, apparently
without the slightest self-consciousness, although just beside her a prim,
school-teacherish-looking little woman, middle-aged, observed her operations with interest. Just when her cheeks presented their customary
velvety appearance, her eyes suddenly welled up again with tears. She
closed the lids tight. No use. The tears oozed out, streaked her cheeks
again.

"Oh, darn it!" she whispered into the hollow of her hands as she pressed her fingers hard against her eyeballs. "Oh, Lollie, Lollie, darn it, darn it!"

Twice she was forced to repeat her operations, and at last gave up the struggle for perfection, satisfying herself with a bit of powder on her nose, trusting that the white veil would suffice to conceal her.

She had planned to spend an hour or two in the shops, take a sandwich and a cup of coffee in a candy-shop a little later, and go to a movie afterwards. It was wholly by accident that she ran across Alfred Munn.

The route she selected to the shops carried her through the outskirts of the wholesale merchandise district of the city. Alfred Munn's present business had something to do with leather or hides—or was it cotton—something of the sort. She ran across Alfred Munn (or rather he ran across her—he saw her before she saw him) at a restaurant.

It had occurred to Stella as she walked away from the station that a cup of coffee would probably help to brace her up better than anything else, and, as it was really time for lunch anyhow, she decided to drop into a certain restaurant she knew about, instead of the candy-shop farther downtown. It was a restaurant where Alfred Munn had taken Laurel and her to lunch one day two years ago. She hadn't seen him since. As she entered it, she observed that men predominated.

She hastened to the dressing-room at the rear. Stella Dallas felt as uncomfortable in the restaurant with her face all red and splotchy, as the school-teacherish little woman would have felt in her stocking-feet. It was with no thought of any man in particular that she set to work again to make herself presentable, now that she had herself under better control; or, at least, with no serious thought of any man in particular. She was always playing with the possibility that some old admirer might run across her path at any moment, and always taking necessary precautions.

Prepared as her cheeks may have been, Stella was taken by surprise when somebody leaned across the little table which she had selected beside the wall-mirrors and drawled in a masculine voice, "Well!"

She knew it was Alfred Munn before she looked up. Nobody else in the world could say "Well," like that. All sorts of interesting implications were packed into the single exclamation.

She glanced up and replied briefly, her blue eyes sparkling at him, "Hello!"

She didn't like Ed Munn. Stephen had been right. He *was* cheap. It showed now that he wasn't dressed in his riding-clothes any more. But even if she didn't like him very much, she couldn't be horrid to him. Stella Dallas couldn't be horrid to anybody whose eyes flattered her like that!

"What are you doing here?" he asked in a kind of caressing tone, as irresistible to the lonely Stella as food by whomever offered if she were hungry.

"I'm waiting for *you!*" her voice caressed back at him. Oh, a little harmless flirting was the one thing she needed to restore her wilted spirits!

Alfred Munn smiled at her, showing a row of little crooked yellow teeth. His face crackled up into a hundred pleased wrinkles. Attention from the opposite sex was as welcome to him as it was to Stella.

He drew out the chair opposite Stella, thinking, as he did so, "What have I got on for this afternoon anyhow? Only two appointments; I can cancel 'em." What he *said* was, as he sat down, "Where's the offspring?"

Stella thought, "Dear me! How thrilling! He's going to stay!" But out loud she said, "Just shipped her to New York."

"You alone?" Alfred Munn exclaimed. "Unattached? No string tied to you?"

Stella, pouting a little, looking pathetic on purpose, nodded. "All alone. No string. Not a thread."

Alfred Munn drew in a deep breath. Let it out audibly.

"My! This is my lucky day, I guess," he ejaculated. "We're going to have lunch together—you and I, and go to a show afterwards. Did you know it?"

Stella, casting down her eyes, and toying with the silver, shook her head. No. She didn't know it.

"Well," masterfully, "you know it now. Here, pass me that menu."

She obeyed with exaggerated docility. "Have your own way. I'm helpless when you're around. Do with me as you wish," her manner implied.

It pleased Alfred Munn. He summoned a waiter with an arrogant motion of his hand, tossed the menu aside, as wholly beneath his notice, and frowningly ordered cocktails—this was before prohibition—oysters, and soup. Then he leaned across the table and suddenly became all soft suavity. The contrast was effective.

"How've you been?" he asked.

"Oh, pretty well," Stella purred. Any one could make Stella purr, who stroked her like that.

"How are things going?" he inquired in his terribly intimate manner.

"Oh, pretty well, I guess," she purred again, and glanced up, her big Delft-blue eyes gazing straight into Alfred Munn's little pig-like spots of brightness, rimmed round with the puffy lids.

"I don't care," Stella thought to herself in defense of the things she was allowing her bold eyes to imply to Alfred Munn. "It's only for today, and I'm perfectly aware of what he is—dissipated, rotten old thing, probably. Doesn't hurt me any if he is. I'm beyond hurting now. He's better than nobody."

Stella had almost forgotten what a cocktail tasted like. How it did bring back the good old happy days, when everybody admired and flattered, just as Alfred Munn was doing now. For he was doing *just* that to Stella—overdoing it a little. Well, she could stand a little overdoing in that line. It had been *so* long since any man had found her attractive! Or, at least, since any man had told her so. She had begun to fear that age had got a grip on her at last which she couldn't loosen, however much she strained. Men hated old women. Alfred Munn restored her self-confidence wonderfully. *He* found her pleasing. *He* found her desirable. He told her the very sight of her made him feel young again. Asked her how in the world she did it. How she managed to keep her wonderful peaches-and-cream appearance. She didn't look to *him* a day over twenty-five!

"Oh," thought Stella, feeling all warm and comforted inside, "if only he could see me in an evening gown!"

As she preceded him out of the restaurant she was as pleased with the present-moment excitement, the present-moment attentions, as a young girl of sixteen on the way to her first matinee with an admiring suitor. Her pleasure was almost as innocent too.

2

Alfred Munn selected for the afternoon's entertainment a popular musical farce. Stella adored a musical farce with all the bold gay costumes. The seats he bought were aisle seats—the best in the house, three rows from the front. As Stella settled herself for the two hours and a half of pleasure in store for her, she was keenly conscious of her nearness to the stage, to the orchestra. How good it did seem to be right down in the midst of things again! When the curtain rolled up on the first act amidst a loud fanfare of trumpets, which Stella could feel tingle inside her, she was filled with gratitude to Alfred Munn. Why, she calculated, already his kindness to her had cost him something like fifteen dollars—twenty possibly. How much were cocktails and wines now, anyhow, and Porterhouse steaks? She mustn't be disappointing to him. She mustn't edge away from Alfred Munn's overlapping arm and shoulder. She must remember her age. Nineteen can afford to be as stand-offish as it chooses, but not thirty-nine. Besides, in one way it was gratifying to Stella that Alfred Munn wanted to sit so close. She had been afraid of late that there was nothing but tiny wrinkles and double chins left of her. But there was—there was! Alfred Munn knew women. Alfred Munn made Stella feel that there was lots else left.

She talked and laughed, eyes shining, and cheeks hot and flushed beneath the powder. Occasionally Laurel's serious face, crowned with the unfamiliar toque with the berries on one side, interrupted, shoved itself between her and the stage, between her and Alfred Munn.

The toque made her look frightfully like a young lady. She was growing up. No doubt about that. Stella hadn't seen her cry since—she couldn't remember since when. Funny kid. Just got silent and horribly quiet instead of letting the tears of a year or two ago well up in her eyes and spill over. Of late she, Stella, was the one who did the crying for the two of them. But she mustn't get teary, *here, now,* for heaven's sake!

Laurel would be about at New London now, Stella calculated, New Haven, Bridgeport later, New York pretty soon, walking up the long granolithic walk, with the bits of mica in it, sparkling like tiny stars beneath the white artificial light; looking for Stephen; seeing him; greeting him; sitting in a taxicab beside him. They always took a taxicab.

Queer, thought Stella, how the very sight of her present escort used to irritate Stephen. It would be interesting to Alfred Munn, she guessed, and flattering to him, too, if he had a notion how much he used to be discussed between Stephen and herself. Stephen was always making such queer mistakes about her little affairs, picking out somebody she really didn't care a straw about, like Alfred Munn, for instance, to get stuffy over, and remaining undisturbed by the attentions from men who *really* interested her. Alfred Munn, indeed! A riding-teacher! That was what he had been, in Milhampton seven years ago. The smartest women in town took lessons of him. So did Stella. And the smartest women in town were keen about him, or pretended to be. Naturally they weren't any of them seriously keen about Alfred Munn. The other women's husbands understood. But Stephen wouldn't. It was ridiculous, absurd. Stella told Stephen so dozens and dozens of times. But he would persist in a making a mountain out of a molehill.

That was how Mrs. Holland described Stephen's attitude. There was no woman in Milhampton more the fashion than Mrs. Holland at that time. Stella had been immensely pleased by her friendship. Every word she uttered was to Stella like the wisdom of an oracle.

"Husbands need a lot of training, my dear," she had told Stella after a burst of confidences from Stella one afternoon. "Don't let yourself become a doormat. Husbands don't respect doormats, in the long run. Teach him that you can look at another man without wanting to elope with him. And get him used to the idea that you aren't blind to every other masculine creature in the world but himself. Such an attitude keeps them lovers, makes them alert, attentive, my dear."

But it didn't seem to keep Stephen a lover. It didn't make Stephen alert and attentive. It worked just the other way with him.

3

These reflections did not possess Stella in the theater. It was later, alone on the train, returning to her beach hotel that she glanced into her past. She didn't allow herself to do so frequently. It didn't make her any happier. Things had been so rosy, so promising ten years ago—so far beyond her most extravagant girlhood dreams. And now—*now!* Resolutely she turned her thoughts to other things. She was to meet Alfred Munn again the following Saturday for lunch and another matinee. What should she wear? The sudden necessity of a new early-fall hat gave her a little thrill of delight.

There was nothing in the world Stella enjoyed more than a morning spent in Boston at the expensive uptown shops, pricing and trying on hats, followed by an afternoon in the downtown department stores buying buckram, wire, velvet, feathers, ornaments, flowers, and whatnot, and the long inspiring day afterwards shut up in her room moulding with her clever fingers a copy of some little gem that a far-away artist in Paris had conceived.

When Stella said good-bye to Laurel, her plan to spend two hours in the shops had not been an exciting prospect to her. It was stupid to shop if you had nothing you had to buy. The chance meeting with Alfred Munn provided Stella with the necessary incentive to start the machinery of her creative genius going. She would have to have a new dress, too. Perhaps she could pick up some summer silk thing marked down, and pep it up with some black bead trimming, at present on an old chiffon evening gown of hers she scarcely ever wore. Bead trimming was being worn again this fall. Possibly it would be a good idea to overhaul her entire wardrobe immediately, even if it was early in the season. Men like variety, and it looked as if Alfred Munn meant to see her rather often during Laurel's absence.

When he had put her aboard her train, he had told her that if she didn't object to leaving the seashore for the city frequently he was going to keep her from getting lonely, if she'd let him, while the kid was away.

She wished he wouldn't call Laurel "the kid" and the "offspring." She wished his linen collar hadn't been grimy round the top edge. She wished he hadn't chanced to omit shaving that morning. A man who shaved every morning without reference to the day's programme, and put on a clean collar without reference to the old one, was one of Stella's tests of a gentleman. Alfred Munn never was guilty of any such offenses when he was the vogue in Milhampton. Yes, yes, Stephen was right. Second-rate—that was the term he used to apply to Alfred Munn. Well, she didn't care. It didn't rob orchestra seats at the most popular shows in town of their attraction for Stella, or luncheon-tables in the most popular restaurant in town of their luxury and joy. Alfred Munn was going to take her for lunch next Saturday to the newest and most expensive hotel in the city.

4

Stella spent that evening packing her trunks (there remained two old-fashioned hump-backed affairs), and again it was early morning before she lay down in the battered white iron bed to go to sleep.

Stella never stayed on at the expensive summer resorts after Laurel went. Fifteen miles nearer Boston, along a sandy beach, there was a stretch of board-walk, with the ocean on one side, and on the other, a row of cheap amusement places. Behind this row of amusement places there was a nest of lodging-houses. By occupying a room in one of these houses, and taking her meals outside, Stella could save enough money over what it cost her to live at the expensive summer hotel, to buy several Permanents for Laurel, and a wrist-watch, and a fur coat, too, if Stephen still persisted in books.

You'd think, perhaps, you wouldn't have to economize on three hundred and fifty dollars a month, if there was only yourself and a child to take care of. But gracious, try it! Try it with a little queen like Laurel to bring up and educate, and give half a chance to. When a twelfth of your yearly income went to the private school your little queen attended, for five days a week; and two-twelfths to a decent hotel roof to put over her head in the summer; and several other twelfths for a decent roof to put over her head in the winter (Laurel couldn't live in a tenement), and a big chunk was eaten out of another twelfth by riding-tickets, at the rate of fifty dollars for twenty rides, and completely gobbled up by private dancing-lessons, and private golf and swimming lessons, and heaven knows what not; I tell you what, you have to stretch every single penny you have left to clothe the child properly, to say nothing of yourself, and your own rags.

"I suppose forty-two hundred dollars a year sounds plenty enough to Stephen," Stella said to her old friend Effie McDavitt. "But Stephen and I have probably got different ideas about how the child should be brought up. Well, I'll never ask him for any more. I'll never go grov-elling to Stephen Dallas for money as long as I live! I'll tell you that! No, sir-ee! I've got some pride, even though he has acted as if I hadn't any feelings."

The boarding-houses at Belcher's Beach, as the amusement boulevard was called, were not attractive. The people who patronized them were not attractive either. The women were loud-voiced and loud-mannered, and spent a good deal of time walking to and from the beach, in bathrobes and canvas sandals; and the masculine element, if one existed, was likely to be found sitting in his shirt-sleeves on the boarding-house porch, ready to make remarks to the robed ladies as they came trooping up the steps munching peanuts or popcorn cakes.

Stella did not confide this particular economy of hers to Laurel. Laurel mustn't know that her mother mixed up with such society. Stella didn't in fact mix up with it, but Laurel mustn't know that her mother slept under the same roof with people of that sort.

Laurel, at thirteen, was not a prolific letter-writer, but whatever mes-sages she did send Stella she directed to the summer hotel, where she supposed her mother was to remain. These were forwarded by the clerk at the hotel, according to Stella's instructions, to Milhampton, care of

Second-rate — that was the term Stephen used . . . . Well, she didn't care.

a certain Effie McDavitt. Stella didn't object to Effie's knowing about the cheap lodging-house—poor worn-out, down-at-the-heel Effie. Effie was the only one of her girlhood friends whom Stella hadn't managed to lose. She had tried to lose Effie. Had succeeded for a while, too, during the height of her social success in Milhampton. But Effie hadn't stayed lost. Effie was the sort of woman whom you can grind your heel on in the dirt and it won't kill her loyalty. Like a worm. Cut her feelings of friendship for you in two, and the parts will still wriggle.

Of course Stella might have gone back to the little red cottage house outside Milhampton during Laurel's absence and stayed with her father, if she could have endured the eccentricities of his old age and the lack of any attempt at a self-respecting existence. (He let the hens come right into the kitchen now, and he'd dragged his miserable bed in there, too—all rags, and no sheets.) And Stella *could* endure much to save a little money, but the danger of discovery was great. Ever since her marriage Stella had been struggling to cover up her early connections with the little red cottage house. She had an idea she had succeeded fairly well, too.

At Belcher's Beach Stella never met anybody whom she knew, nor who knew her. It was only fifteen miles away from the big summer hotel where she and Laurel had spent the season, but it was an entirely different world. The guests from the big summer hotel never left the automobile highway, a half a mile inland, to seek out Belcher's Beach. There was another amusement boulevard of bigger proportions and of less tawdry appearance a few miles farther on.

This wasn't the first time Stella had successfully hidden herself at Belcher's Beach, during Laurel's absence. She had tested its advantages for some three or four years now. It *had* advantages. For one thing, it was near enough to Boston so that when the "dirt-commonness of the hole" got too unbearable she could dress up in her best clothes and escape to the Boylston Street shops without the price of the ticket hurting too much.

It was cheaper than living in Boston itself. Take just the food, for instance. Stella had always liked hot frankforts embedded in a soft biscuit, slimy with mustard. There were several night-lunch-carts at

Belcher's Beach. At Belcher's Beach it was not conspicuous, in the least, for a lady to buy a meal at the door of one of the night-lunch-carts, and carry it away, hot, in a damp brown paper, under her arm. It was not conspicuous to return from Boston at a late hour with Ed Munn after one of his grand parties. It was just as well, Stella supposed, not to be seen with Ed Munn too much, after all the silly talk there had been about him and her in Milhampton years ago. Even if she could have afforded to stay on at the expensive hotel, she would have been obliged to have foregone too many parties with Ed. There were some compensations, and, ostrich-wise, she stuck her head in the sand of Belcher's Beach and proceeded to enjoy them.

One late Saturday night Ed Munn, who had seen Stella decently inside the front door of the boarding-house at Belcher's Beach, after one of his parties in town, had asked her with an insinuating smile, glancing towards the stairs, "Sure you can unlock your door alone?"

Stella hadn't taken offense. Ed was like that.

"Of course I can, you goose." She flashed back. "Do I look feeble?"

You can just bet she didn't let any masculine escort trail up any inside stairs behind her! Some women in the boarding-house did!

Too bad Ed had that common streak in him. Some men would know when and where it was good taste to spring a joke of that sort.

Stella was blissfully unaware, as she climbed the stairs alone to her room that night, that at the same moment, a touring car, with two excited women in its rear seat, was slipping smoothly away from under the arc light that hung on the tall pole outside Stella's boarding-house.

The automobile had stopped under the light for only a moment. The chauffeur had wanted to find out how much gasoline he had. It was unfortunate for Stella that the car hadn't stopped longer. The two occupants in the back of the car had seen Alfred Munn follow Stella Dallas into the boarding-house, but they hadn't seen him come out!

One of the women in the back of the car was Mrs. Henry Holland. The other was Mrs. Kay Bird. They both lived in Milhampton in the winter. Mrs. Kay Bird occupied rooms directly opposite Stella in the same apartment hotel.

"It was she! I can swear to it!" said Mrs. Henry Holland, as she clutched the arm of her companion.

"It was he. I'd know him anywhere!" said Mrs. Kay Bird, as she clutched back.

"Only ten more days," said Stella, half an hour later as she knelt in the dark by her bed. "Gosh! how I miss you, Lollie."

CHAPTER SIX

1

The red cottage house where Stella had lived as a young girl, and until she married Stephen Dallas, was located in an outlying district of Milhampton. The district was known as Cataract Village. The little settlement of houses was named after the Cataract Mills, and the mills were named after a fall of water hidden inside them somewhere, over which they crouched like some great vampire and sucked the strength that made their wheels go round.

Cataract Village was the home of the Cataract Mill employees. Stella's father had worked in the mills ever since he was a boy. Stella was born in one of the ugly three-deckers, close to the mill gate. She was ten years old when her father bought one of the red cottage-houses on the river-bank. She had been proud of the cottage then, and proud of it, too, as she grew older. On each side of the little porch over the front door, every spring, for years, Stella planted morning-glories and wild-cucumber vine, which climbed a string trellis of her own making.

The first time Stephen went to see Stella at the red cottage her vines were profuse with leaf and blossom. She had trained the docile vines to run all over the picket fence that surrounded the little house, and had shrouded the back porch with them; had shrouded with them, too, a latticed summer-house which stood in the side yard. Stella had copied the summer-house, with much the same genius with which she copied hats or dresses, from a summer-house she had seen in a garden in Milhampton across the river. Stella's summer-house was made of plasterer's laths painted white, and criss-crossed. The summer-house in the garden at Milhampton, designed by a landscape-gardener, had been covered with Dorothy Perkins roses. But sunlight shining through the chinks of Stella's morning-glories and wild-cucumbers, was just as prettily dappled with shadows, as sunshine shining through rose-vines. At night the darkness was just as dense inside Stella's summer-house—a little denser, perhaps. Stella had been particular to plant her seeds thick. Inside Stella's summer-house there hung a Gloucester hammock!

The first night Stephen called on Stella, he had sat in the hammock alone, while Stella had curled herself up on the low step of the summer-house, leaning her head against one of the upright posts, so that the searchlight moon could shine full upon her face, and her caller could observe from the darkness of the hammock how pretty she was.

She was pretty—she was very pretty in those days. But it was not Stella's bright eyes and bright cheeks that Stephen Dallas thought about most, after that first call. It hadn't been quite dark when he arrived. Before he was sure that the red cottage was the house where Stella lived, he had noticed the morning-glories and wild-cucumber vines.

When later that first evening he discovered that Stella had planted the vines herself, had built much of the summer-house, driven all the nails in the diamond lattice-work, done all the painting, it had set him to thinking. Out of a bundle of plasterer's laths and a handful or two of common little seeds, she had created a charming spot. As he leaned back in the Gloucester hammock, and gazed at Stella on the step below him, the simplicity of her setting, the absence from it of everything that required accumulated wealth to possess, had been soothing and comforting to Stephen, suffering as he was—suffering as he had been for the last year and a half.

2

Stephen was young then, barely twenty-three, but for eighteen months he had felt nothing but the resignation of old age, and the bitterness of disappointed old age. It had never occurred to Stephen Dallas that disgrace, disaster, utter and complete ruin, could befall *him*. He had taken it for granted always that he would fulfill, to a greater or less degree, his expectations for himself, and his family's and friend's expectations for him, too. Whether as a doctor or lawyer, or business man of ability, he didn't know which, before he went East to school, but in some capacity he would fill a position of responsibility in his home city. It had always been understood that when Stephen's education was completed, he would return to that home city, where he had been born, and where his father had been born before him, and continue to add honor to the family reputation.

It was a reputation to be proud of. The Dallases of Reddington, Illinois, were a respected and honored family. The Dallas house, built by Stephen's grandfather, was quiet and unostentatious in appearance, but solid, substantial—a big, square brick affair, painted dull brown. There was something so solid and substantial about everything connected with the Dallases, that people in Reddington supposed them to be infallible, as immune to panics and market fluctuations as an oak to the varying antics of the elements.

This attitude of the people toward the Dallases was partly responsible for their ruin. Stephen's father prized and treasured his reputation for indestructibility. To a man of his special brand of pride, it was galling to allow his fellow citizens even to suspect that the roots of the oak tree were not as healthy as the proud and upstanding trunk signified. And so it was not until the great tree fell—was pulled over by its own weight, and lay sprawling on the ground, a mammoth and pitiful wreck, for every curious passer-by to gape at—that the decayed and rotten condition of the roots was discovered by the astonished public.

When the brief telegram from home reached Stephen (he had completed his college course by this time and had nearly completed his post-graduate course—he had decided to follow in his father's steps and become a lawyer) the message gave no details. Simply stated the fact of his father's sudden death and summoned him home immediately.

It was not until he was within a few hours of Reddington that he learned of the manner of his father's death. He read it in a Chicago paper.

His father had committed suicide! He had locked himself up in his office downtown, one night, and shot himself with a revolver!

"For a number of years," the article stated, "Mr. Stephen Dallas, who was a lawyer and one of Reddington's most respected citizens, has acted as trustee for various estates, and sole legal and financial advisor for a number of charitable institutions. It is feared that the various funds entrusted to him may have suffered and an investigation of his affairs is now under way."

Stephen learned upon his arrival home that the fears hinted at in the papers were justified. His one desire was to escape, to get away from everybody and everything familiar as soon as possible, after the details of burial were disposed of. He had no forgiveness, no charity, for his father. He told his mother and his older sister Fanny that he wished they could dispose of the ruined thing his father had made of the Dallas reputation as easily as they could dispose of the ruined thing he had made of his body. But no, the reputation they must wear tied round their necks for everybody to see, and stare at, and keep away from. Obliged as he was to bear his father's name (why had his parents handicapped him thus?) he could never hope to succeed in any large way, he said; for who would ever trust a man with the name of Stephen Dallas? It spelled suicide and dishonor now.

His mother tried in a weak, feminine sort of way, Stephen thought, to excuse his father's act. He had never let them even guess at home, she said, that the big house and all the servants, the stable full of expensive cars, and the proportionate demands in way of clothes and entertaining, and contributions to various charitable institutions, were eating into his capital—had been for years.

But why hadn't he? What kindness had it been to them? It was beyond Stephen's young comprehension that his father, like some weak, inexperienced bank clerk, could be tempted into "borrowing" even a portion of the funds entrusted to him.

"Borrowing!" That is what his father's friends and associates called it, when they talked to Stephen. They tried to soften the facts to him, these kind, old, pitying men, who felt sorry to look upon the destruction of so young a man's career, Stephen supposed. Well, there was one satisfaction. Thank heaven, his father hadn't taken liberties with the legacies left to him and Fanny by their grandfather, nor touched the solid securities packed away years ago in his mother's safe-deposit box. By scraping everything together, none of the estates which had been entrusted to his father need to suffer at all. The kind old men told Stephen that he and his mother and sister were under no obligation. Stephen was glad that his mother and Fanny felt, just as he did, that the only thing for them to do was to wipe out his father's dishonesty as far as possible.

Stephen was glad, too, that his mother and Fanny agreed with him that it would be unbearable to continue to live in Reddington. As soon as the big brown house, and the automobiles, and the servants were disposed of, they would disappear as quietly as possible. Fanny and his mother would go to Chicago and conceal themselves there as best they could. There would be little for them to live on. Only the insurance policy. Stephen would, of course, get a job somewhere, as soon as he could. Oh, no, he wouldn't finish at the law school! He couldn't afford the time. He never wanted to see the law school again! He never wanted to see anything again, or anybody that recalled to him his old bright hopes and ambitions, he said.

"Oh, no, least of all Helen Dane," he shuddered, replying to his mother's timid reminder that Helen had sent her card to him, with a message written on it to come and see her.

Stephen was thankful that there had never been anything serious between him and Helen. There might have been. It had seemed last summer as if there probably would have been, but not now—*never* now! There was no girl in Reddington, no girl anywhere, whom he would ever ask to bear the name of Dallas.

3

Stephen first heard of the Cataract Mills in Milhampton, Massachusetts, through an advertisement in a paper. He answered the advertisement. He had never been to Milhampton. He had no friends, no acquaintances there, that he knew of. It was well removed from Reddington. It would serve his purpose as well as any other place in the United States. His mother had begged him not to put the ocean between himself and her, when he had mentioned Australia or South America.

Upon his arrival in Milhampton, Stephen hunted up a lodging-house in Cataract Village close to the mills, and hired a room. He worked hard for his eighteen dollars a week. But there was little joy in his work. Even the raise in his position, and pay, at the end of the first three months, gave him no thrill. What was the use of his rising in the world? Wasn't oblivion what he desired more than anything else? Wasn't the feature that he liked best about his new job, the fact that it hid him, covered him up? None of the men who ate breakfast and supper with him—who softened their bread-crusts in their coffee, and prepared their meat and potatoes as Stephen had seen the dog's meat and potatoes prepared at home, chopped all up and covered with gravy—had heard of Stephen Dallas of Reddington. Success, too many raises, would mean exposure finally, opening up the old wound again. Stephen had suffered enough for a while.

Stephen believed he would suffer always. But he didn't take into consideration his youth. There is something about twenty-three that struggles and fights all by itself—never mind how indifferent the soul, how sick the body—and accomplishes its purposes and designs without help. The same month that Stephen's mother's age came to her rescue, Stephen's youth came to *his*. Early in September, before a year had passed since the Dallas oak had fallen, death delivered Mrs. Dallas from her suffering. It was two or three weeks before his mother died that Stephen met Stella.

He met her at a church-sociable, in the vestry of the Congregational Church in Cataract Village. He had gone to the church sociable with the shipping-clerk at the mills, who had told him, with a wink, that he had met some peaches there at the last shindy, and invited him to come along, if he wanted to. Stephen had never in his life before passed a whole year practically void of feminine society.

It so happened that the night before the shipping-clerk invited Stephen to the church sociable, Stephen had drifted into a musical show downtown. The musical show started him to thinking about Helen Dane.

All the way back to Mrs. Bean's lodging-house he had dwelt upon Helen's loveliness, longed, as he didn't suppose he could ever long again, for an hour with her. A wave of despair had swept over him. Helen Dane was miles away, barriered and forbidden now. Stephen had fallen to sleep in his bare, bleak bedroom very miserable and unhappy. But in reality his state of mind was healthier, more normal than it had been since his father had died, and that night Stephen's youth danced a little delighted jig of triumph on the dingy pillow-case beside him as he slept.

4

Stella Martin was an acknowledged belle in Cataract Village. Her lips were cherry-red, her cheeks peach-blossom pink, and without paint and powder in those days. She had, too, as her girl friends expressed it, "stacks of style." Stella Martin could drape a straight piece of cloth about her hips and shoulders, and it would assume fashionable lines all by itself! She far outshone the other young girls in Cataract Village. She was far better educated than the other girls. Stella had gone all the way through the high school, and graduated in a white dress with ruffles. When Stephen met Stella she was completing a course at the State Normal School on the other side of the river.

Not that Stella meant to make teaching a life-work! By no means! But it happened that next to the State Normal School there was located a technical school for young men. Stella had heard that students at the two institutions of learning sometimes made friendships that led to an interchange of ceremonies that sounded attractive to her.

Stella was ambitious. She couldn't help but see she was different from the girl friends of her childhood. Most of them were content to take a job in the weaving-rooms at the mills, as soon as they had finished the ninth grade, or a year or two in the high school; or else to marry some raw, half-awake young man, from the mills, and live in one of the Cataract Village three-deckers, and have children, and children, and children! Not Stella, however! Nothing like that for Stella Martin!

There was a little brown spot on Stella's neck. It showed when she wore summer dresses cut in a low V in front. She was on the point of having it removed when a certain old woman, a sort of half-witch, told her it was a sign that some day she would make a brilliant marriage. So Stella kept her little brown spot, and though she laughed and flirted with almost every young man who admired her, and generously let them hold her hand, and take advantage of the dark, she had no notion of marrying in a hurry.

Stella had a streak of common sense in her, and she didn't leave it entirely to the magic power of the brown spot upon her neck to bring about the brilliant marriage. After providing herself with a few possible candidates for the marriage, the enterprising Stella spent long laborious hours making the yard surrounding the red cottage attractive, with morning-glory vines and wild-cucumber; and built herself a little temple that was very becoming to her type of beauty; and when the young men from the technical school came, in their clean collars, and dark suits, with beautiful creases down the front legs of their trousers, to call on Miss Martin, she usually chanced to be sitting in her little shrine. Therefore, during the spring and summer and early fall these young men seldom caught a glimpse of her mother in the ugly mouse-colored wrapper and flat shoes shuffling about in the kitchen, washing dishes, or mixing bread. They never had a chance to discover that the red cottage lacked a dining-room. Later, after Stella's charms had worked their blinding enchantment, it was her theory that the skeletons inside the house were less to be feared.

5

The first night that Stephen Dallas went to see Stella she exerted herself more than usual in behalf of her caller, for though he was one of the spurned Cataract Mill employees, she was aware that he was as far ahead of the technical school students of her acquaintance, as to requirements for a brilliant marriage, as the technical school students were far ahead of the Cataract Village young men.

Stella had an eye for details. This Mr. Dallas, she observed, wasn't too spick-and-span. He didn't look as if he had just stepped out of the barber's shop round the corner, and he didn't smell so. His cheeks didn't shine. His collars didn't shine, and his clothes seemed to have been worn by him long enough to fall naturally into *his* lines, instead of retaining those of the wax dummy's with the black mustache in the gentlemen's furnishings shop on the corner of Main and Webster Streets downtown. When he leaned forward his waistcoat (but Stella called it vest) clung to him, instead of sticking out and making caves and caverns, in which glimpses of lining and suspenders could be seen; and straight across the vest, rather low-down, where it wrinkles a little (just where it ought to wrinkle when a man leans forward), Stella observed the slender watch-chain made of gold and platinum shafts, linked together.

She observed, too, Mr. Dallas's handkerchief. He had pulled it out of his pocket and offered it to her to sit on, when she insisted upon occupying the low step of the summer-house. She had taken it from him just to feel of it. It was made of finest linen. It had a narrow hemstitched edge, and hand-embroidered letters in the corner.

"What's S stand for, Mr. Dallas?" Stella had asked with the time-worn coyness of her sex when first touching upon so intimate a subject as first names.

"Stephen," Stephen had replied shortly, from the Gloucester hammock.

"Stephen, Stephen," Stella had repeated two or three times—in a dainty, sort of experimental fashion, as if she were tasting some new kind of candy. "Stephen." Then, "It's nice. I like it," she exclaimed and glanced up at Stephen from under her long lashes.

"Really? Do you?" Stephen had laughed, just a little disconcerted. Stella liked the way he said "Really?" and "Do you?" and later, "Delightful," and "Int'resting." He spoke like an actor on the stage, she thought.

When Stella discovered that her caller was a college graduate, and a college graduate from the same university which Harold Miller and Spencer Chisholm had attended, as well as a half-dozen other young Milhampton blue-bloods, who lived on the other side of the river, and

71

whom Stella knew by sight and reputation, and by their fine houses on upper Webster Street, she was aware that this Mr. Dallas was the biggest opportunity she had ever had.

You might have thought she would have been a little awed, but Stella had confidence in her personal charms. Experience had convinced her that the same upward glances, intimacies, reservations, shynesses, boldnesses, what-not, were attractive to the genus "young man" whatever his species. When Stephen Dallas bade Stella good-bye that first night, he had held her willing hand a moment longer than is conventional and had asked if he could come again.

Later, when Stella went to bed, she tipped the little high square mirror on her bureau well forward and, gazing up into it, at her bare, fair expanse of gleaming neck and shoulders, she placed her forefinger on the little brown beauty-spot and pressed it gently.

"I wonder," she whispered.

6

The distance between Mrs. Bean's lodging-house and the little red cottage was only a quarter of a mile. It took Stephen less than ten minutes to walk it. Mrs. Bean's boarding-house was an impossible place in which to spend the evening. The walks around and about the boarding-house had come to seem impossible, too. So also had the bare, white-lighted, white-walled reading-room at the Milhampton Public Library.

Ever since Stephen had come to Milhampton (up to the time he met Stella), each night, when he finished his supper in the boarding-house dining-room, he was faced with the problem of killing two and a half hours somehow till a civilized hour for sleep arrived. But after he met Stella, and found the straight, easy way that led to the red cottage, there was no more problem as to how to spend his evenings—at least as to how he wanted to spend them.

If Stephen's mother hadn't died just when she did; and if, on top of that, Stephen's sister Fanny hadn't received, in reply to an application she had made to teach in a girls' boarding-school in Japan, summons to sail immediately, Stephen's infatuation would probably have burned itself out before he was in a position to consider additional financial burdens of any sort.

Suddenly Stephen found himself free and unfettered. There was no more need to send weekly checks to Chicago. There was no more need to send letters there, or to go there from time to time himself. Stephen was entirely cut off from his old associations, his laboring boat had lost even its dragging anchor, and was touching the shores of a country on the other side of the earth.

CHAPTER SEVEN

1

Stephen married Stella in January, four months after he first saw her. He thought he loved her. Most sincerely he thought he loved her. He desired to be with her—terribly, terrifyingly—more than he had ever desired to be with any girl. Moreover, he felt very tenderly towards her. He was aware of her limitations, of her little crudities, but what if she did make a few mistakes in grammar, a few mistakes in taste, occasionally. She was wonderfully sweet-tempered, always amiable, always gay, as easily pleased as a child, as easily guided, he believed.

Once, when he corrected her for one of her grammatical offenses (she *would* say "somewheres"; and "would of" for "would have"; and "got *a*" for "got *to*"—"got-a-laughing," "got-a-going"; and "lay" for "lie"; and "how does it suit," and "how do you like," without an object), she replied good-naturedly, "That's right, Mr. Harvard of Bawston, teach me to talk like you do. I'm crazy to learn."

Stephen thought that he could make her over, rub down the rough edges once they were married, once he had her alone to himself. Alone, to himself! Blinding possibility! Well, well, he must use his head, too!

Of course she was different from the girls he used to know. But he was different from the man he used to be. He required somebody different. Stephen did not want a girl to step down to him. Stephen did not want pity from the woman he married. Stella was not stepping down to him. Stella did not pity him.

When he first told her about his father, she replied, lightly, laughingly, "Mercy, I don't care what your father did, Stephen, nor your

74

Stephen married
Stella in
January, four
months after he
first saw her.

great-grandfather either." Then, with disarming honesty, "Gracious, you'd never have looked at poor me unless something had knocked you off your high horse."

No girl who belonged to Stephen's former existence would look upon a hundred and fifty dollars a month as a fortune. Stella did. Nor upon five rooms and a bath in an apartment house in the upper Webster Street district in Milhampton, as a palace. Stella did. Nor upon himself, dethroned, cast out, and disgraced, as still a prince. Stella did.

Stephen experienced no crude and sudden awakening. During the first year of their married life, there were surprises for him, gentle shocks almost every day, but nothing shattering. For instance, he was amazed to discover how little education a girl can absorb, and go through a high school and two years of normal school besides. Why, Stella didn't know Thackeray from George Eliot!

"Oh, I suppose I learned about those old fellows once, but you know how things of that sort slip in and out, unless they're dinged in everlastingly."

But didn't normal schools "ding in" such things? Apparently not. Stephen had been counting on the normal-school experience. He had dwelt with emphasis upon it when he had first written his sister Fanny in far-away Japan, about Stella.

It was another shock to Stephen to discover how little interest his precious resurrected library aroused in Stella. Once before they were married she had told him she would simply adore to live in a room with books to the ceiling! But her only passion, as far as books were concerned, seemed to be in their decorative quality. One day she spent three hours changing Stephen's careful arrangement of his books, so that all the bindings of one color should be grouped together, irrespective of subject. One evening, when Stephen started to read out loud to her from one of his favorite authors, in an attempt to lure her inside the books, she told him good-naturedly, for goodness' sake not to spout any more of that dead, old-fashioned, high-brow stuff to her. It gave her the fidgets.

She had no love at all for music, it appeared, although during the short period of their courtship she told Stephen she was "crazy about it," and in fact seemed to him to be. She was a beautiful dancer. "I just can't keep still when there's a tune going on." But after her first real musical concert with Stephen, one Saturday night several weeks after their marriage (Boston artists often came to Milhampton), she frankly confessed herself as horribly bored. A violin made her want to scream. It was so squeaky, like filing finger-nails with a steel file, she thought. Of course if musical concerts, Kneisel quartettes and the like were "the thing," she was game for them. But really a good vaudeville show (movies were then in their infancy) was much more entertaining. And a good play, where you saw modern actors, kept you so much better up-to-date, and rubbed the green moss off you in rolls. The beauty of out-of-doors had no attraction for her, nor flowers either, her morning-glories and wild cucumbers notwithstanding. She spent a good deal of time outdoors, walking; not, however, for the physical exhilaration of it, but simply "to reduce" (even then Stella was inclined to be a little plump) or to save the price of a car-fare, which she usually invested in candy. She was always nibbling at candy.

Often during the first few months of his marriage, grave doubts and misgivings assailed Stephen, but he was able to send them slinking away usually by comparing his present existence with that of a year ago. A year ago his evenings had been awful stretches of loneliness and unloveliness. *Now* each night there was a very pretty and always good-natured Stella waiting for him in a little sweet-smelling apartment; and after his evening meal there were distant sounds, far from unpleasing to him, of running water and rattling dishes, as he sat smoking and reading in his old Morris chair, wrapped round with his books and his rugs and a few treasured pieces of furniture unburied from a storehouse in Reddington.

Later, there was somebody sitting on the arm of his Morris chair, pressing against his shoulder, somebody soft and warm and alive, and his—all his, to do with as he pleased. No; he was not sorry that he had married Stella.

2

If time had not been steadily at work performing its gentle cure upon Stephen, he might never have been sorry he had married Stella. But old hopes, old ideals began to reassert themselves. In spite of himself, gradually, slowly, Stephen became interested in his job at the Cataract Mills. More than once that spring, Stella, coming in from the kitchen of the little apartment after the supper dishes had been put away, found Stephen poring over one of the sheepskin-bound volumes from the bottom shelf of the bookcases he had had built around the living-room, his precious Trollope or Meredith (Lord, what *did* he find in those old birds?) pushed aside, discarded.

The sheepskin-bound volumes were Stephen's law-books. He told Stella he wanted to satisfy a curiosity he had, as to the legal right or wrong of certain affairs at the Cataract Mills. Stephen was in the Complaint Department at the mills at that time. This curiosity of Stephen's percolated through the man immediately above him, and through the next man, and the next, and the next, and so on to the general manager finally. Once the general manager discovered Stephen, it was every night *then* that he pored over the law-books.

Stella did not begrudge the late nights Stephen spent with the big volumes.

"Gracious," she had exclaimed, eyes aglint, when Stephen confided to her that the general manager had suggested that he pass his bar examination, so as to be able to assist in the legal end of the business, if occasion arose. "Gracious, a lawyer! My! Won't I feel just grand? Oh, Stephen, I knew I'd picked a winner. I wouldn't be a bit surprised if I found myself a governor's wife some day, or a president's! Gosh, wouldn't I be thrilled?"

"Oh, Stella. Not 'Gosh!' Please."

"Oh, well—Jiminy then—What's the diff? Lord, I'm excited!"

"Poor Stella," thought Stephen. "Poor Stephen, too!" For it occurred to him suddenly, sickeningly, gazing at Stella, listening to Stella, that there were two reasons now instead of one a year ago why he should avoid the smiles and favors of success.

But he didn't. He couldn't. Much in the same way as water seeks its own level, so Stephen had a level he, too, involuntarily sought. He had been born with the love of success running in his veins and it wouldn't be denied.

Mr. Palmer, the general manager of the Cataract Mills, became very much interested in Stephen Dallas. He had no son of his own; he had no protégé in whom to feel pride and pleasure. He could well feel pride and pleasure in Stephen. Stephen was by nature very adaptable, very approachable. His father's act had only temporarily crippled his graceful self-confidence. He was tall and slight, more aristocratic than rugged in appearance; forehead high, eyes well-set, chin and mouth strong and distinctive. His dark, close-cut hair grew thick on top of his head, but receded on either side like so many American boys still in their twenties. The mustache, restrained and close-cut, which he had allowed to grow when he first came to Milhampton, in order to make him forget whom he had been before, gave him a foreign look.

"English," delightedly whispered some of the Milhampton women, to whom everything English was desirable.

Mr. Palmer suggested his name for membership at the Milhampton City Club; at the River Country Club; introduced him to a group of young lawyers. Stephen ran across some old college acquaintances, some old law-school contemporaries. Swiftly, with amazing speed old lines of communication were established between himself and the world to which he belonged. The impression he made upon Milhampton was distinctly favorable.

One day Mrs. Palmer invited Stephen and his wife to dinner. Others invited Stephen and his wife to dinner. Stephen became very anxious to feel pride in Stella, now that he had begun to feel pride again in himself. Stella became very anxious that he should feel pride in her. To appear the lady Stephen's wife should have been born became Stella's greatest ambition. On the first few occasions when she appeared with Stephen before the footlights of the social life in Milhampton—a stage she had gazed upon with longing eyes for years—she would do nothing, say nothing, almost think nothing, until it was first approved by Stephen. At first she invited his criticism, responded with eagerness to his constant drilling and grilling, welcomed his slightest suggestion. Of course she made progress. She was a clever mimic. At first Stephen had great hopes for Stella.

4

But success went to Stella's head like wine, even a small amount of success. Stella never became the belle she thought she did in Milhampton society, but she was, for a period, received and accepted by certain of its high prelates and officials, for Stephen's sake. It puffed her all up; it filled her with disastrous self-confidence. Within a period of a few weeks the limelight of recognition made of the soft, pliable clay Stella had been in Stephen's hands, something hard and brittle that would fly to pieces at his slightest touch.

Stella's first dance at the River Club was a bitter occasion for Stephen. She, a stranger, an invited guest of Mrs. Palmer's, had allowed one man to dance with her for the entire last half of the evening. Afterwards in their bedroom, when Stephen spoke to her about it, to his amazement she laughed and scoffed.

"Oh, gracious, Stephen, don't think you can give me pointers on how to treat a man at a dance! There are some things *I* know more about than *you*, my dear."

It was when Stella began to think that there were some things she knew more than Stephen, and to act upon that superior knowledge, that the seed of the trouble that ended so disastrously for her first began to grow.

"But, Stella, for *you*, a stranger, to dance so much with one man is conspicuous."

"Of course! Of course, it's conspicuous," Stella replied. "Oh, *I* know what I'm about, stupid! That man was Spencer Chisholm! Gracious, think of it! *The* Chisholms, Stephen! Think of it! An affair between *me* and Spencer Chisholm!" Her eyes sparkled.

Stephen turned away. It was going to be as difficult to stamp out Stella's vulgarity as to rid a lawn of the persistent dandelion once it gets its roots down. Stephen despised kowtowing.

"*The* Chisholms! My dear Stella, I hope you'll avoid that attitude toward people hereafter. You're my wife now."

"And can't look at another man?" she flashed.

"That isn't the point."

"Mercy," she went right on, "I can't help it if a man wants to dance with me. I should think you'd be pleased to have your wife popular. Most men would be. Most men—"

"I'm not pleased to have you talked about. Please don't give any one occasion to again, Stella."

"Good Lord, Stephen, you're not going to turn out to be the jealous kind, I hope, if another man *looks* at me."

Stephen winced.

"I hate a jealous man," she went on. "I always have!" And she threw down her comb upon the dressing-table. It screeched as it struck the plate-glass protection.

Stephen winced again. Throwing things! His wife! Accusing him of jealousy! Very quietly he went out into the hall, and stood a moment in the darkness, waiting till his jarred nerves stopped tingling.

"I must be patient," he thought. "It isn't her fault. It is only that she has been bred differently. She doesn't know."

5

There were many late-night discussions in the bedroom after that. Stephen hated wrangling, constant argument, constant controversy, but he was willing to endure much if he could prevent Stella from cheapening herself, and him, too, by promiscuous flirtations. But he couldn't. It was a futile attempt. It was as instinctive for Stella's eyes to brighten up, and for her manner to brighten up, too, when a man appeared who might admire her, as for a puppy's tail to wag when a possibly appreciative human being approaches. Stephen might as well have tried to discipline the puppy's tail as Stella's eyes and manner.

Stella's fondness for attention from men was not deep-seated. If her response had aroused any great depth of feeling or desire, red danger-flags would have appeared to warn her. As it was, her very innocence worked to her disadvantage. She could see no reason for not taking a little harmless fun as it came along, especially if it improved her social prospects. Because it was harmless she persisted in it, until Stephen's patience was worn out, and his pride and self-respect torn and tattered.

It was not only in regard to her relations with men that Stella turned deaf ears to Stephen. Under the head-turning effect of attentions paid her by such women as Phyllis Stearns and Myrtle Holland (Myrtle Holland took up Stella Dallas as a sort of fad that spring, her friends said) she came to consider all Stephen's ideas as old-fashioned, and out-of-date.

She could see nothing but advantage in forming alliances with such women as Phyllis and Myrtle. "They're in everything. They go everywhere." Nothing but distinction in entering into every activity and amusement that they suggested. "Gracious, how little men know how to get on in society." Stephen was harping morning, noon, and night, on the dangers of too intimate friendships, and too rapid progress. "If I followed your advice I wouldn't get anywhere. You'd make out of me just a prim, stupid, little stay-at-home. Myrtle says she'd just die if her husband tried to dictate to her the way you do to me."

" 'Myrtle says'! Oh, Stella, you don't talk over our affairs with your women friends, do you?"

"Oh, no! Of course not. We talk just about the weather!"

"But, Stella, surely your sense of good taste would prevent you from telling any one of our differences of opinion?"

"Our 'squabbles,' you mean? Oh, Stephen, a saint couldn't please you. Finding fault with the things I talk about with my girl friends! Honestly!"

"They'll only ridicule you afterwards. I don't like those women. I wish you'd avoid them. I don't think they're real friends of yours."

"That's right. Run them down. Have friends of your own, you lunch with and play cards with, and golf with, and have a regular good time with, but don't let *me* have anybody! Myrtle says some men are like that—jealous even of their wives' women friends. Oh, Stephen, why *will* you try to take the joy out of everything so? Why don't you let me have a little fun in life without all this argument? I get sick to death of it.''

"Oh, very well.''

"Yes, you say 'very well,' but you'll be at me again to-morrow. I don't find fault with *you*, do I?''

"No.''

"Well—?''

Stephen was silent.

"That's right, now get glum and sulky, and don't say anything to me but stiff formal things for a week. Oh, gracious!''

Stella could forget all about such a discussion as this by the following morning. "I'm blessed with a good disposition,'' she was fond of boasting. "Dad used to say it was almost impossible to worry me cross when I was a kid. Come on, Stephen, cheer up.''

If Stephen didn't, if he couldn't "cheer up,'' Stella would fling down her comb, or slam a door, and five minutes later be heard humming a song in her bath. Stephen suffered.

6

"Why did you ever marry me, Stella?'' once despairingly he inquired.

"Why, because I was crazy about you. I thought you were perfectly great.''

"How can a woman be crazy about a man—care for a man, and not be willing to adapt herself somewhat to him, to give up a few things for him?''

"How would it do for *you* to do a little of the adapting, Stephen, a little of the giving up? Why did you ever marry *me?*'' she retorted.

83

CHAPTER EIGHT

1

It was an ironic coincidence that the same cause that killed the last bit of struggling love Stephen had for Stella (if indeed love it had ever been) should also bind him to her more closely.

Suddenly in the midst of Stella's first year of social success in Milhampton, she found herself facing the dismaying possibility that she might soon become a mother. She didn't want to! Not now! It would be a terrible tragedy just when she was making such headway in Milhampton. It would wipe her off the social map for a whole year, or more! When the possibility became a certainty, it seemed to Stephen that all there was left sweet and fine in Stella disintegrated suddenly and completely into futile and unbeautiful protest.

She fought the frightening fact day after day, night after night, with violent attacks of crying, with uncontrolled fits of rage, self-pity, and despair, as if in frenzied resistance lay possible escape. Her one desire was to escape—somehow, *anyhow,* from the horrible trap that had snapped on her, and held her in its grasp.

She talked in a way during this time that made Stephen want to go into another room and close the door. He did, sometimes. Her complaints were worded in the parlance that came easiest to her tongue. She was in no mood *then* to pick words and choose phrases. All that Stephen held most sacred and precious about marriage went to pieces under the constant fire.

He took many long lonely walks into the open country around Milhampton that fall to escape from Stella, to get out of sight and sound of her and purify himself, if he could, under the open sky. His thoughts were bitter ones as he tramped and tramped. It seemed as if life was determined to grind its heel upon him, and crush him. He didn't believe in fate; he didn't believe ill-fortune or good-fortune was planned and sent to helpless victims. He believed staunchly in the unchanging law of causation. But oh, it did make a man wish there was some other reason than his own fault, for disaster following him, wherever he went, whatever he did. It had been in an attempt to escape the horror of his father's last act that he had come to Milhampton. And now the horror of finding himself married to a woman he did not love, had never loved (it was to get away from Mrs. Bean's boarding-house that he had married) was his to bear. He wished he might go back to Mrs. Bean's boarding-house. There are some kinds of unloveliness more difficult to endure than mere dirt and grime. The apartment was no longer a refuge.

Stephen made no effort to reason with Stella. In the beginning he told her briefly, sternly, that she must accept the fact of the coming child, unwelcome as it was to her (unwelcome as it was, therefore, to him). They must both accept it. There was no escape. Absolutely. Having delivered himself of this dictum, he treated her as kindly as he knew how, as he would a sick and unreasonable child—tolerated, indulged, and endured.

Stella's protestations quieted down. Her attacks of crying and abandonment to despair grew less violent, less frequent. They disappeared completely after a month or so. That was nature's way. Stephen knew that no emotion can continue long in intensity, in the consciousness of a human being. It runs a course, like a disease. Mercifully. Recuperation begins its gentle work, once facts are comprehended and accepted. Stephen expected that in time Stella would acquiesce and submit to "her inevitable." But he did not expect her acquiescence and submission to become interest and delight.

One evening in January she showed Stephen a little dress she had been working on in secret, daytimes, when he was absent, she explained. As she held it up by the arms for him to see, she gurgled with amusement and pleased satisfaction.

"Isn't 'he' cute?" she laughed delightedly.

Stephen stared at the little dress, amazed. Why, six weeks ago Stella had declared she wouldn't take a stitch for the baby! He couldn't refrain from reminding her of that.

"Well, what of it?" she shrugged. "I said all sorts of things then, in the beginning, when I was scared, I suppose. Oh, Stephen," she laughed good-naturedly, "you don't know beans about women. Why, I'm getting quite crazy about the baby *now!*"

Stephen looked at her sharply. Did the maternal instinct come alive suddenly in some women, like that?

"Really?"

"Certainly," she assured him lightly. "Of course it will tie me down, terribly, for a while, but Myrtle says" (she was constantly quoting Myrtle to Stephen), "Myrtle says I'd be awfully out of things in the long run, if I didn't *ever* have a child. All the young married set talk babies—at least the women; and, after all, it *is* sort of fun to dress the cunning little things up, and send them out rolling, with a nurse-girl. Myrtle has got a baby. She dresses her in darling things, and Phyllis" (Phyllis was often quoted to Stephen, too) "told me something is going to happen to *her* next summer. I'm really quite in the swim."

Stephen turned away, no longer dismayed. Only a little more disillusioned.

2

Laurel was born in June. Stephen named her Laurel—at least it was the name he applied to her the first time he saw her. He had come across some clumps of mountain-laurel in bud a day or two before, when out on one of his long tramps. The buds were clusters of sticky little spurs of deep pink and red. The first morning the trained nurse brought Laurel to Stephen for inspection, the baby was wrapped up in layers upon layers of flannel. Only the tip of her little pink head was showing.

"Hello, you little mountain-laurel bud," Stephen had said to her, at a loss to know what to say.

He never would have called her a laurel-bud again. It was the nurse who insisted upon the term. Every morning when she took the baby to Stephen for inspection (a ceremony she never failed to perform), she remarked, "Here's your little mountain-laurel bud, Mr. Dallas!"

Laurel's real name was Hildegarde—it was as Hildegarde that she was enrolled on the city's records—but she was never called anything but Laurel and "Lollie," and sometimes "Lolliepops." Myrtle Holland had suggested Hildegarde to Stella. It was a name that had style and distinction, she had said. Stella fully intended to adopt it as soon as Lollie was old enough to go to school. But by the time Lollie was old enough to go to school, she had ideas of her own upon the subject: She didn't like Hildegarde.

"It's big and ugly, and has corners," she announced.

3

During the first few weeks of Laurel's existence Stella gloried much more in the pleasing curves her own figure assumed than in the exquisite beauty of Laurel's perfect body. Oh, yes, it was a cute little thing, she acknowledged, but she had wanted a boy—always preferred the opposite sex. She nursed the baby for a week or two, but she warned the doctor, with a gay little nod of her head, she wasn't going to be "a cow" once she got up. How Stephen had cringed when she referred to herself as "a cow." Honestly it was funny how the English language could hurt Stephen.

Laurel was barely five weeks old when Stella donned an evening gown—("Look at me, Stephen," she had exclaimed delightedly; "I'm a perfect sylph.")—and went to an evening dance.

She didn't look pale and tired and wistful, the way most mothers of young babies looked, and go home early. "See," her bright cheeks announced, her ecstatic manner proclaimed, "it hasn't made any difference. I can dance just as well, I can flirt just as well!" She and her partner had been one of the half-dozen couples still dancing on the ballroom floor to the music of a solitary piano at 3 A.M., when the janitor began turning off the lights. Stephen, waiting patiently below, outside the ladies' dressing-room, had been the parent who was wondering—and wondering bitterly too—if the baby had slept through.

Stella returned to the arena of her ambitions with a determination to make up for lost time as quickly and as emphatically as possible. And Stephen returned to the valley of shame and humiliation. During this period the cloak he wore to cover the shivering nakedness of his mortification concealed at the same time much of his natural *camaraderie*. It was impossible for him to participate in mild hilarities of whatever kind, in Milhampton, under the constant ban of his relationship to one whose hilarity was so often overdone. He became extremely subdued in manner, reserved, short of speech, disinclined to respond to friendly approaches. Some people in Milhampton called him glum and ill-humored.

Outside Milhampton, however, there was nothing glum and ill-humored about Stephen Dallas. In another city he met amiability more than half way. His old charm, of which he possessed no small amount, returned to him shining and bright the minute that he escaped his relationship to Stella. He bore himself with more confidence and effective self-esteem with business associates, too, who were far enough removed from Milhampton to know nothing of his home life. Every week's or two weeks' absence from Stella became oases of refreshment to Stephen. Mr. Palmer, accompanying Stephen on one of his business trips, had witnessed the metamorphosis, and he opened up as many business opportunities out of town for his protégé, as possible. Stephen's reputation for ability in the law spread.

The year Laurel began going to school, a New York law firm asked Stephen to become one of its members. Mr. Palmer advised Stephen to accept the invitation. It would mean, of course, a loss to *him*, not only a business loss but a personal loss too. Stephen had come to seem to him almost like a son. "But go," he said, "go. It's your big chance, my boy. Go."

It happened that, during the time that Stephen had the New York proposition under consideration, Stella was carrying on a rather more obvious flirtation than usual with a man of a very offensive personality to Stephen. Stephen had told Stella how distasteful this particular man was to him; but Stella had paid no heed to his objections. Stephen was always objecting.

The man's name was Alfred Munn. He was a stranger in Milhampton. There had sprung up in Milhampton an interest in horseback riding the preceding summer. The River Club had filled its stables with a dozen or more Kentucky thoroughbreds obtained from a Southern hostelry. They were somewhat worn-out animals for the most part, but they were safe and steady for beginners, much safer and steadier in fact than their owner—or keeper. (It was never definitely known which Alfred Munn was.)

Alfred Munn became almost as much of a craze at the River Club as the sport he taught. It was difficult to get an hour's instruction from him, if you hadn't engaged it weeks in advance. He was busy every day from six in the morning till six at night, instructing women and children mostly. Certain women of the younger married set began paying Alfred Munn ridiculous attention. It was discovered that it was not only on the back of a horse that he was skillful, and the epitome of grace and rhythm; he could also excel on the ballroom floor. One of the younger married women, bolder than her sisters, invited him to a River Club dance. He was soon attending all the River Club dances. He was taken up by a certain set of women in Milhampton like some new exotic food.

In spite of the report that he belonged to an aristocratic Southern family of reduced financial circumstances, most of the women who paid him attention were aware of his lack of breeding. They were simply amusing themselves. But Stella couldn't see why Alfred Munn wasn't a gentleman, she told Stephen. Other women like Edith and Rosamond (it was Edith and Rosamond *then,* instead of Myrtle and Phyllis) didn't seem to find anything so horribly objectionable about him. Why in the world should Stephen expect *her* to be so particular!

Stephen used to find Alfred Munn sitting with Stella over a kettle and tea-cups, in the living-room, when he came home in the late afternoon. Stephen and Stella had moved from the apartment by then, and were living in a detached house with a lawn and garden.

Afternoon tea was an effort and affectation with most of the young married women in Milhampton, in those days. It was served on low tabourettes, before open fires, in overheated and underlighted living-rooms. It was the Milhampton custom, at that time, for the hostess to dangle a perforated silver ball, filled with tea-leaves in individual cups of hot water, and to inquire, while dangling, as to the cream and lemon and sugar. When Stephen found Stella coquettishly dangling her silver ball for Alfred Munn, as he sat comfortably ensconced in one of the big Dallas arm-chairs, it was more than irritation he felt. It was disgust.

Why, the man left his teaspoon in his cup! He had the habit of drawing air through the spaces between his teeth after eating! And Stella could endure him! When he was not disguised in his riding-clothes, his coarse-ness was obvious in such details as shirts and waistcoats. He wore conspicuous jewelry too! On his little finger there appeared usually a huge gold ring with red, white, and blue stones in it. Occasionally he wore a gold scarf-pin representing Psyche asleep in a crescent moon. He was that sort of man. Sometimes Stephen found Alfred Munn smok-ing his cigarettes, handling his precious books. Sometimes he found him fondling Laurel! Laurel didn't seem to object to it. Why should she?—Stephen asked bitterly. Stella was her mother.

4

The reason Laurel didn't seem to object to Alfred Munn's fondling her was for the sake of a marvelous watch he carried. He used to show it to her if she would come and sit in his lap. Laurel never forgot the wonders of that watch. When she grew up she thought of them whenever she thought of Alfred Munn.

It was a gold watch, big and heavy, and very thick. There was a horse's head engraved on the back of it with a diamond eye that twinkled. His bridle was studded with tiny red stones.

Beneath the horse's head on the inside of the back cover (which Mr. Munn had to pry open with his thick thumb-nail) was a picture of another horse. It was a pure white horse with a lady in short skirts standing on tiptoes on his back!

Underneath the white horse, way, *way* inside, next to the little gold wheels and blue screw-heads, was another picture. It was a colored picture. It was a picture of a lady with long hair. She had no clothes on at all!

5

One day (and it was that day Stephen had decided to go to New York) he had come upon Stella and Alfred Munn in the corridor of the Milhampton City Club. They had been having lunch there in the ladies' dining-room.

The City Club was strictly a man's club. There was a ladies' dining-room, to be sure, but women did not make a practice of lunching there without an escort who was a member. This club had been the one place outside his office where Stephen had felt safe from Stella in Milhampton.

Stephen wasn't alone when he met Stella and Alfred Munn. There was a lawyer from Boston with him, an older man with whom he had been conferring all the morning; and upon whom he was anxious to make just the right impression. Stella had greeted Stephen with enthusiasm when she met him, and he had had to introduce the Boston lawyer to her, to present her impossible escort to him as well.

It was with a sinking heart that Stephen noticed that Stella had probably ordered something in the way of liquor to go with the luncheon she had just been enjoying with Munn. She was particularly vivacious. Stella never drank enough of anything to lose her self-control, but she did like getting her tongue unloosened, once in a while, she said, and her "flirting spirit up." Her "flirting spirit was up" now, Stephen observed. She made an arch attempt to flirt with the Boston lawyer, as she gave him her hand!

Stephen could feel himself grow red with mortification. He hastened the meeting to as speedy an end as possible, but brief as it was, it unpoised him, sapped him of all assurance and self-confidence. He didn't want to look the Boston lawyer in the eyes after the meeting with Stella and Munn.

That night he wrote to the New York law firm and definitely accepted their proposition. Stephen was in a mood to accept any proposition which offered him relief from Stella.

CHAPTER NINE

1

It was only temporary relief he contemplated, then. It was his intention, when he first went to New York, to establish Stella somewhere, sometime, within commuting distance of his business. Not within too easy commuting distance, however. "In New York a man's business-life and his home-life," Mr. Palmer had once said to Stephen, avoiding his eyes as he did so, "can be made two distinct and separate affairs, which is difficult to accomplish in a place the size of Milhampton."

When Stephen first went to New York, he consulted several real-estate agents, and listened to many confusing arguments, about the desirability of this suburb over that, its commuting advantages, its unexcelled schools, its unusually "nice" set of young people. Stephen fully expected that Stella would join him in the spring in some suburb or other best suited to her peculiar susceptibilities. Or if not in the spring, in the summer. It would be unwise, he concluded, to take Laurel out of school until the end of the year. Laurel had just started in at Miss Fillibrown's in Milhampton, an excellent school for little girls. Stephen had no idea of leaving Stella permanently when he first went to New York.

But until he went to New York, Stephen had no idea what release from Stella would mean to him. He had no idea what possibilities for success, what resources for enjoyment, had been growing in the dark within him, unencouraged, all these years. He went out among people very little the first winter, but he was able to devote himself to work as never before. When he did seek recreation, the freedom to follow whatever whim or fancy his nature dictated was actually exhilarating.

Between October, when he first went to New York, and the New Year, Stephen spent three Sundays with Stella. Each one was an ordeal to him, and each one a more difficult ordeal than the one before. The long period of absence tended to make him more sensitive to Stella's offenses, he supposed. It seemed to him as if she almost delighted in doing the sort of things he disliked over those week-ends; indulging in all the striking slang of the day; indulging in all the striking styles of the day (she knew how he disliked her in conspicuous clothes); carrying on long giggling conversations over the telephone with "one of the girls," gossiping, tale-bearing; carrying on long giggling flirtations over the telephone with one of her male admirers, going through a series of smiles and smirks, shrugs and arch expressions, as if the man himself were present to see her, ignoring Stephen behind his book at the other end of the room as if he were a plant or piece of furniture; dashing off for her riding-lesson at ten o'clock Sunday morning with Alfred Munn, while Stephen read the paper or went to church or took a walk by himself. Going back on the train after his third week-end with Stella, Stephen asked himself why he persisted in these self-inflicted periods of torture.

To what end? To what purpose? The idea of separation or divorce had always been distasteful to him, but some things were worse—a thousand times worse, after love had turned to contempt, and respect to scorn. Of course there was Laurel. But wasn't it better for Laurel not to grow up beneath the shadow of constant chafing and irritation? He could see Laurel. She could come to New York occasionally. He could have his child alone.

On a certain week-end in January, which Stephen forced himself to spend in Milhampton, he had found upon his arrival some cigarette ashes in a tray upstairs in the little sitting-room off Stella's bedroom. Stella didn't smoke. At that time few of the women in Milhampton smoked. Stephen didn't refer to the cigarette ashes to Stella. He was too listless, too desireless to care who had left the ashes there. He didn't doubt Stella's fidelity. Not then. It was just another offense in taste. She'd be sure to argue, to harangue, to acclaim in a tone, that would

Laurel could come to New York occasionally. He could have his child alone.

become loud and harsh, that she could see no difference between a man's smoking *upstairs* and *down*. And the pity of it was she couldn't see the difference.

A month slipped by. Two months. Stephen wrote only the briefest notes to Stella and they were far between. Oh, how easy it was to drift out of the troubled waters! What a comfort and relief!

2

At first Stephen's periods of absence were a comfort and relief to Stella, too. It was simply wonderful, she told Effie McDavitt, to go about unhampered, when, where, how, and with whom she pleased, and have a little harmless fun in life, without being preached to for hours afterwards. It didn't seriously occur to Stella that Stephen's absences portended anything permanent. When Effie suggested such a possibility, she "pooh-poohed" the idea.

"Oh, goodness, no," she said. "It would just about kill Stephen if his domestic affairs got aired in the newspapers. I know Stephen. I never could even mention divorce, or separation, in our squabbles, even as a joke, without his sort of turning away, as if I'd said something indecent. No. We'll stick—you'll see."

In early March, Stella wrote to Stephen and asked him when he expected to come home next. She'd like to know so as to be there. There was a good deal going on and Rosamond was planning a house-party out at her country place, over some week-end soon.

Stella was unprepared for Stephen's reply. He told her that he had no definite plan as to when he was coming to Milhampton next. She was not to worry about expenses, the letter went on significantly. He would see that she and Laurel were always provided for. Had he known in January that he was not coming back again for so long a while, he would have told her. But after all they had already had their discussions.

"Isn't that the coolest?" Stella exclaimed to Effie. She made frequent trips across the river to Effie's tenement now. She always made frequent trips across the river to Effie's tenement when she had "something on her mind."

"You'd think we'd had a row or something, the last time he was here, but we didn't. In fact, it seemed to me, if anything, he was a little more friendly than usual. I can't imagine what he's got up his sleeve. I think he had a right to kick up a little dust, don't you? Puts me in a pretty position! It wasn't bad, for a while playing around alone, and calling myself a grass-widow, as a joke. But the real thing is an entirely different matter. It's no fun being an extra woman of *any* kind for long, in society. If you don't own a husband, or a brother, or some two-legged article in trousers, you drop out of things—out of *evening* things, anyhow. Of course, there are luncheons, and teas, and women's shindies left, but I get on best with men, and I look best in evening clothes, too. I'm the kind, anyhow, who wants to take in *everything* that's going. The more places you're seen at the more you go to, and it's just *life* to me to keep going! Why, when I don't go out for a week— have a wave and a manicure and a hot bath and get all dressed up in my best clothes, and set out for a real little party of some sort some-wheres—I get horribly depressed. Listen here, Effie, I haven't eaten a dinner outside my own house for three weeks now! I haven't been to a River Club dance since Alfred Munn took the horses South in December! I've known for quite a while it was time for Stephen to come back and get Laurel and me."

Effie wanted to know why Stella didn't write to him, and urge him to come back and get her then.

"Urge him to come back!" Stella exclaimed. "Indeed, I won't! I've got a little pride left, I hope. I never urged a man to come back to me yet, and I don't intend to begin. Oh, I'll manage somehow. Don't worry. You'll see."

She herself worried a good deal. What was she to say? She couldn't go on indefinitely, telling people that Stephen had arrived so late on a Saturday and been obliged to go back so early Sunday, that he hadn't seen any of his friends. Nor could she repeat many times the subterfuge she had successfully carried through once, of stealing across the river, and burying herself for three or four miserable days in the little red cottage with her father, returning with the story that she had been in New York.

It had been necessary to practice involving deceptions in explaining her absence from such generally discussed functions as the River Club costume dance, and the Annual Charity Ball. Once she had pretended a turned ankle, another time a headache. But the truth was that on both these occasions she had stayed at home and had gone to bed at ten o'clock, because no one had invited her to a dinner-party beforehand. She couldn't go to a dance without either a man or a party!

She had tried to get up a party of her own before the ball. But everybody's plans seemed to be made. Rosamond might easily have included her in the dinner-party she gave. She had two extra men. Neither Edith nor Rosamond had had her to a single dinner-party since Stephen had gone to New York! And they were her "best friends" in Milhampton now. She had had *them* one night, with two other couples. A real party! Ten in all. She had given them two cocktails apiece and a generous amount of Stephen's champagne. Not one of her guests had reciprocated yet by an invitation of any kind.

The possibility of an empty engagement calendar, the consideration of long stretches of idle days with no climaxes at their ends, filled Stella with alarm. Frightening ghosts of various kinds filtered through the cracks of Stella's bedroom, during this time, woke her up every morning about five, and kept her awake until it was time to get up and dress. The tragic idleness of a certain new gown she had bought in January haunted her day and night. Never had a new dress of hers remained new so long. For three weeks it had hung in the closet, just as it had been lifted from its box. Stella longed to wear the gown. It would make an impression. Now that she could no longer contribute a man to society it was necessary for her to contribute at least an impression. A conspicuous gown could do a lot for a woman at a dance, Stella believed.

"But it can't if it hangs in the closet," she sobbed into her pillow.

When Alfred Munn returned from Florida with his horses for another season at the River Club, he put many of Stella's ghosts to flight. He filled her engagement calendar; he provided climaxes to her days; he saw to it that there was never a week when Stella didn't dress up in her best clothes and set out for "a real little party" of some sort somewhere. He broke the back of the worst goblin of all—her fear (her almost conviction now) that when a woman's husband goes out of town for any length of time and people begin to wonder why, all her old admirers turn tail and run, too, to avoid any possible danger of being mentioned in a scandal. Life wouldn't be worth living, Stella felt, if she had no admirers.

Riding was still popular in Milhampton that spring; Alfred Munn was still popular. Stella grasped at his attentions eagerly, instinctively, as she would at a rope flung to her from the basket of a balloon that offered to rescue her from some unfortunate fate and carry her aloft. But the balloon of Alfred Munn's popularity in Milhampton had already begun to lose its buoyancy. It couldn't carry Stella far. Alfred Munn should have been throwing off ballast instead of taking more on. For a while, though, it lifted Stella out of the valley, and diverted her attention from its shadows. Under the excitement of Alfred Munn's attentions, Stella took heart.

Alfred Munn invited her to every dance there was at the River Club that spring. People began to talk. Women, she told Effie, began to envy. She knew of at least a dozen who would give their eye-teeth if Alfred Munn would ask them to dance with him. He already was as good as a professional. He had asked her to be his partner in one of the new fancy dances last Saturday night. They had been the only two on the floor. Everybody else had sat around and stared, and applauded afterwards! Oh, she was really managing to make quite a splash in Milhampton with Alfred Munn. At the Luncheon Club she belonged to, "the girls" had discussed little else last Friday. Rosamond was simply green with jealousy. Stella could tell she was, because she acted so cool and offish. Lots of people were "jollying" her about him. She got it from all sides. Even that nice old tabby-cat, Mrs. Palmer, had heard the talk. She had stopped her, on the street, one day, and given her a little motherly advice. Too bad nobody ever invited Ed to dinner, or to anything small or private. He would be so much more useful. She couldn't see why they didn't. But never mind, he was convenient just as he was, and oh, *awfully* kind! She was getting a little tired of him, she must confess. But then, she always did, when "the new" wore off, and "they got a little slushy."

Effie wondered if there wasn't danger of Stephen's hearing about the splash Stella was making in Milhampton with Alfred Munn.

"Why, of course," Stella exclaimed to that. "I *want* him to hear about it. I don't intend to give Stephen the satisfaction of thinking I had to go into seclusion the minute he cleared out. He had an idea I couldn't get along in this town without his telling me how to do it. He meant to use his importance to my position here as a kind of gun to point at me and make me do just as he wants, when we get together again. Good gracious, having a good time, being successful all by myself, is the only gun I've got to point at *him,* my dear."

But Stella was inexperienced in the use of fire-arms. Her gun exploded when she didn't expect it to. And she herself became the victim.

4

It's possible to receive a bullet wound, even a fatal bullet wound, and be unaware of it, until you put your hand to the spot where it tingles a little. You're surprised when your fingers come into contact with something warm and wet. You're shocked when you draw them away, and find them red! Laurel was the messenger who brought the first sign of red to Stella's horrified attention.

Stella sent out a dozen invitations to a party for Laurel in June. All Laurel's schoolmates were having parties this year. Stella intended that Laurel's party should surpass them all. There was going to be a tailess donkey, and a peanut-hunt, and a cobweb contest, and a Jack Horner pie, and creamed chicken, and ice-cream, and paper caps.

CHAPTER TEN

1

It was several weeks before Stella knew how serious her bullet wound was. She was calm by that time. She could talk over its details with Effie McDavitt with perfect composure and with a touch of brusque humor, too.

"Why," she said, "Ed bores me. He never gave me a thrill in his life. Oh, Milhampton makes me sick! Narrow-minded, evil-minded, nasty-minded, I think. I'll tell you just how it was. I was down there in Boston, for two days, shopping, getting favors and things for Lollie's party. Naturally, when Ed suggested that he run down and take me to the theater in the evening, I was pleased to pieces. Wouldn't you be? I love the theater in Boston. We didn't stay at the same hotel, though for the life of me I don't see why we shouldn't. There were a hundred or so other men staying there. Glory, how I hate all this winking and shoulder-shrugging stuff about hotels and bedrooms! When Ed suggested, after the theater, that he drop around and have breakfast with me, why, I said, 'Sure, Mike,' quick as a wink. It never entered my head but what that was all right. I didn't care if somebody from Milhampton *did* see me. Married woman like me! Breakfast! Right in a public dining-room! What's there so horrible about that, I'd like to know! I didn't want anything of Ed but a little fun, and a little advertising. When Stephen wrote to me in that iceberg-y way of his, and asked if I would like my freedom so as to be able to marry Alfred Munn, I could have screamed! Marry Ed? Why, I'd commit suicide first. I don't want to marry Ed! Hasn't *anybody any* understanding of

Laurel had been told all about the elaborate plan
select the invitation-cards with the pretty colored pic
and the thrilling announcement underneath, "I am
party." She had stood close beside her mother when
had been filled in. She had watched the addressing of
little pink envelopes. Afterwards, standing on tiptoes,
them, one by one, into the green box at the corner.

Laurel mailed the invitations on a Friday night. All
Sunday she was full of the exhilarating consciousness
sharing the wonderful secret now. When she started to
day there was a sparkle beneath the calm gray surface
made them look almost black—like the pools of me
mid-morning sunshine. When Laurel came home at
seemed to have faded like the pools when the sun is
clouds. Instead of the blackness and the sparkle there
wondering, bewildered look in them.

"Nobody can come to my party, mother," she annou

All day Sunday the mothers of the recipients of the p
had been busy at the telephone.

Twice Laurel had to tell her mother that nobody could
party before Stella grasped the significance of the announc
fiercely she threw her arms about Laurel, and held her to

"We don't care. We don't care!" she burst out. "L
away! We'll have our party by ourselves! Don't you mind, I
have the party just the same—you and I and Uncle Ed N
Just because father runs off and leaves us all alone! Well–
each other, Lollie, anyhow. *I* won't ever run off and leave
oh, Lollie, *you* won't ever run off and leave *me,* will you—ev
Stella was crying now.

Laurel did not cry. She stood very still, and listened, and
remembered.

the human animal? A woman can have other reasons for liking a little attention than just the one the shady stories are all based on. I'm no worn-out old man whose appetite for everything but just indecency has gone dead. I like a little dinner and theater-party just for *fun's* sake. Honestly, Effie, sometimes I think I'm the only one who's got a clean mind in this town."

Stella took rooms, for the season, at a fashionable hotel on the coast of Maine that summer. She had never spent a summer at a hotel. It might prove diverting. She certainly needed something diverting, she thought. But whatever it proved, the arrow of direction pointed her out of Milhampton for a while.

"I'll give the mud-slingers in this town a rest for a month or two," she said to Effie. "By the end of the summer perhaps their muck will have all dried up. Of course, it would be rather nice if I could fall into some harmless, but showy 'little affair' this summer, with some attractive gentleman or other, up there at that fashionable hotel. That would prove there wasn't anything serious in this Alfred Munn business. It would be rather nice, too, if some of the cats in this town could hear that I was having a wonderful time this summer—being taken right into all sorts of inner circles, and select groups. Oh, there are lots of possibilities in this summer hotel scheme of mine, Effie, my dear."

Stella equipped Laurel with a dozen new frocks, replenished her own wardrobe, and, stout-heartedly, set forth to new fields and untried country, in search of fresh laurels with which to cover up the dried and dead ones.

That was the beginning of her summer hotel era. In the fall, not even Effie was told, in detail, of the disheartening experiences of the first experiment.

"You can drill forever for oil in some places, but unless oil is there, it won't do you any good," was how Stella briefly summed it up. "Next summer, I'll try the Cape—or the mountains possibly."

Stella didn't go back to the detached house when she returned from Maine. Instead she took two-rooms-and-a-bath in an apartment hotel that had lately been built in a residential section of Milhampton.

The apartment hotel offered her more companionship than the detached house. There would at least be the necessity of getting out of a kimono when you went down to meals. Besides, she could have people to dinner more safely. The invaluable Hedwig, whom Stephen had engaged six years ago, and taught and trained, had left to be married. Stella was afraid to trust a new servant with all the hard-and-fast rules. In an apartment hotel, all you had to do, if anything went wrong, was to shrug and say, "Oh, dear, isn't the service in this place dreadful?"

Moreover, there were social advantages. The King Arthur (that was the name of the new apartment hotel) was to be patronized by what Stella called "the right people." She needed all the advantages that she could get from close proximity to the right people.

Stella was determined not to let her injury of the preceding spring incapacitate her. It isn't always necessary for a man to go to bed and stay there even if there is a bullet embedded in him somewhere. Stella wasn't going to become a social invalid just because she'd been unfortunate and the target of a little disagreeable gossip.

Alfred Munn had left Milhampton by the time Stella and Laurel returned from Maine. He had gone into another business in another city. Somebody else had taken over the horses. In time people would forget about Ed. Bullet wounds heal. Scars can be covered up. Of course it was a handicap not to have a husband if he was still in the land of the living; at least it was a handicap in Milhampton, Massachusetts. In California single married women were as plentiful as sunshine, and as welcome, Stella had heard—Oh, she did wish it had been in some place in California that she and Stephen had happened to put down their roots. But it couldn't be helped. It was only common sense, of course, to keep on growing in the same place where they'd started. Stella appreciated her own limitations to the extent of realizing that it would be difficult, even in California, to work her way up alone to anything like the position that she had attained with Stephen in Milhampton.

When Stephen's business took him to New York, Laurel was enrolled as a pupil in the exclusive school of the community. She attended the exclusive dancing-class, and she attended the exclusive Sunday-school. Stella belonged to a few helpful organizations herself. Her name was in the Blue Book. She had at least a bowing acquaintance with almost everybody "worth-while." She had lots of men friends. She believed she had quite a few women friends of value. There was, besides, Stephen's membership at the River Club, an asset indeed to her now, since she had no house of her own in which to entertain crowds, and pay back social debts.

It was a very unhappy day for Stella when she first learned that Stephen had resigned from all his Milhampton clubs. She thought it was the cruelest blow he could deal her. At that time Stella was mercifully unaware how many more cruel blows were to follow, not from Stephen alone, but from *everybody*—from *all* sides. They didn't come all at once. If they had, she must have been convinced of the futility of her effort, and given up her fight early.

Her defeat was gradual. She lost ground by degrees. Her various points of vantage and fortresses of strength fell slowly. This season she failed to received an announcement of the Current Events Class; next season, her name appeared to have been dropped from the Charity Ball list. The season after, the small Luncheon Club she belonged to was reorganized and she was omitted. Every year there were personal slights of various kinds, coolnesses, intentional inattentions from all quarters. Laughing—bitterly, too—she told herself that the people in Milhampton must be having some sort of chronic eye difficulty. So many old friends and acquaintances failed to recognize her, lately. But Stella didn't lose hope. She didn't, anyhow, *show* that she lost hope. She managed to keep her eyes bright, and her lips smiling, and her head erect, in spite of repeated rebukes.

"Why, I've got to. For Lollie's sake," she said. "Lollie mustn't know her mother has got anything to look sour-faced over. Oh, we'll be all right after a while—Lollie and me," she told Effie McDavitt. "We'll come out on top in the end. You watch us."

It was always "Lollie and me," always "we," and "us," by that time. Stella didn't even think in the singular number, once her maternal instinct had worked its way up through her vanities and self-interests and appeared in her consciousness. The seed of it must have been planted deep, for it took a period of years to appear. In vain Stephen had looked for it when Laurel was a baby; and later when she was in the helpless, toddling stage.

For the first half-dozen years of Laurel's life, Stella took her lightly. Not that she neglected her in any obvious way. She couldn't. There were certain manners and forms in the modern bringing-up of a child that had to be observed. She had an excellent nurse-girl for Lollie; she spent hours in the selection of Lollie's clothes; she had a Mother-Goose cretonne at Lollie's windows; a Noah's-Ark paper on Lollie's walls. There were low chairs, and low shelves. Stella loved to show Laurel's room to guests, when occasion arose. Laurel benefited by many an attention from Stella in those days that did not spring from the maternal instinct. However, the maternal instinct must have been growing underneath the surface, and growing according to Nature's own methods—sending down tough wiry roots in the dark, all the while it was sending up its tender arrow-pointed shaft of life, for when it did shoot through into light, the plant was strong and vigorous.

Perhaps the first time that Stella was aware of the new insistent force within her was the day Laurel came home from school with the news about the party.

"Gosh, Effie," she had said afterwards, "I don't care what people do to me, but to stick hatpins into Lollie—into *my baby!* Say, that's more than I can stand. I'm ready to use my claws on anybody who hurts Lollie."

During the years between Laurel's sixth birthday and her thirteenth there were many times for Stella to use her claws. There were many times that Laurel was hurt and Stella knew it. "Though the funny little kid doesn't think I do. She never lets on to me. I just have to guess at it from the way she acts."

If she came home from school especially quiet and uncommunicative, and was not very hungry at dinner, Stella would begin to be suspicious. "What's the matter?" she would demand with a piercing look.

"Nothing," Laurel would reply, feigned surprise and wonder in her voice.

"Has anything happened at school?"

"No."

"Who'd you play with at recess?"

"Nobody special."

"Did you play all alone?"

"No."

"Look here, Lollie. Answer me. Has somebody been horrid to you? Has somebody hurt your feelings?"

"No."

If Stella stared at her hard enough, probed long enough, Laurel might reply, "My stomach aches a little bit," and pay the price of two shredded wheat biscuits and no dessert for dinner.

It would never be from Laurel that Stella would get the first wind of a party in prospect from which Laurel was omitted. Laurel would never tell her that the girls in her class were meeting every few days at each other's houses to work for a fair, or to rehearse a play or fête in which she had no part. When information of an event of this sort did reach Stella, she knew then what had been the cause of Laurel's quiet, brown-study day a week ago. And yet she couldn't use her claws after all. It would be the worst policy in the world. For the sake of Lollie's future, for that dim, far-away, full-of-promise time when Lollie would "come out" (girls "came out," now, in Milhampton), she must be as nice and purry as she knew how to the women she knew who could help her daughter.

Laurel could see through her mother's little shams and deceits, devised to spare her pain, much quicker than Stella could see through Laurel's. At thirteen Laurel was an odd mixture of artificiality and truthfulness, of craft and naïveté, of grown-up woman and little girl. She could deceive her mother without flickering an eyelash, and could repeat to strangers the little white lies Stella taught her, with the finesse of a woman of the world, but at school in her work and play, she was never anything but strictly honest.

As experienced as Laurel was in certain of the world's cruelties, and as mature in her calm manner of acceptance of whatever befell, she was amazingly young and innocent about many of the facts of life. Another antithesis. Much younger and much more innocent than the group of sophisticated little girls in her class at school. They were constantly spending days and nights with each other. Their intimacies led to easy discussions of all sorts of subjects. By the time they were twelve their activities out of school were closely resembling their mothers'. And their conversations, too. There were already conflicting invitations for every Saturday. Laurel could catch bits of conversation, now and then, as the various competing parties and entertainments were reviewed afterwards, and their details discussed and criticized. Most of these girls became perceiving and canny little critics before they had finished playing dolls.

Laurel had no intimate friends, belonged in no group, joined in no daily gossipings. Her critical faculty went through no such course of training. She was still groping for the whys and wherefores of many of society's verdicts long after her dolls were put away. Why had she no intimate friends? Why was she never asked to lunch, or to spend the night? Why had she been dropped from the Widow's Mite Club which met Saturday mornings at Stephanie Holland's? The worldly-wise little girls at school could have told her.

"It's your mother."

"What's the matter with my mother?" she would have asked, surprised. Laurel thought her mother beautiful. The little girls would have shrugged and said, "Our mothers don't 'know her.'" With just the same shrug and inflection that had silenced them.

But Laurel never asked questions of the little girls. She passed through her childhood blindfolded, picking her way cautiously along, sensitive fingertips stretched out before her to avoid sharp corners and unyielding walls, clinging close to the protection of solitude and isolation.

There were other questions besides those connected with social values to which she didn't know the answers, big questions like, what becomes of dead people, and what God is like, and if He really hears you pray, and knows when a bird falls out of a nest, and where babies come from, and what doctors carry in their mysterious leather bags, and how kittens are born, and if there was ever actually a George Washington, and a Polyphemus, and a Jesus Christ, and a Noah, and a Noah's Ark, with a pair of every kind of animal there is in it, even a pair of mosquitoes, and why there had to be a pair.

Laurel never asked her mother questions about big things. She had discovered that her mother always changed the subject ever so quickly if she did. And once she had exclaimed, "Oh, my! Laurel, nice little girls don't talk about things of that sort!"

Until then Laurel had thought that perhaps she might ask her father. He liked talking about big things, about certain big things, that is— like beautiful music, and beautiful sunsets, and how wonderful nature is, and being honest and a good sportsman, and all that. But Laurel was shy with her father during the short periods she spent with him. She usually listened more than she talked. He always introduced the subject of their conversations. She'd sooner die in ignorance than to ask him a question that wasn't "nice."

CHAPTER ELEVEN

1

When Helen Morrison caught the timid, butterfly-like little creature that Laurel was at thirteen, in her soft deft hands, and cautiously lifted one scooped palm from over the other, as it were, and peered into the dark, domed chamber to see what sort of creature was there, her interest was instantly aroused. She had never seen a little-girl specimen of Laurel's sort—so composed and self-possessed in speech and manner, so at home in smart, up-to-date frocks, so skilled in smart, up-to-date sports, so familiar with smart, up-to-date beauty-shop secrets—but underneath like a child who has lived on an island, alone somewhere, untold and untaught.

"She's like a book I bought in Florence once," Helen Morrison told Stephen one day, after Laurel had been visiting her. "It's a beautifully bound book, in full leather, and hand-tooled, in old blue and gold. But its pages are blank. I bought it to write odd bits of poetry in. Yes. Laurel is a little like that—beautifully finished on the outside, but full of pages as white as snow that never have been written on."

2

On a small table beside Helen Morrison's bed there was a picture of a little girl whose pages also had never been written on. Often Helen Morrison would take the lovely little miniature of her dead child close to the strong light, and gaze at it hard and long, in a hungry attempt to recall how the soft cheek used to feel when she brushed her own against it, how the limp little body used to melt into her arms when she held it close.

It was a beautiful baby's face that smiled back at Helen from out of the ivory, but it was always a baby's face. That was the pity of it. What would she have looked like to-day? (Oh, never to know. Never to know!) What strength and confidence and beauty would that weak little body have attained? What strength and confidence and beauty would that spark of fine intelligence, shining so steadily in her baby's face, have kindled under constant caring and tending? What had they both lost—this little daughter and herself, in way of rare companionship and human love?

Sometimes as Helen gazed at the picture, it seemed that she caught a wistful expression in the eyes, as if, she sentimentalized, her little girl had become tired of waiting, waiting, waiting, so long to grow up. It hurt, even after years it hurt Helen Morrison, to feel the stab of her uselessness to this child who had so trusted her. Oh, if she could only do something to rescue her from that eternal loveliness of babyhood—give her back the gift of life again, even though it might hurt her sometimes, even as life had hurt her mother.

Helen Morrison had worshiped her gentle, flower-like little daughter. She had been more than just a precious baby to her. She had been a symbol, a manifestation, a gift from heaven. For years and years Helen Morrison had longed for something feminine of her own. She had never had anything feminine of her own. No sister, no mother. Her mother had died when she was born. Her father had never remarried. Helen had been brought up by nurses and governesses, under the strict régime of an elderly and masterful housekeeper.

Helen used to plan by the hour what she would do for a daughter if she ever had one of her own. Even before she thought seriously about marriage, she built air-castles about that little dream-girl of hers. She should have all the joys and delights which her own childhood had lacked. She should be surrounded, day and night, by feminine tenderness and comprehension. She should have a friend always waiting for her at home, to play with her, or to work with her, to walk and talk with her, or to love pretty clothes with her, or pity wounded bugs with her, or to hold hands with her when it "thundered and lightened." Later, when life itself seemed to "thunder and lighten" about her, there would still be somebody holding her hand, reassuring her, making facts lucid and clear, and truth beautiful. Helen had ideas about girls and what made for happiness in their lives. She would have filled the blank pages of her little daughter's book full of inspired and lovely things.

When that little girl was born, Helen Morrison had been married several years. She had already had two boys—fine sturdy specimens—but soldier-material, American business-man stuff. When a little girl, a little feminine creature of her own, was placed in the curve of Helen Morrison's arm, she could not speak for joy. It seemed as if a bit of heaven itself had slipped through the clouds. Her cup was full and brimming over. That precious relationship that she had lost so long ago, the day she was born when her mother died, had been given back to her again!

She spent two radiantly happy years with her daughter (Carol, she named her. It became the sweetest word in the English language to her), and then suddenly, with the arrow-like directness of a bolt of lightning from the skies, disease struck straight down into the holy of holies of her heart and killed her darling. By a mere accident the realization of her lifelong hope was broken into fragments—disintegrated into a thousand poignant little memories. Her little girl became a dream again, an ideal, a picture on ivory. "There were her boys." That is what people said in way of comfort. Yes, yes. Of course. Thank heaven she had her boys! But, oh, her boys must be made stalwart and bold, strong and tough-muscled. The image she would have modeled out of her bit of little-girl clay was to have been as graceful as poetry, as delicate as violin music, as perfect in detail, as fine and exquisite as an etching.

After Carol died, Helen Morrison offered her services to a certain charitable institution for working-girls in New York City. She was living in New York then. She had been living in New York ever since she married. She thought, perhaps, if something of the young and tender ideals she had had for Carol was given to other girls, then everything about her lovely baby would not remain in that state of undevelopment which hurt her so every time she looked at the miniature.

It was soon discovered at the working-girls' home that Mrs. Morrison possessed rare genius with girls. She knew just how to approach them—just how to talk with them. She could hold the attention of a whole roomful of factory hands reading poetry—Browning and Whitman—out loud to them, and telling them what it meant to her. She could interest a dozen lively little errand girls for an hour at a time, gathered around an ant-hill in operation, at the edge of one of her garden-paths at her summer place on Long Island. Frequently she had groups from the Home come out from the city during the summer, and spend a day with her in her garden, among the illuminating bugs and bees and flowers.

Helen Morrison usually talked with her working girls in groups. She seldom came in contact with the girls individually. That was probably why they failed to satisfy her, why they remained, always, simply a worthy charity dedicated to the memory of the little girl beside her bed. It wasn't until Laurel came to spend a week with Helen Morrison that she felt the same heart-string, which Carol had pulled so hard once long ago, gently touched again. It hurt a little at first—brought back the pain. But it also brought back a little timid thrill of the old joy and ecstasy.

There was something of the same pristine beauty about Laurel at thirteen as about her own child's crystallized innocence. There were areas in Laurel's soul, big white expanses, untouched by experience, unsullied by life. It was almost as if those parts of Laurel had disappeared into a picture also, when she, too, was just learning to walk alone.

Laurel was nearly the same age as Carol. She was dark like Carol. Graver than gay, like Carol. She wore the same sort of clothes Carol would have worn. She had slept at night, it occurred to Helen with a little twinge, in the same bed where Carol would have slept, sometimes, now her father was gone. Even her name was something like Carol's.

After Helen Morrison said good-bye to Laurel at the end of her first visit, wrapped her own coat about her, tucked her in beside her father in the automobile, and laughingly, playfully kissed her good-bye, she hurried away quickly to her own room and closed the door. Taking the miniature close to the light, she gazed at it till the slow tears ran down her cheeks.

CHAPTER TWELVE

1

At the same moment that Laurel, high up above the rumbling traffic of New York, was packing her trunk on the last day of her never-to-be-forgotten visit to her father (never to be forgotten because of the wonderful Mrs. Morrison), Stella several hundred miles away, was also packing a trunk.

There was no sound of traffic outside Stella's window, only the distant pound of the surf and a distant glimpse of a deserted board-walk. By the end of September there were only three or four people left at the boarding-house at Belcher's Beach. By the middle of September at least half of the amusement booths on the board-walk had been closed for the season.

Stella had remained until the literal eve of Laurel's return, because she had been very lucky this year, and had found a tenant for her rooms at the King Arthur for the month of September. Laurel could have her fur coat and wrist-watch, too, now! My, though, but Stella was glad her job was over! She did hate horrid places so, and horrid people, and run-down, second-rate boarding-house styles and customs—loud talk and loud laughter and loud women, and flies and dirt, and bathing-suits hanging out all the front windows to dry (that is, when the season was still on), and bathing-corsets, and bathing-garters. (''Honest, Effie, you'd think some people had had no bringing-up.'') And all sorts of queer questionable things going on at night—doors opening softly and closing—whispers—giggles. The walls were like paper. Lord, she'd be glad to get away from Belcher's Beach! Thank heaven, the four weeks were at an end.

To-night she'd be sleeping at the King Arthur! To-morrow night Lollie would be sleeping with her at the King Arthur! She hummed deep in her throat as she packed. Nothing gave Stella the blue doldrums like this month of Belcher's Beach. Nothing gave her the spring-song feeling like release from it.

This year Belcher's Beach hadn't been quite so bad as usual, though. At least it ought not to have been. Ed Munn had done his best to brighten it up. Funny, though, Stella would be about as glad to get away from Ed as from the boarding-house. What ailed her? Ed had been ever so generous. Every single Saturday since Laurel had been away, and *one* Sunday, he had planned some diverting form of entertainment. It must have cost him a pretty penny! Stella was filled with remorse that she couldn't work up any real excitement over Ed. He was paying for "all wool," and deserved it, not the imitation stuff she gave him. It was all pretense with her when she returned his various little signs and signals. How pitiful to be so old one isn't even tempted to flirt any more! How amazing to be so crazy about your own child that being crazy about a man loses all interest and excitement in comparison.

Sometimes, looking straight into Ed Munn's little red hippopotamus eyes, trying her utmost to pay for his expensive entertainment in the harmless coin that he liked best, the vision of Laurel would appear back there in the dark cavern behind her eyes, down there in the mysterious cave where her heart beat, like a sudden shaft of light. And the shaft of light would seem to be pointed like a sword, and pierce Stella. Her eyes would become suffused with sudden tears, and tenderness. Dear dear Lollie, with her big gray eyes and her dark hair, and sharp-pointed, little-girl shoulders breaking through the hair as it fell to her waist, over her slim white body when she slipped off her nightgown in the morning. Dear precious little Lollie! In a little while they would be together again! What a zigzagging thrill of joy the thought gave Stella! Good Lord, how she worshiped the kid!

Once, when Stella's eyes had become suddenly soft with the thought of Laurel, Ed Munn had mistaken the cause of her emotion, and grasped hold of her hand, of her arm, of as much of her as he could reach across the small table that divided them; and that sort of mouth-watery look which always turned Stella's pleasure in a man's attentions to disgust—if he persisted in it—came into his eyes.

It had been Stella's intention to keep up her masquerade with Ed Munn to the end of the month (she did admire a good sport), but, my goodness, she wasn't a Sarah Bernhardt. Ed got terribly insistent that day she let her mind trail off to Laurel. She simply had to come out with the truth.

"I'm sorry, Ed," she sighed, as she drew away her hand with a little jerk.

At that he simply imprisoned one of her feet under the table between two of his, and leaned towards her, his eyes still gobbling her up.

She drew away her foot, too, and perched it safely on the rung of her chair.

"Nothing doing, Ed," she shrugged.

"What's the matter?" he inquired. She hadn't shown squeamishness before. "What's got into you all of a sudden?"

"I guess it's age, Ed," she confessed, "and it isn't all of a sudden."

He merely laughed at that and tried to grasp her hand again. But she wouldn't let him. He frowned. Flushed a little.

"I don't wonder you're mad, Ed."

"I didn't say I was mad."

"But you aren't pleased, I guess. I know. Ed, listen. I don't blame you a bit. I'm disgusted myself with the way I act, with the way I feel, or the way I *don't* feel. But don't, please, think it's anything personal. There's no man living could get me really going now. It isn't your fault. It's Lollie's. It's that darned little Lollie's fault!" she brought out fiercely. "I'm no good for anything any more except to be her mother. I'm so crazy about Lollie that she uses up all the emotion I've got, so I'm just sort of dead ashes with everybody else in the world."

"You're alive enough for me."

But Stella was deaf to flattery now. "Ed," she exclaimed, "I simply worship Laurel!" And the expression that forced its way through the make-up on her face had something sublime about it. A tear splashed down her cheeks. "You see!" She shrugged and shamelessly began to wipe her eyes. "Oh, it makes me so mad!"

Ed Munn leaned over and patted her on the arm, big-brother fashion. "That's all right. That's all right."

Stella blew her nose. "I'm terribly sorry."

"You needn't be. I'm satisfied. I'm not asking you to get excited over me. I like a woman all the better for being fond of her own kid."

"Oh, Ed, you *are* nice!" She warmed towards him.

"In fact," he went on (he knew *now* what tack to pursue), "the few times I've seen the offspring I've thought to myself, what a peach of a kid she was."

"Oh, she's wonderful, Ed. I'd die without her!" And again the tears welled up in her eyes.

"Sure you would! Well, I've no intention of kidnaping her."

You see, as Stella told Effie McDavitt afterwards, she and Ed had a *perfect understanding*.

3

When Stella paid her bill of indebtedness to the proprietor of the boarding-house at Belcher's Beach, for allowing her to economize for a month on his property, it was with a feeling of triumph and with the comforting sense of a disagreeable job well done. There were those, however, who regarded Stella's sojourn in a different light. Stella was blissfully unaware that any one except Effie and Ed even knew of the sojourn, any one who had any connection with Milhampton.

As the train sped along towards that city, at the end of her ordeal, she was happy with the simple joy of release. She smiled and her heart sang, automatically almost, a little as a kitten purrs when it comes in out of the rain and sees the warm fire on the hearth. She had no premonition of the nest of bombs lying in her letter-box among the other letters and communications that had arrived too near the date of her return to be forwarded. Stella had not seen the automobile standing on the opposite side of the street from the boarding-house at Belcher's Beach the late Saturday night when Ed had brought her back and left her as usual at the foot of the stairs that led up to her room. She had not seen the same automobile the next morning on the Boulevard as she and Ed had started out for lunch in Boston.

The day after Myrtle Holland and Mrs. Kay Bird had seen Alfred Munn follow Stella Dallas into the boarding-house—but had not seen him come out—they had driven to Belcher's Beach again. Myrtle Holland was occupying a summer cottage, that year, thirty miles inland. She had never been to Belcher's Beach before. It was only because the chauffeur had lost the road that she happened to be driving through such a place at all. Myrtle Holland wanted to inspect Stella's boarding-house by daylight. She told Mrs. Kay Bird she wanted to point it out to her husband so he might look it up and see what sort of a place it was.

It chanced to be over the only week-end of Laurel's absence, when Ed Munn had both a Saturday and Sunday engagement with Stella, that Myrtle Holland and Mrs. Kay Bird made their two visits to Belcher's Beach. On the second visit they had been almost as excited as on their first. They had seen Ed Munn and Stella Dallas again! The pair were leaving the boarding-house this time! It was eleven in the morning! It looked pretty bad, didn't it?

It looked still worse when Mrs. Holland called at the fashionable hotel, where Mrs. Kay Bird had heard Stella Dallas was spending the season, and discovered that Mrs. Dallas hadn't been there for three weeks! And that her forwarding address was care of a Mrs. Effie McDavitt, in a very queer part of Milhampton, way down by the mills somewhere. Obviously Stella Dallas had done her best to cover up her tracks. Oh, wasn't it all too shocking for anything?

"Probably those two have been carrying on their little affair, off and on, ever since the scandal about them when her husband left her. I wouldn't believe then that she'd really gone the limit (I'm always slow at jumping to conclusions of that sort); but *now,* I do not see that we can very well help thinking the worst. My husband says that Belcher's Beach is full of questionable places. He didn't care to go into an investigation of that particular one, but you could see by looking at it—so dirty, and run-down, and ramshackle—and by observing the women who came out of it, what sort of a place it was. Stella Dallas herself looked a little more common and ordinary than ever—paint just piled on, and that riding-teacher—Munn—has degenerated terribly. Oh, it makes my blood boil to think that the mother of one of the girls, with whom our daughters associate daily at the little private school we're all supporting and protecting to the best of our ability, should be carrying on an affair of that sort with a man of that sort in a place of that sort. As one of the trustees of Miss Fillibrown's School there's only one course open to me. A thing like that cannot be known about a woman, and countenanced, can it?''

''Certainly not,'' was the general dictum.

''I for one won't countenance it anyhow,'' announced Mrs. Kay Bird, with emphasis. ''Either Mrs. Dallas moves out of the King Arthur or *I* do. I had to play bridge with her twice last winter!''

''And either her child is removed from Miss Fillibrown's or mine is,'' another voice proclaimed.

This conversation took place in Myrtle Holland's living-room a few days after her return to Milhampton, in late September. There were half a dozen women gathered around the tea-table.

''But,'' feebly observed one of them, ''there's just a possibility that you're mistaken, Myrtle, isn't there?''

''Oh, sweet protector of the innocent, virtuous defender of the maligned,'' laughed Mrs. Kay Bird.

''My dear Mabel,'' Myrtle replied, ''there's just a possibility a man who frequents corner saloons doesn't drink, but it's rather slight, I fear; and anyhow, whether he drinks or not, the fact that he enjoys the company and atmosphere of corner saloons is sufficient to bar him from certain drawing rooms. Dear me, Mabel, haven't we all endured Stella Dallas years enough in this town to satisfy you? I, for one, don't enjoy torturing animals even though some of them don't seem to mind it very

"Such a woman doesn't deserve to have a child."

much. That woman is in for a lot of disappointments when that child of hers she's always using, to boost herself into some sort of prominence, is older. The time has come, for her sake, as well as ours, to put an end to all further suffering."

"The child seems quite a nice little thing."

"But how long will she stay quite a nice little thing with a mother like that? Really, Mabel!"

"And nice little thing or not," spoke up somebody from the other side of the hearth, "I'm sure I don't want my son meeting her at dances, and things, as he grows up, and run the risk of having him fall in love with a girl with such a mother!"

"Oh, isn't it sad?" deplored Phyllis Stearns, with a sanctimonious sigh, "that women exist who care so little for their children as Stella Dallas? I used to know her very slightly, when she was fist married, and before her child was ever born she didn't want her. And now she goes off with a man like that! Oh!"

"Such a woman doesn't deserve to have a child," exclaimed Mrs. Kay Bird, who had successfully avoided ever having had one herself.

4

Stella was safely in the haven of her two-rooms-and-a-bath at the King Arthur when she opened her mail. She had just come up from luncheon in the dining-room below, where she had greeted everybody she knew with her usual cordiality. "Be it even an apartment hotel, there's no place like home!" she had laughed to Mrs. Kay Bird. "Gracious, but this place seems good to me!" she had thrown across to the young doctor who ate at the table next to hers; and to the two white-haired old ladies who occasionally asked her of an evening to make a fourth at auction, "All ready for a game, any time," she had exclaimed.

She was still purring as she moved about the three rooms which were hers and Laurel's alone, humming in a low tone to herself, delighting in their luxury and their comfort, as she laid away her hat and veil and gloves, bag and umbrella, in their old familiar nooks and corners.

She sat down on the edge of her bed to open her mail. There was a postcard from Laurel. She read that first. There was a note from Miss Simpson, verifying the hour of Laurel's arrival. She read that next. After Miss Simpson's note there were two announcements of fall openings; a bill; a receipt; then suddenly occurred an explosion of one of the bombs! Miss Fillibrown regretted that, owing to the unexpected increase of pupils in Laurel's class, there would be no place for her next year!

Stella's low humming ceased abruptly. She read the note again. She read it a third time. She was aware of a certain familiar heart-burning sensation which usually followed announcements of this sort. No place for Laurel at Miss Fillibrown's? Oh, that was cruel. There was no other private school in Milhampton. Laurel couldn't go to a public school. Nobody did—except foreigners. No place for Laurel at Miss Fillibrown's! There must be some mistake. But deep in her heart Stella knew there was no mistake. Experience had taught her there never was a mistake in the cruel stabs dealt her.

It was fully ten minutes before the second bomb exploded. The letter immediately underneath Miss Fillibrown's was a note from the proprietor of the King Arthur. The proprietor of the King Arthur regretted that he would be unable to accommodate Stella the following season! He had rented her present apartment, he explained, to a party who had offered almost double what she was paying, and there would be no other space available.

Stella got up and walked over to the window, folded her arms, as if to hold herself under better control, and stood staring out into the street below. What did it mean? What had she done? Why were people so unkind? What was to become of Laurel and herself? It wasn't as if there were other apartment hotels in Milhampton. The King Arthur was unique. The other places were boarding-houses, pure and simple. All sorts of people lived in them. She could no more take Laurel to a boarding-house than send her to a public school. Good heavens, this was a serious situation! Stella had received blows before, but the combination of these two, occurring both at once, and striking such vital parts of the anatomy of her social position in Milhampton, she knew would prove fatal. A wave of physical sickness swept over her.

It was fully half an hour before the last bomb shattered the frail scaffolding of another of Stella's air-castles. The last letter in her pile was from a lawyer in New York. The lawyer stated that he was writing for Mr. Stephen Dallas. Stella's eyes skipped over the introductory sentences. She caught the word "divorce." Stephen wanted to get a divorce!

Hope had never died that sometime she and Stephen might live beneath the same roof again. The possibility that when the golden harvest-time arrived when Laurel was old enough to come out, Stephen, too, would wish to give his child every possible advantage, and resume at least the semblance of a conventional relationship with his wife, had been for years a sort of secret candle Stella would take out and light whenever it seemed dark. But a divorce, a separation would rob her of her candle. Besides, she couldn't say "my husband" any more, could she, to her friends and acquaintances? Nor refer to her husband's absence as temporary. Oh, no one knew what a protection the uncertainty had been to her all these years.

At one o'clock the next morning Stella lay wide awake in her bed beside Laurel's empty one, tossing and turning in the darkness, reviewing the contents of each of the three cruel notes that had swept so bare her little hill of hopes, and left it bleak and desolate. At two o'clock she was still awake, and again at three she heard the chimes ringing in the Episcopal Church belfry, a half a mile away. At half-past three she got up and went into the bathroom. She poured herself out half a glass of gin, and filled the glass up with hot water from the faucet. She placed two sleeping-tablets on the back of her tongue and washed them down with the strong hot drink.

Laurel was due to arrive the next morning at nine o'clock. Stella simply must pull herself together before Laurel arrived.

CHAPTER THIRTEEN

1

"I shouldn't think that Simpson woman earned her salt. She's let your nails get into a terrible condition!" scolded Stella.

"Oh, but Miss Simpson never does my nails, mother," laughed Laurel.

She and Stella were seated opposite each other at a card-table in their bedroom at the King Arthur. There was a bath-towel spread over the table. Laurel held the finger-tips of one hand in a bowl filled with warm water, while her mother worked over the other. It was early afternoon of the first day of Laurel's arrival.

"Gracious, Laurel, this cuticle hasn't been pushed back once since you've been gone, I'll bet. I don't know what will become of you if you don't take more pains with yourself. These nails of yours are all split and broken to pieces."

"But I've been camping, mother."

"I should think you'd been mining, and using your fingers for pick-axes!"

A cat no more vigorously sets herself to work over the deplorable condition of her kitten after a visit to the coal-bin than did Stella over Laurel after her visit to New York and the Maine woods, "where they lived like animals," according to her way of thinking.

Stella was thankful this time, with all her heart, that she could work over Laurel, for when she had anything to conceal it was always easier to talk to the funny little perceiving creature, if she could keep her eyes down close on some sort of fine careful job, like cutting a bit of cuticle, or filing a nail to just the proper arch.

When the manicuring was well under way, Stella inquired, "How is your father?"

She always asked that question before Laurel had been back many hours.

Laurel always replied, "He's all right."

"Didn't seem different any way?"

"No."

"Didn't refer to me, I suppose?"

"No."

Laurel wished he would refer to her sometime, so she might tell her he had.

"Goodness," exclaimed Stella, "I should think he'd ask after my health once in a while!"

Laurel was silent.

Stella applied the blunt end of a steel file to the half-moon just appearing out of the pink flesh of Laurel's thumb.

"I should think he'd have some interest in my welfare."

Still Laurel was silent.

"I never did anything to have him treat me as if I was dead."

"You hurt, mother."

Stella laid down the file. But it was somewhere inside where Stella was really hurting Laurel. Laurel always suffered when her mother talked like that about her father.

"You'd think from the way he acts such a thing as a marriage ceremony had never taken place between him and me."

"Mother," Laurel interrupted—she *must* change the subject somehow—"I've learned to use a shotgun."

"I hope, Laurel," Stella went right on, *"you'll* have more respect for the promises *you* make, than your father seems to."

Laurel made another desperate attempt.

"Oh, mother," she exclaimed brightly, "I saw that lovely lady again in New York."

She was successful this time.

"What lovely lady?" asked Stella.

Laurel had been too busy so far answering her mother's questions as to what restaurants and theaters she had visited in New York to tell her about Mrs. Morrison.

"The lovely lady who gave me my silver pencil."

"Oh, yes, you met her at afternoon tea last year. I remember. You said she had on black broadcloth with broad-tail trimming then. What did she wear this time?"

"She isn't wearing black at all this year, but palish colors when she dresses up that you think are white until you see her up against a white wall or something, and then you see they aren't. They're usually pale yellow, or faint blue. She never wears pink."

"Good gracious, how many different rigs did you see this person in?"

"Oh, lots!"

She had not referred to Mrs. Morrison in her letters to her mother. That was not strange. Laurel was not fluent with her pen. Her letters were labored little notes, usually, that mirrored her personality imperfectly. Laurel's father used to say he could scarcely catch a glimpse of Laurel in the stilted notes she wrote to him. Once Laurel had tried to write to her mother about Mrs. Morrison, but Mrs. Morrison was like the Maine woods. There was so much to say that you just didn't know what one or two things to choose to cramp into half a dozen proper little sentences that must begin with a capital, contain a subject and a predicate, and end with a period.

"You'd love her clothes, mother," Laurel now went on. "She's got the loveliest negligée, she's got two or three lovely negligées, but I think my favorite was a yellowish one, made of a most beautiful crêpy stuff, with not a speck of trimming on it anywhere."

"Negligée!" exclaimed Stella. "Did she spend the night with you?"

"Oh, no, I spent the night with her. I spent almost a whole week of nights with her, while father was in Chicago."

"Oh, you did, did you?" said Stella, speaking thickly through an orange-stick which she held between her teeth. Stella often used her mouth to hold small tools, when she sewed or manicured. Lucky for her now! A sudden suspicion had shot up and gripped her in the throat.

The orange-stick helped to disguise the tenseness in her voice. "That was a funny arrangement, I should think."

"I didn't want to go a bit, at first," said Laurel. "I was frightened at the thought of visiting a stranger. But I needn't have been. Mrs. Morrison was perfectly lovely to me!"

"Oh, she was, was she? How?"

"Just every way there is to be lovely. For one thing—she thought I had lovely clothes, and that you had awfully good taste. She said so. *She* talked about you, mother. She thought you must be simply beautiful when I told her what you looked like."

"What does *she* look like?"

"A little like an Indian Pipe," said Laurel reflectively. "That's a sort of flower that grows in dark places up in the Maine woods. It hasn't got any color at all."

"Oh, gracious. I mean is she tall or short, dark or light, fat or thin. I don't care what kind of a flower she looks like."

"Well," Laurel began slowly, methodically. "She's dark—at least her hair is—and tall—at least she looks tall until you see her beside somebody taller like father—and slim, and cool-looking and pale—oh, ever so pale. And the queer thing is, she doesn't use any rouge at all. She does her hair," Laurel went on, "with only five hairpins, and no net. And once I saw her put soap right on her face! And she goes out in the broiling sun and lets it beat down on her without any veil or sunshade, or anything."

"What's her age?"

"She doesn't seem to be any special age. She's like one of those goddesses in my Greek Mythology Book that way."

"Oh, come. You can tell me whether she's twenty or forty, I guess."

"Oh, she's not forty! She can touch her fingers to the floor without bending her knees just as well as I can. We tried it one morning. And she rides horseback, and swims and plays tennis and golf. Father said she could almost beat him at golf. I guess she's about twenty-five."

"Oh, she and your father play golf sometimes."

"Sometimes."

"How in the world did your father become acquainted with this goddess?'' Stella inquired, in as light a tone as she could muster. "Happen to know?"

"Yes, and it's like a story. Father found her in Central Park! He saw her there riding horse-back one day. He was on a horse, too. She passed him. He didn't like to run after her, and try to catch her, so he went by another path, and cut her off when she came round a curve later on. Con told me about it.''

"Who's Con?"

"Con is her oldest son.''

"Oh, son! Married is she?"

"She used to be. Her husband is dead now."

"Oh, dead, is he? That's convenient," murmured Stella.

"Oh, no, it isn't. It isn't a bit convenient. Mr. Morrison left a whole lot of money and horses and houses and things, and Mrs. Morrison has to look out for them all alone. She says she wouldn't know what to do without father to help her and advise her.''

"Oh, I see, I see.'' Stella was still polishing, still keeping her voice light and inconsequential with the help of the steadying orange-stick. "A whole lot of money and horses and houses, has she? And what house did you visit her at?''

"I visited her at her house on Long Island. Oh, mother, it's wonderful! It has a beautiful lawn and garden all around it, and on the first floor out of all the rooms there are long windows, like doors, which are always kept open, so you can walk out onto the grass any time, just as easily as walking out from underneath a tree. Upstairs in the house there are the loveliest bedrooms and little tiled bathrooms hidden away like jewels on the inside of a watch. And all the bedroom doors stand open all day. Nobody ever thinks of locking the bedroom door. And in the pantry off the dining-room there's a big tin box with rows of thin cookies on each shelf. You can take one whenever you're hungry. Sometimes you can go into the kitchen and make candy! Oh, mother,'' Laurel broke off, "would it cost too awfully much for us to have a house all of our own somewhere—not a great big expensive one, like Mrs. Morrison's, but a little tiny one with a front door that's just ours, and a dining-room that's just ours, and a warm sleepy-looking kitchen that's just ours, where I could make candy sometimes (Mrs. Morrison and I made fudge one rainy day in the kitchen), and a guest-room so I could ask girls to come and stay all night with me sometimes? Mrs. Morrison asked a girl my age, whose mother she knew, to come and stay with me one night. And she came, and when she went she asked me to come and stay all night with *her!''* (No girl had ever asked Laurel to stay all night with her before.) "But I couldn't because I had to go back to New York the next day. I hated to go back to New York to Miss Simpson. Mother, next to you I think Mrs. Morrison is the loveliest lady I ever saw." Laurel's voice actually trembled.

Stella removed the orange-stick from her mouth and laid it down on the table beside the buffer.

"There," she said, "how do those look?" And she held up Laurel's fingers for her to see. She spoke harshly. She had to or the child might discover the tremble in *her* voice too.

Laurel gave the fingers a hasty glance. "They're all right," she remarked. Then dropping her hands on the bath-towel, and gazing out of the window, she added, and a glow stole into her eyes—into her voice also, "Mrs. Morrison has the most beautiful hands—long and white and slim like the rest of her. I wish I could have hands like hers!"'

2

Stella got up and went into the bathroom. She closed the door and locked it, then turned on both faucets, so that Laurel would think she was busy washing up. She stood staring at herself in the mirror over the wash-stand, while the water gushed into the basin.

Laurel had never glowed about a woman before. Stella didn't know what to make of it. It perplexed her. It hurt her. It hurt her more than the possibility that Stephen might be glowing about the same woman. Who was she, anyway—this tall mysterious siren, who was bewitching Lollie with her youth and beauty and prosperity, buying the kiddie's affection, by bestowing luxuries and attentions upon her in a single week which Stella would give her eye-teeth to be able to give Laurel in a lifetime.

Laurel was sensitive to beauty. Stella was aware of it—cruelly aware of it, as she stared at herself in the mirror before her. She saw all the tiny wrinkles. She saw the coarseness and the flabbiness. She saw the unmistakable yellow cast of color. It was as definite now as that of a white China silk waist after half a dozen washings. Good gracious, how could she hope to compete with a woman of twenty-five? It seemed lately as if nothing would cover up the defects and blemishes for any length of time. Often within so short a period as half an hour after she had left her bedroom, glancing into some unexpected mirror, she would discover the horrible old look sneaking out of hiding. A wave of discouragement swept over Stella. She had never required youth so much as now.

She pulled open the door to the medicine-closet in the wall beside the wash-stand with a determined jerk. She produced a large jar of cold cream, and began smearing great globs of it over her face. "A cold-cream bath, and a good hot steam is what you need," she announced to her reflection, and with a practiced rotating motion she proceeded to massage cheeks, chin, neck, and forehead vigorously, furiously; admonishing herself the while in the mirror—exhorting, and inciting with fresh courage.

This wasn't the time to lie down and submit. What if the world was treating her like a bunch of cruel boys a dog—kicking her from all sides, all at once? She mustn't put her tail between her legs and yelp and hug the ground. She must stand up and bristle her back, and snarl, and show her teeth, if necessary. And she would, too! Oh, there was a lot of fight left in her yet.

She didn't know exactly how a dog managed to fight so many boys at once. No sooner did she consider lowering her head to offer resistance to one of her tormentors than another hit her from behind. Seemed as if. Really, within the last twenty-four hours it seemed as if everything in the way of sharp-cornered missiles had been thrown in her direction, and struck her somewhere. It was confusing. It was alarming. But she mustn't show she was confused or alarmed. Lollie mustn't guess. Good Lord, no!

Half an hour later Stella emerged from the bathroom, with all her war-paint on. Her cheeks were a little rosier than usual, her eyebrows a little more distinctly emphasized, and her lips a little more definitely bowed.

3

Three days later Stella took the early morning train to Boston, "to do a little fall shopping," she told Laurel, but really to meet Mr. Morley Smith, the lawyer who had written to her from New York about the divorce. Mr. Smith had suggested in his letter that he would like a personal interview with Stella. Stella had replied that she would meet him at the appointed hour, at the office of the Boston law firm which he had mentioned.

You may be sure she had on all her war-paint when she sallied forth that morning, all her war-feathers too. She had selected a costume of wide black-and-white striped foulard in which to combat this particular adversary (the stripes wound sleekly around her. She resembled a zebra somewhat), and she had made herself as formidable as she knew how with all her loudest finery. A hat with sharp futurist angles, a shadow veil that hung unsecured and diaphanous to her shoulders; pearl earrings, filbert size; around her neck a long noisy chain of imitation amber beads. Her shoes were French-heeled, and steel-buckled. She carried several dangling articles on her left wrist that clattered every time she moved her hands.

When she was ushered into the private office placed at Mr. Morley Smith's disposal, he had to make an effort not to allow himself to betray his amazement. Stephen had not prepared him for anybody of this sort. The truth is Stephen himself would have been surprised at Stella's appearance. In the days when he had advised plain dark dresses, and no decorations, she had not used rouge, lipsticks, and eyebrow pencils. She hadn't needed to. Stephen didn't take into account that there had

been no one to advise Stella since he had given up the enterprise, no friend or protector to care what mistakes she committed during that critical period when her volatile prettiness began to evaporate like ether into air.

As Morley Smith drew up a chair and asked Stella to be seated, he looked at her closely and catalogued her forthwith. Morley Smith had known Stephen Dallas for years. How could he ever have married this woman? How could any man, who was attracted by the gentle, genuine charms of Mrs. Cornelius Morrison (and had been attracted by them, too, according to his story, before he ever met this Stella Martin), have contemplated matrimony with such an absolute antithesis? What a Quixote Stephen Dallas must have been, in spite of his insistence that he had married the pretty Normal-School student of his own free will and in the pursuit of happiness.

"I am glad, Mrs. Dallas," Mr. Morley Smith began from his high place of authority in front of the flat-topped desk, glancing across to Stella in her low place at the side of the desk (three feet and an armchair make all the difference in the world), "that you found it convenient to meet me here to-day. It is so much more satisfactory to talk a matter of this kind over quietly together."

"Oh, that's all right," said Stella. She wished *her* chair had a deep seat and arms so that *she* could lean back and assume a position of command.

"It is my hope," Mr. Smith went on suavely, "that I may be performing a service for both you and Mr. Dallas in arranging this affair without publicity, to your mutual satisfaction. I want you to feel, Mrs. Dallas," he smiled, "that I am here, not only as Mr. Dallas's friend and attorney, but as your friend and attorney, too."

"I don't need any attorney," said Stella.

"I agree with you, you do not. This affair should be, and can be settled without contest—between ourselves. That is your husband's wish, too. He and I have gone into the details of this matter and there lies open to us a line of procedure, which, if pursued, will cause almost no unpleasantness, as far as you are concerned."

"And what's that?"

"Why, you are to bring suit against Mr. Dallas for desertion. He will not contest the grounds of your suit, and the divorce will be granted without disagreeable controversy."

"I don't want a divorce," said Stella.

"Really?" Mr. Morley Smith raised his eye-brows in surprise. "Surely, you want your separation of seven years' standing legalized, do you not, and enjoy the advantages thereof?"

"I don't want a divorce," Stella repeated.

"The word has an unpleasant sound for some women, I know," Mr. Smith smiled. "It shouldn't. Let me explain. Perhaps you haven't thought in detail just what the benefits would be of a settlement of the relations existing between you and Mr. Dallas—just what hardships you are inflicting upon yourself, unnecessarily, in allowing them to continue in their present state."

And in the next ten minutes he laid out before Stella, as attractively as he knew how, all the fine arguments, moral, social, and financial, for her consideration, that he possessed.

But his display apparently made no impression upon Stella. For when he had finished all she said was, just as if she hadn't been listening, "I don't want a divorce, and," she added, "what's more I don't intend to have one."

Mr. Morley Smith frowned and shrugged. Then, balancing the tips of his elbows on the arms of his chair, and the tips of the fingers of his left hand nicely against the tips of the fingers of his right, he said, "That's a pity."

"I'm sorry to disoblige Stephen, I'm sure," said Stella, shrugging too.

"I meant a pity for you," flashed back Mr. Smith. And the smile and suave manner had disappeared. "Mr. Dallas can obtain his divorce without the least difficulty in the world, by another method. Don't have any doubt on that point. But the other method will not be exactly to your liking, I fear," he announced, fastening his keen shrewd eyes upon Stella. "I always feel sorry for any woman," he went on, "whose mistakes and misdemeanors of a dozen years are dragged out by opposing lawyers from the little hiding-places where she thought they

were safe, and held up for the curious public to gape at and glory in. Your husband, Mrs. Dallas, in allowing *you* to bring suit against him, instead of the other way round, is acting chivalrously. He is offering you an avenue of escape."

"I don't want any avenue of escape," Stella retorted. "I tell you I don't want a divorce."

Really it was annoying. Mr. Morley Smith couldn't make the least indentation on her.

"It looks to me, Mrs. Dallas, as if you will be obliged to have a divorce whether you want it or not."

"I don't know why. I don't pretend to know anything about the law, but I've got some common sense, and I never heard of a woman's being forced to get a divorce from her husband because he happens to want to go and get married again. Stephen does want to get married again, doesn't he?"

"That's entirely a side issue in this case, Mrs. Dallas. I am unable to inform you."

"Well, he does. I know he does."

"I should think under the circumstances he would wish to feel free to marry again."

"Well, he can't do it, and that's all there is to it. You can go back to New York and tell him that I refuse, with thanks, his chivalrous offer. Gracious. I don't call it exactly chivalrous for a man to walk off and leave his wife for seven years, and then, when he gets good and ready, give her the privilege of suing him for a divorce, so he can go and marry a rich young widow, and kick the high spots with her."

"You will, then, as I said before, force Mr. Dallas to bring suit against you."

"I never deserted him."

"No, your offense is graver."

"I never knew what my offense was. I've been ransacking my brain for seven years to find some good reason for Stephen's clearing out the way he did."

"Oh, come, Mrs. Dallas," half-laughed, half-sneered Mr. Morley Smith.

"What do you mean by that?"

"Don't try and pretend innocence with me. I've handled too many cases of this nature, dealt with too many women placed in your unenviable position. It won't work."

He looked straight into Stella's eyes, as he spoke, piercingly, drillingly. It was a horrid look. It was a look not to be endured from a man who was your enemy. Stella could feel the blood throbbing up into her throat.

"Are you trying to be insulting to me somehow?"

Mr. Morley Smith's sneer deepened. "That's right. You're acting consistently. It's quite the right tack—surprise, indignation, rage, tears, confession finally. Mrs. Dallas, allow me to spare you further attempt at evasion. I have facts—unalterable, unescapable facts. You were seen." He lowered his voice. "You were seen at Belcher's Beach," he brought out.

"Well, what of that?" flashed Stella.

"You were seen at the boarding-house, with Munn," he added, still keeping his sword-pointed eyes upon Stella.

Oh, so that was it! That was why there was no room for Laurel at Miss Fillibrown's! That was why the proprietor at the King Arthur had rented her apartment.

"Oh, what a rotten, rotten world!" she exclaimed.

Mr. Morley Smith shrugged and looked away. There was a silence. Then, "Well, you understand me, now, I think. You have your choice. Think it over. Either the generous escape Mr. Dallas offers, or the public exposure of acts you have taken such pains heretofore to conceal and cover up."

Stella stared at Mr. Morley Smith speechless, helpless for a moment. Every word he uttered, every glance of his eyes, every pharisaical shrug of his shoulders shamed and degraded her. She would simply have to get out of his presence, or she would do something horribly common and crude to him, like slapping him in the face, or calling him something unladylike, like a cur or a skunk. She stood up.

"I'm going," she said.

He stood up too. He smiled.

"You will cooperate with us, then? You will accept our proposition?"

"Cooperate? Accept your proposition? No, I won't. I'll fight! That's what I'll do. I'll prove to the world whether I'm guilty or not of the filthy things rotten-minded people have said about me. And I'm glad of the chance, too. I hope Stephen *will* sue me for a divorce. I said I didn't need a lawyer, when I first came here, but I need somebody to defend me against such a pack of muck-rakers. Why, Mr. Smith, I have no more done the thing you come here and accuse me of doing than your own wife, or, if you're not married, your own mother, or the woman you honor the most in this world, whoever it is, and I'll get the best lawyer in this country to prove it."

Behind the belying paint and elaborate make-up the white image of this woman's innocence stood out before Morley Smith clear and defined, for an instant, like a white-sailed ship, when the fog lifts a moment—a white-sailed ship in distress. He saw it. He recognized it. He turned away from it.

"You're going through the usual motions, Mrs. Dallas," he commented with another sneer.

CHAPTER FOURTEEN

1

The same chaste charm that pervaded Helen Morrison's summer home was even more striking in her New York house. A feeling of space and fresh air is more of a triumph in the city than in the country. In both Helen Morrison's houses there was delicious freedom from deleterious overcrowding of possessions beneath a roof. She knew how to make walls backgrounds, instead of boundaries, as unconfining as the sky behind a mountain, or the sea behind a sail. Yet neither of her houses could be called large. Much as nature conforms itself equally happily to decorating a mountain-side, or a salt-water pool no larger than a baptismal font, so Helen conformed herself instinctively to whatever proportions were offered her. Never for the sake of displaying some beautiful work of art would Helen disturb the nice equilibrium and fine composition of a room. Never were the space and air necessary for the spiritual well-being, as it were, of one rare treasure robbed for another. She possessed a nice sense of harmony, too. She could no more have placed Tiffany glass beside old luster than have mixed people of discordant instincts at her dinner-table. This discernment was not acquired. It was as effortless with her as breathing.

When she married Cornelius Morrison and came as a very young bride to the New York house, filled with its chaotic collection of treasures picked up from all over the globe, not only by her widely traveled husband, but by his father before him, she felt little of the delight which beautiful things had given her before. On the contrary, she was possessed of an incessant desire to escape them, to get outdoors, and breathe deep, and look upon broad spaces.

Finally she asked her husband if he would object if she cleared out just one of the rooms in the house of every single thing that was in it. He told her she could clean out the whole house, for since Cornelius Morrison had obtained *her*, his other treasures had sunk into trivial insignificance. Therefore Helen Morrison had had the entire top floor of the house built into a single room which she called the Museum, and into which she moved the wealth of two generations of collectors.

Cloisonnée no longer rubbed shoulders with Copenhagen in the Morrison drawing-room, nor futurist touched frames with early Italian. Such jarring juxtapositions gave Helen somewhat the same feeling of displeasure that a discord on the piano gives to a sensitively musical child when he is still too young to understand why. Helen Morrison could understand her recoil but imperfectly. She knew little about schools and periods and values in art in its various forms when she married Cornelius Morrison. She warned her husband that she was an expert judge concerning only the merits of table-linen, lingerie, and flat silver. But he soon discovered that if an article was really fine and genuine, the something fine and genuine in his wife recognized it and responded to it. He made her curator of the Museum without hesitation.

Underneath the Museum, Cornelius Morrison's house was like a barn at first. At least so the aunt who had lived with Cornelius before he married told Helen, when she saw it.

Helen had exclaimed, "Isn't it? All beautiful space and shadows, and room enough to dance a spring song in, if you feel like it."

The house didn't remain long like an empty barn, however, though according to the aunt it never seemed "like a really furnished house."

Helen spent hours browsing in the Museum, assimilating it slowly, piece by piece. Gradually various treasures began appearing in the rooms below. When Helen discovered, or believed she had, an affinity between some empty niche downstairs and one of the objects of art in the Museum, she united them with delight. "Trial marriages," she called them humorously to her husband. Many of them proved permanent, but there were certain corners, tables, old chests, and secretaries, "that enjoyed a constant state of polygamy,'' she laughed, ''that adjusted themselves happily to various of the temperamental objects of art in the Museum.''

You never could be sure what would be the dominant note in the long room with the old-ivory tinted walls in the front of the house. This room was Helen's own. Here, she changed the ornaments as she would the flowers, with every changing season and mood. Therefore there were few of the objects of value in the Museum that, one time or another, didn't descend to the rooms below.

Cornelius Morrison discovered his collection all over again. As Helen isolated one piece of it after another and placed it in a sympathetic environment, he was constantly finding new beauties in form and line and color, heretofore unseen. He liked to boast that he had never enjoyed his collection until Helen came with her unerring intuitions. She gave it new birth. Helen gave new birth to everything he possessed. He told her that she gave new birth to *him,* too.

2

Helen had known Cornelius Morrison ever since she was a little girl. He was her father's friend—not so old as her father by a decade or so, but a younger brother of the same generation. He used to come occasionally and spend a night in her father's house in Reddington, on his way farther west, or else on his way back to New York from some protracted journey to China or Japan. He was one of the few honored guests for whom the wine-glasses were always produced and the little liqueur set. Helen used to examine his baggage in secret—his umbrella, his overcoat, his toilet articles—for they were permeated with the same vague fascinating cosmopolitanism of which she was aware whenever he opened his mouth to speak. In those days he was ''Mr. Morrison'' to Helen. He was ''Mr. Morrison'' to her up to the day she told him she would marry him. One of the hardest things she had to do was to learn to call him Cornelius.

Helen spent the first half-dozen years of her long boarding-school career in a small town in Connecticut. But she finished her education at a boarding-school in New York. Judge Dane wrote to his friend Cornelius Morrison, when Helen went to New York, and asked him if he would look up his little daughter sometime, and see if she seemed happy in her new environment.

Cornelius Morrison was very kind to the little daughter. He became a sort of fairy godfather to Helen and her group of friends at the New York school. He sent them flowers. He sent them candy. He gave them theater-parties, and afternoon-tea-parties, and college football-parties—all properly chaperoned, all properly discussed and arranged with the mistress of such affairs at the school.

Helen was old enough to appreciate that Mr. Cornelius Morrison was something of a personage in New York (her friends left her in no doubt on that point), but she was not old enough to appreciate that the friendship between Mr. Morrison and her father scarcely warranted so much time and thought spent in her entertainment. She accepted his attentions with enthusiasm, and with the simple joy of a child accepting the bounty of a generous Santa Claus. He bestowed them with no more thought of return.

Cornelius Morrison had never married. In spite of the prominence of his name and family in New York, he had always been shy with women. Helen and her friends were an entirely new adventure to him. He became very fond of Helen Dane. At first he believed he was fond of her as he might have been fond of a younger sister, and he mourned the fact that he had been an only child. Later he believed he was fond of her as he might have been fond of a daughter, and he mourned the fact that he had never married. Then suddenly Cornelius Morrison discovered that he was fond of Helen—that he *loved* Helen—as only a man can love the woman he wants to make his wife. And she was nineteen, and he was fifty-two!

He started for India a few weeks after his discovery. He didn't return for three years. When he came back he stopped off at Reddington as was his custom when returning to New York from the Far East. His old friend, Judge Dane, had died during his absence—he had been dead a year—but he wished to pay respect to his memory and also to find out if the little daughter, who had finished school now, was well and happy.

He was disturbed about the little daughter when he saw her. The death of her father must have cut deep. She had suffered. This tender creature was still suffering, Cornelius Morrison believed. It struck him, as he sat opposite her at dinner in the big ponderous dining-room where he had often sat opposite her father before, that she was like an abandoned kitten in this great empty place, with only paid caretakers to see that she was fed.

After dinner in the drawing-room he said to her, "Helen, I believe you are lonely here."

Calmly, with no tears (Helen had shed all her tears), with no raising of her voice—she might have been a woman of forty who spoke—she replied, "I *am* lonely, Mr. Morrison, and I *am* unhappy, too. I wish I could leave Reddington forever. There's absolutely nothing for me here now."

A wave of tenderness swept over Cornelius Morrison. A wild delirious hope sprang alive within his heart. Could it be that he had anything to offer Helen that she wanted?

3

Cornelius Morrison had arrived in Reddington a few months after the Dallas tragedy. He had reappeared in Helen's life at a time when every waking moment was dull pain to her, and the days and the months and the years stretched ahead of her like a long, dark, dreary road with a blind end.

Helen Dane had loved the son of the man whose last act had cast such a shadow upon the boy who bore his name. Helen had loved Stephen from the first time he had come to call on her the night after the dance her father had given her when she returned to be the young mistress of his house. He had danced with her half a dozen times that evening. He had claimed her for "Home, Sweet Home." Well, who had a better right? They had known each other as children, years before they went East to school. Their fathers served on several same boards of directors together. During "Home, Sweet Home" Stephen asked Helen if he might "call." Such was the custom in those days. He was returning to his law school shortly. He asked if he might call the next evening, that is, if she was going to be at home, and if she hadn't too many other bookings. She was going to be at home. If she had other bookings, she canceled them. Stephen found her alone.

They sat in Judge Dane's big quiet drawing-room, one on each side of the rose-shaded table-lamp and discussed such impersonal subjects as the football game in New Haven last November, and the boat-race on the Thames last June, and the plays they had seen last spring in New York, and the places they had dined and danced there; and Shaw and Ibsen and Arnold Daly and Nazimova. It was a typical call for that era. Helen had carried on conversations of the same sort with many a young man before. But never had her hands been cold, and her face hot, and never had she lain awake afterwards for three hours and a half.

The truth was that Helen, with the same unerring instinct that later guided her in recognizing kinships between objects of art, was aware of something of the sort between Stephen and herself on her first evening alone with him, and it was exciting. It wasn't only that they were both young, with traditions that were not dissimilar, and tastes and ideals that were were not antagonistic. For such was the case between Helen and many of the young men she had met. It was something deeper, more vital. Why, even when this Stephen disagreed with her, now and again, as he had that first evening, she had experienced as sharp—as glowing a sense of pleasure, as certain sharp contrasts in color gave her. No. It wasn't that Stephen was like her, any more like her than a cup is like a saucer (but one without the other is incomplete—broken) or the tallow candle like the silver stick to hold it (but one is the perfect complement of the other, even though made of such different stuff).

Stephen also had been awake a good many hours of the night after his first call on Helen. He wouldn't have been, probably, if he had been in his own bed at home, instead of on the train speeding East. (Stephen was less given to contemplation than Helen.) But every time a stop, or jolt, or sudden application of brakes shook him awake, he was conscious of Helen Dane. "By George, she's a pretty girl"—"I'll write to her to-morrow"—"I'll order her some flowers as soon as I reach Boston"—"I'm going to see something more of that girl. She has beautiful eyes—and a brain too"—"I don't know when I've met such a girl"—"I wonder if she'll want to settle down in Reddington."

The world took on a new interest and significance for Helen after that. The sound of the mailman whistle would often make her heart jump up in the region of her throat. The sight of a certain-shape envelope on the hall table, sometimes bearing two and three stamps in its corner, would fill her with such a choking wave of emotion that she couldn't answer questions coherently until she had closed herself in her room and had devoured the letter contents. And why not? Wasn't it written by the man she was going to marry (though he might not yet be aware of it), and didn't it discuss thrilling things about religion and philosophy, and art and music, and all sorts of foundation-stones of a life together?

They didn't refer to that life together in their letters, not directly. They didn't refer to it at Easter-time when the discussions continued by the roseshaded lamp. Of course not. Stephen's education was not finished yet. He had a whole year and a half at the law school still before he could even start upon a self-supporting career. But Helen was not impatient. She liked prolonging the sweet adventure. It couldn't possibly come out but one way. Stephen's eyes had told her over and over that she was the only girl in the world for him, and her eyes had replied, shiningly, mistily, that she knew it—she knew it and was glad! At least she thought that was what his eyes had said. She thought he understood what she had replied.

When his father did that awful thing, Helen's love for Stephen burst into a blinding desire to help and comfort and share. Her own father had died a few months before. She was alone in the world. If Stephen had need of her, she had need of him, too. She must tell him so when his long torturing journey home was over and he came to her.

Helen waited for three days for Stephen to come to her. Finally, convinced that he was waiting for a sign from her, she stole out quietly, one evening, by herself, and called at the Dallas's big brown house, shrouded in its silent and solemn horror. She stood on the doorstep and rang the bell, and without explanation asked for Stephen. He was out. She left her card with a hasty pencil message written on it, "Please come over to-night. Helen." But he didn't come.

4

Helen didn't see Stephen Dallas again until one day, fifteen years later, sauntering along one of the bridle-paths of Central Park, she glanced up and there he was standing before her (on horseback also) with his hat off, smiling and saying, "Do you remember me?"

Her heart had jumped up into her throat in the same old young way it used to at sight of him a lifetime ago.

5

When Helen told Cornelius Morrison that she would marry him, she felt that Stephen was as definitely lost to her as her father. When the doctor had come to her just after her father had died and said "It is all over," his words were no more final than Stephen's letter, which Helen received a long three weeks after she had called at the Dallas house. The letter was in answer to her note of consolation. For Helen had written to Stephen an outburst of sympathy at the first possible moment.

He thanked her for her note in a formal punctilious manner which she scarcely recognized. He thanked her for the card she had sent over to the house at the time of the funeral. He appreciated her kindness in offering to see him, but it was difficult for him to talk to his friends. He had left Reddington forever. He never wanted to see Reddington again. He was going away—very far away, to Australia, possibly, where he was unknown. He was thankful that Helen's and his friendship was still in its infancy. He was thankful he had formed no business alliances. He was thankful that his father's act cast no shadow of shame on any one outside his own immediate household.

Helen read Stephen's letter until every word of it was graven on her heart. Then she put it away and faced the world without him. There was no recalling him. One cannot recall that which one has never had. One cannot pursue that which does not exist. Stephen was aware of no special bond, of no insolubility. That which to her had been one of those rare relationships that occur once in a long, long while in various groups and communities, had been to him but a "friendship in its infancy." He classed it with a dozen others. She was just a girl he had fancied for a season.

6

There was only one small light to relieve the darkness of Helen's solitude that winter. She had always loved children. One of her aunts had a little girl—a baby barely three, who took a fancy to Helen. The baby would clamber up into her arms, and cuddle down contented like a kitten in the sun. When Helen told Cornelius Morrison that she would marry him, it was with the distinct image of a little girl of her own, clambering up into her arms and cuddling down contented.

When he asked her when she would like to be married (he waited a whole week before he broached the question: not for anything would he frighten Helen, would he seem to hasten her), she replied, "I would like to be married soon, within a few weeks."

Her voice did not waver. The pallor of her cheeks was as steady as that of a petal of a white rose. It was Cornelius Morrison who was trembling. He could scarcely trust himself to speak. A few weeks! Did she know what marriage meant? He didn't think so. Well, he would never teach her. It would be more than he had even hoped for, just to have her to be kind to, to take care of for a little while.

"I'll do my very best to make you happy, Helen," he said quietly.

There was something in his voice that struck through the wall of Helen's personal suffering behind which she had shut herself for so long. She leaned toward him. She grasped one of his hands with both of hers.

"I'll do my best to make you happy, too," she said fervently.

Neither of them ever forgot their promise.

CHAPTER FIFTEEN

1

Although Cornelius Morrison was always aware he was not the perfect mate for Helen, and Helen observed her marriage with wide-open and seeing eyes, they both did much to enrich and beautify the life of the other. All happy marriages are not "made in heaven," Helen discovered. Some are the result of wise human effort, and long steady adaptation.

Cornelius Morrison was thirty years older than Helen. He was never free from the fear that some day a younger man, a more appropriate comrade for his wife, might supplant him in her affections. If a younger man devoted an evening to Helen, if she seemed to respond to his attentions with interest and vivacity, a deep melancholy would take possession of Cornelius Morrison—unreasonable, perhaps, but uncontrollable and terribly painful.

Helen needed no explanations. With her intuition she saw as clearly as through a microscope into the reason for her husband's occasional waves of depression. Not for anything in the world would she hurt him. She might not love him in the romantic way that she had loved Stephen. She knew that she didn't; but there was something fine and untarnished to be preserved about their relations, beside which passing and personal pleasures were trivial and unimportant. She became as careful to spare her husband the secret ignominy of jealousy as to guard her children from groundless fears and premonitions. In spite of her youth, in spite of her natural impulses, she avoided all intimacies that might even indefinitely disturb Cornelius.

With gentle consideration, too, she abandoned all forms of pleasure that emphasized the difference in their ages and placed him at a disadvantage. Cornelius spoke no word of complaint on the several occasions when she danced half the night away on a ballroom floor while he waited for her in a smoky anteroom, but quietly, without comment, Helen gave up dancing after a little while. Cornelius liked to give dinners. Helen learned to like to give them. Cornelius liked to go to the opera. Helen learned to like to go to the opera. Cornelius liked to ride horseback. Helen learned to like to ride horseback. It was when Helen was riding horseback in Central Park one morning alone that she met Stephen Dallas.

2

When Stephen had said, "Do you remember me?" Helen had replied with a little puzzled look, as if she wasn't quite sure, "You're Stephen Dallas, aren't you?"

"You *know* I'm Stephen Dallas," he exclaimed in the old sure way with her he used to have.

There was joy in his eyes. There was gladness in his voice. He had the queer sensation that the intervening years since last he saw this girl were a bad dream, and he had just waked up, as keenly responsive to her as the day he lost consciousness.

He leaned over and they shook hands. The sort of ecstasy swept over Stephen that any victim of a nightmare feels when he returns to the realm of realities and his physical contacts register properly.

They exchanged a commonplace or two—Helen sweetly, but coolly. Stephen with an impetuosity he didn't try to conceal.

"I saw you, half a mile back," he confessed. "You passed me. I didn't think at first it could be really you. Chance isn't usually so kind to me. By the time I had decided it couldn't possibly be anybody else, you had gone too far ahead for me to overtake you with proper park decorum. So I've been contriving ever since how I might head you off. Again chance has favored me. You might have made half a dozen wrong turns. Or, perhaps it wasn't chance at all. Perhaps it was mental telepathy."

To this boyish outburst of Stephen's Helen replied, still sweetly, still coolly (long practice had made her skillful), "I'm delighted we met, but I scarcely think it was due to mental telepathy. I let my horse choose the turns this morning. I usually ride with my husband and we always come this way."

"Oh, I know you're married, Helen," laughed Stephen boldly, as much as to say, "I suppose you think I ought to be told, I seem so glad to see you."

Helen was not to be perturbed by boldness. She was not a young girl to betray a pounding heart which she had reason to wish to conceal.

Politely, calmly, she inquired, "Are you living in New York now?"

He nodded, smiling. (What a beautiful woman she had become!)

"If two rooms in bachelor's apartments is living, yes, I am," he said.

"Have you been here long?"

"Three years."

"Three years? Really!" She raised her lovely brows.

"Oh, people may say the world's a small place, Helen," Stephen exclaimed. "But New York isn't. I've been trying for three years to run across your path, and I haven't succeeded until to-day!" He simply couldn't resist being personal with her at every turn.

Helen replied prosaically, "Well, I'm glad we've met at last. It's always a pleasure to see any one from Reddington."

She was almost convincing. Stephen looked at her sharply. Was it pretense, or was she actually unaware of any special significance in this meeting? "Don't you remember the talks we used to have, Helen?" he asked.

"Why, of course," she answered him, but she managed to sound more tactful than honest.

Stephen looked into her well-remembered eyes. "I've never forgotten them," he told her quietly.

Helen would not give him the slightest sign of response.

"I suppose," she went on serenely, "like most young people of our time we tried to settle all the weighty questions of the day, didn't we?''

Stephen felt a pang of disappointment. The years since last he saw Helen had not been a dream. They were real—every one of them was real, and Helen was as far removed, as beyond recall, as his youth. There she sat opposite him, graceful, lovely, beautifully poised upon her horse (beautifully poised in speech and manner, too), as impervious to him as a picture. She looked at him kindly, graciously, but disinterestedly as if he were a part of the landscape. He turned away from her tranquil face.

"You must come to dinner with us some day," he heard her saying in that cool, smooth, impersonal voice of hers.

"Thank you very much," he replied perfunctorily, not looking back at her. Oh, he, too, could be cool and smooth and impersonal if that was what she really wanted.

3

It was what she really wanted. When he dined for the first time at the Cornelius Morrison's there were half a dozen other guests present. He sat nowhere near his hostess, nor did she give him any chance for conversation after dinner. It was always like that. As time went on, Stephen was frequently in the same drawing-room with Helen, and often one of the same party, but she always contrived to avoid all opportunity for intimate conversation.

Stephen was hungry to talk to Helen. He had no intention of making love to her. She needn't have been afraid. He was scarcely less free than she. He simply wanted to sit occasionally, for short periods, in an outer circle of the warm sunshine of her radiating sympathy. But she wouldn't let him. Her insistence upon a purely impersonal basis of intercourse made anything but the merest superficialities impossible.

When Cornelius Morrison met Stephen Dallas, he took a fancy to the young man. They had several interests in common. Cornelius and Stephen went on a fall fishing-trip together six months after Stephen met Helen in Central Park. Stephen was often at Helen's house after the fishing-trip. Cornelius would bring him home to dinner unannounced. After dinner the two men would play long games of chess in the library, while Helen read to her boys in a room above. Of course Stephen saw Helen alone sometimes, but never for longer than a passing moment or two. Helen always had something to call her away. And during those passing moments or two she was always clothed in her armor.

Stephen made no attempt to pierce that armor. Convinced that it was not only her wish, but her determined resolve to treat him merely as a friend of her husband's, to whom she extended the courtesies of her position, but nothing more, he acquiesced. He even tried to help her. Finally Stephen avoided all chance for intimate conversation with Helen as delicately and adroitly as herself. Through Helen's skillful management Cornelius Morrison never experienced a moment of the cruel suspicion that he was unwelcome in the company of these two creatures so many years younger than himself.

For over half a dozen years Stephen came and went to and from the Morrison home. He was constantly moving before Helen's eyes—vivid and alive, but, as far as she was concerned, apparently divested of all reality.

When Cornelius Morrison died, and suddenly Helen was released from all fear of hurting him, she did not immediately alter her attitude towards Stephen Dallas. Habit was so strong—or was it respect for Cornelius that was so strong?—she contrived to maintain with Stephen for many months the same remote relations which she had established when her husband was alive.

Stephen had a great deal to do in settling Cornelius Morrison's affairs. Cornelius Morrison had concluded that, of all his friends who were members of the bar, Stephen Dallas, who had known Helen as a child, could work with her to the best advantage. He named Stephen as one of his trustees. Therefore Stephen and Helen were necessarily alone together frequently.

At first Stephen treated Helen as she had indicated she wished to be treated. He was almost formal with her unless the children were present as a safeguard. It was difficult to strike a happy medium after Stephen had been alone in Helen's presence for longer than half an hour. For he loved her! He believed he had loved her ever since that day he had met her in Central Park, and his own eagerness and joy at sight of her had so startled and surprised him. No. He believed he had loved her longer. Occasionally a look would pass between Helen and himself— a vague, indefinite look that recalled to Stephen the picture of a girl sitting by a rose-shaded lamp, and a boy opposite her toying with a little bronze which he had picked up from the table near by. Stephen believed he had loved Helen ever since that first night in Judge Dane's drawing-room!

When for the first time Stephen pursued one of those vague illusive looks, gazed straight at Helen in the gray depths of her eyes, and by sheer mind-energy captured that will-o'-the-wisp impulse that had drifted like vapor between them, she had drawn in her breath quickly and her eyelids had flickered and closed for a moment; and color, ever so faint, ever so indefinite, had tinged her cheeks.

It was no picture of a girl that Stephen saw then! It was the girl herself! She was not the wife of Cornelius Morrison. She was his, to love and to win! And again Stephen had the queer sensation of waking up from a bad dream. Again his father's suicide, the black days that had followed, Milhampton, the boarding-house, the little red cottage and Stella, were all parts of a nightmare. Helen alone was real. She was made for him. She was meant for him. All that had happened to prevent nature's plan was a mistake, an abortion.

At the time of Helen's betrayal of her real feelings for Stephen, he made no comment. He seemed not to notice the sharp intaking of her breath, the faint color, the closed lids. He began talking quickly about a certain exchange of property they had been discussing. And he left her very soon. Stephen made up his mind he would not speak a word of love to this beautiful woman until he was free to do so, with no fear of casting reflection upon her reputation.

Divorce, public acknowledgment of failure in the most sacred department in a man's or a woman's life, had always seemed hideous to Stephen. But wasn't it the failure, after all, that was hideous, rather than the acknowledgment? His and Stella's failure had already been demonstrated. They had already made the slow embittering descent from confidence and hope to doubt and despair. For years their marriage had been absolved. To place the law's decree upon dead hopes is not the saddest part of the experience. It is not the required death notice in the city's records that remains graven forever in the memory of the watcher by the bedside. Thus Stephen reasoned.

4

It was in September, shortly before Laurel's first visit at Mrs. Morrison's, that Stephen called on his friend Morley Smith and started proceedings for a divorce. It was in January when Stephen came to the definite conclusion that there was only one way that he could obtain a divorce; and that one way would defeat the object for it.

Stella was as firm as adamant. Every form of argument that Morley Smith could think of, every variety of persuasion that he could devise, had been brought to bear upon her, but to no avail. Stella would not comply. "If Stephen wants a divorce he will have to fight for it," was her invariable answer.

Stephen's hands were tied. It was unthinkable to expose in court the tawdry and unbeautiful details of his life with Stella before he went to New York, to unbury for the delight of a greedy public her compromising relations with Alfred Munn. He might be granted a divorce (Morley Smith assured him that he would), but of what use would it be to him? Helen's position as Mrs. Cornelius Morrison must be considered. She had always looked upon it as a sort of trust. Besides, there were her boys. They should not be made victims of such a scandal. And there was Laurel. No. A divorce obtained in such a manner was out of the question.

As a last resort Stephen had gone to see Stella himself. It was after that ordeal that he felt convinced that he could never marry Helen Dane. He went to her as soon as possible after he had left the Boston train to tell her of his defeat. He stopped only long enough at his rooms to change, and then hastened directly to her house.

It was nearly twelve o'clock at night before he arrived. As he sat down in the long room two floors above the entrance, he felt a little faint. Helen was not in the room, but it was so peculiarly hers that he could hardly breathe its air lately without feeling her sweet presence. To-night there were fresh logs flaming in the open fireplace. There was a flame-colored porcelain bowl, placed on each of the chests on either side of the hearth. There was a piece of flame-colored brocade, brilliant as a bank of nasturtiums, thrown over one end of the long Sheraton sofa.

When Helen came into the room Stephen was aware that she was in pure white, but there was something as brilliant about her, as flame-colored, as the two bowls, as the brocade, as the fire.

He gazed at her speechless a moment, then went to meet her. He put his arms around her and kissed her.

Afterwards he said quietly, "They're numbered, Helen." And she knew that what she had read in his eyes when first she entered the room was true.

She slipped a firm, steadying arm through his, and guided him to the sofa. They sat down side by side, on the flame-colored brocade. He kissed her again.

In spite of his high resolve to hold himself in restraint, until the law had pronounced him free, he had not done so. As long as there had been hope that he might go to Helen unentangled, some day, he remained silent. But when that hope had grown faint, had all but disappeared, brokenly, despairingly, one day, he had confessed his love to her. That was a month ago. His confession had acted like a lighted match on paper. Once Stephen revealed himself to Helen, her love for him, long concealed, but long realized, flashed into flame, like the combustion of a long-stifled fire once it is given air.

As she sat beside him on the sofa, to-night, her arm thrust through his, she observed with fierce pity his drooping shoulders, his hand lying limp and inert upon his knee. She placed her own on top of it and grasped it hard.

"Never mind, Stephen."

"There's no hope."

"I know. We scarcely expected it so soon."

"Oh, it's final, Helen."

There was a pause.

"Do you care to tell me about it?"

Stephen shook his head. It seemed to him sacrilege to bring even the image he had of Stella in his mind into this room. So long as he remained in Helen's presence, he wished he might erase from his brain the memory of the interview he had just had with the woman who had one day been his wife. (Was it possible that she had one day been his wife?) Stephen closed his eyes an instant. Stella, powdered, painted, perfumed, coarsened in speech and manner as he didn't suppose it possible, her fattened figure covered with cheap trappings from head to toe, flashed into his field of vision. He looked down at Helen's lovely hand. Stella and Helen were as unlike as a wax figure, with highly colored cheeks, glass eyes, and blond hair, is unlike a statue of a beautiful Diana carved in white marble.

"You saw her?"

"Yes, I saw her."

There was another pause.

Gently Helen withdrew her arm and got up. Of course as long as she sat so close to Stephen he could not talk to her. She shoved up her little armchair opposite him and sat down in it.

"Now, Stephen, tell me about it."

Tell her about it? Repeat to her the threat Stella had hurled at him? No! Helen must never surmise that her fair name had been mentioned, even by an unscrupulous lawyer as a correspondent in a divorce case. For such had been the nature of Stella's threat.

It had been torture to Stephen to sit in Stella's presence and listen to her using Helen's name familiarly, daring to refer to her in the same breath that she referred to Alfred Munn. Stephen closed his eyes again an instant. He could hear Stella still. Her speech had grown terribly crude with the years.

"Thank heaven for lawyers, I say *now*. Gracious! I'd never have thought *myself* of getting something on *you*, Stephen, but my lawyer has been right onto his job. He's been down there to New York, and he says that I've got as much grounds to do a little naming as you have. So if you want a divorce, Stephen, go ahead and dig up Ed Munn, and I'll dig up Helen Morrison and we'll give the public something worth reading. Of course, I, myself, don't *want* a divorce. There's nobody *I* want to marry. I'd see myself dead rather than tied up to Ed Munn. And I can't see that it's any advantage to a woman with a daughter she's got to bring out in society to be a grass-widow. I'd just rather have you in New York, on business, the way you've always been. I've taken an apartment in Boston now, and by the time Laurel's old enough to come out, it may strike me as a good idea to have her father in the background somewheres, when we give her a ball at one of the big hotels. Mr. Hinckly, my lawyer, says you'll probably want to do about anything I want you to, just so I don't show up your little affair with that pretty widow down there in New York. My! But I think lawyers are clever. I certainly take off my hat to Mr. Hinckly.''

It was Helen's sweet voice saying, ''You have had a difficult day, Stephen. I'm so sorry,'' that called Stephen back to a brief glimpse of heaven again.

He looked at her long and quietly. Then he said, ''Helen, I gave you up years ago, because I felt I could bring you nothing but shame. I must give you up again for the same reason.''

CHAPTER SIXTEEN

1

A new venture always acted upon Stella like fresh soil in a garden upon seeds. It brought out renewed effort and vigor. An experiment untried possessed all the possibilities of success. Stella never considered failure until it was demonstrated. Even then she would not accept it as such— invariably searching for some hidden advantage in her various disappointments and rebuffs. Even when she had the daunting situation of a forced exile to face, she kept right on spinning her thread of optimism like a spider rudely ejected from her web, falling dizzily at first, but quickly recovering herself and fastening her slender cable to the first solid support that offered itself.

"You never can tell," she said to Effie McDavitt. "It may be the best thing in the world that ever happened that there wasn't any room for Laurel at Miss Fillibrown's this year, and that I've got to get out of the King Arthur. I'd gotten into the way of thinking that the sun rose and set in Milhampton society. I'm going to take an apartment round Boston somewheres! A housekeeping apartment. Lollie is just crazy to have a home of our own, so she can 'entertain,' and I guess it's high time. Mercy, I just wish I'd had sense enough to get out of Milhampton before. The town has always had it in for Laurel and me, ever since Stephen cleared out."

Stella didn't know anything about apartments in Boston. She didn't know anything about where "the right place was to live," nor "whom the right people were to know," nor which was the "right church," nor the "right school." Her knowledge of Boston was confined to the shopping district.

"But that's where this flare-up with Stephen comes in handy," she told Effie. "Before I had to dig up a lawyer to defend me against that Morley Smith creature, I didn't have a soul in Boston to ask advice about desirable locations, and desirable schools and things, that you have to know about to start right in any new place."

Mr. Joseph Hinckly, of the firm of Hinckly, Jones and Hinckly, became to Stella more than a mere legal adviser. His knowledge of Boston was somewhat confined too, although not to the same district as Stella's. However, he never hesitated to give her an authoritative opinion on any subject if she asked for it. That was instinctive with him.

When Stella inquired, "Commonwealth Avenue's one of the best residential streets, isn't it?" he had assured her there was nothing to compare with it this side of Riverside Drive.

"Well, I've found an apartment on Commonwealth Avenue, way out beyond the thousands, and its front windows are just flooded with sunshine."

"Snap it up quick," exclaimed Mr. Hinckly. "The sunny side of Commonwealth Avenue! Great Scott! You can't do better than that!"

Mr. Hinckly was fully aware that the distance between one and one thousand in some instances, in some streets, is as great as between one side of the globe and the other. (He himself had been born at the wrong end of a fashionable street, he once said in a political speech.) But he was also fully aware that his client might live in the very heart of the Back Bay and barriers more forbidding than space would prevent her from ever crossing its thresholds.

Stella moved into her five-roomed furnished apartment just before Christmas. She still possessed some of the old knack in copying department-store window effects. But it had been a long time since she had had "her eye out for that sort of thing." With no one to guide her, and the matter of expense a constant argument for the cheaper article, her results were not successful. As Laurel gazed upon the slowly growing tawdriness of the apartment, the joy she thought she would feel in

159

inviting the vague new friends her mother told her she would make in her new environment, once they got settled, began to fade.

The living-room was furnished in Mission of the Roycroft Style— big oak chairs with leather cushions; a rectangular couch, leather-cushioned also; a table that was strong enough to be used for a carpenter's bench. And all in spite of the fact of a two-toned light-green, satin-finished wall-paper of the 1890 "parlor period," and an ivory-tinted mantel, which, mongrel though it was, showed more strain of Adam than of Elbert Hubbard.

Stella put yellow-flowered cretonne at the windows. She told Laurel that she had seen a colored picture of a Mission room, in a magazine with yellow-flowered cretonne for hangings, and it was perfectly stunning! She knew where she could get some yellow-flowered cretonne for only ninety-eight cents a yard as effective as linen at six-fifty. But, the hangings did not make the room right. Laurel felt convinced at last that the room would never be right.

One afternoon, when her mother was out shopping, she tried to give it just a little of the same look that Mrs. Morrison gave her rooms. But it was hopeless. Afterwards she wandered through the apartment gazing upon all its details with despairing eyes.

The kitchenette with its piled-up breakfast and dinner dishes, waiting for their nightly washing (Stella kept no maid, and she had her own way of keeping house), suggested to Laurel little of the hominess of Mrs. Morrison's big roomy kitchen, basking in the afternoon warmth of a great black stove, the table spread with a bright red cloth, and a cheerful, broad-faced clock ticking lazily on the mantel.

The Boston apartment was very little like the "home all of our own" of Laurel's dreams. There was no garden. There was no lawn. There was no front door with a knocker, and a single bell. The only difference, as far as Laurel could see, between an apartment and a hotel was that in an apartment you ate your meals in your own rooms instead of downstairs, and it wasn't against the rules to use the gas for cooking.

Laurel didn't like Boston. She didn't know of a single winding river, over which to glide upon skates, in and out among alder bushes; nor of a single bare hillside, white with the first snowfall, down which to fly into the sunset, upon skiis; nor of any stone wall to follow for pussy-willows in March; nor rocky pasture-land nor rough woodland, to steal away to, all alone, in April, in search of trailing arbutus.

She didn't know of any corner store where stationery was sold and pencil boxes and return balls and jackstones, and gumdrops, seven for five cents, and cocoanut cakes, three for two. She didn't know of any hump-backed cobbler, whose tiny shop smelled deliciously of leather and was such a cheery place to visit when school was over and her mother was out. Jake, the hump-backed cobbler, would bow and bob at her like a Rip Van Winkle dwarf, whenever she came into his little box, and sweep off a place with his grimy shirt-sleeve for her to sit down upon, and chuckle and spit, and tell her stories about what his father used to do when he was drunk.

Laurel missed Jake. She missed Tony, too—the black-haired, olive-skinned young Greek, who kept a fruit store, and gave her a plum or a pear, or a banana, not the least bit rotten, whenever she went to see him; and, smiling, showing his beautiful white teeth, told her about the lovely dark girl in Athens, waiting for him to send her a ticket to come to America and marry him.

She missed Mrs. McDavitt, who had so many children, and lived in Cataract Village in the top of a tenement house, whom her mother used to take her to see occasionally of late—but whom she must never refer to, any more than to her grandfather—the queer, glum, ragged old man, who lived all alone in a little reddish house, which her mother called "that hovel," on the edge of the river, whom occasionally, also, of late, her mother used to take her to see. She missed Sadie, the chambermaid at the King Arthur, and Michael Dolan, the policeman; and Jim Doherty, the mailman, who knew her father's handwriting; and "peg-legged Eddy," who sold pencils and shoestrings at the corner of Main and Depot Streets. Laurel missed all her Milhampton friends. For

Laurel had friends in Milhampton, although they did not attend Miss Fillibrown's Private School.

Most of all, perhaps, she missed Miss Thomas, the kind, wrinkled-faced, quiet-voiced librarian at the Milhampton Public Library, who let her wander at will, alone, among the book-stacks, and take out and put back any volume she pleased without asking.

She believed she hated the librarian at the public library to which Mr. Hinckly directed her. On her first day there the librarian had spoken harshly to Laurel, and made her blush with shame. Laurel had never used a card catalogue before. It hadn't been necessary with Miss Thomas. In her engrossed interest in the myriads of varying titles she had drawn out and piled on the table beside her at least a dozen of the little drawers that contained the luring cards.

Suddenly somebody at her elbow exclaimed, "You mustn't do that!"

Laurel gave a little startled jump. She had been a thousand miles away.

"It's not necessary to remove but one drawer at a time." There was displeasure in the voice.

Laurel flushed.

The librarian began returning the drawers to their places with emphatic little jerks and shoves. Then, glancing at Laurel sharply, she remarked, "Why, you've picked them from A to Z! What book is it you're hunting for, anyway?"

Laurel was forced to answer. "I wasn't hunting for any special book."

"What were you doing, then?"

"I was just looking at the titles for fun," Laurel murmured.

The librarian gave her a withering look. "The card catalogue is not fun. It's for use," she reprimanded. "It's not a toy. It's a tool. Don't ever play with it again."

Once out on the street Laurel said to herself, fighting with tears she could not control, "I'll never go near it again! I'll never go into the building again!"

It was six months before her hunger for books overcame her fear of being recognized, and humiliated a second time.

Laurel spent many hours in the trolley-cars in Boston. Her mother decided it was too late in the year to attempt to place her in any private school (of course public schools were no more to be considered in Boston than in Milhampton), but Mr. Hinckly said Boston was full of splendid institutions that specialized in about every subject that existed, and he could arrange for Laurel to take up courses of instruction in almost any of them.

Therefore Laurel traveled from one side of Boston to another, pursuing music in one building, French and German in another, Art in a third, Current Events in a fourth, Filet lace-making in the top loft of a fifth. She chafed beneath the incoherent routine. She longed for Miss Fillibrown's, although she hadn't been very happy there. She thought it was the familiar classrooms and familiar faces she was homesick for, but really it was the coördination and consistency of an organized unit. The pupils in Laurel's classes in Boston were as varied in age, race, sex, and station as are a chance group gathered together in the elevator of a public building.

Night after night Laurel cried softly into her pillow after her mother had fallen safely to sleep. Day after day she struggled with tears that seemed always to be just beneath the thin surface of her smiles.

She tried to reason with herself. She had been away from Milhampton before. Why, almost every summer since she could remember, she had been lonely in some unfamiliar place. But it had been bearable, she supposed, because it had been only for limited periods. And, besides, there had always been bellboys to speak to, elevator-men, and chambermaids. There had always been a game of billiards to watch, or an auction-table of women to listen to.

Once, on the sidewalk outside the apartment, waiting for her mother to return from a shopping-tour, Laurel fell into shy conversation with a dark little girl, a few years younger than herself who lived in the apartment below. The possibility of a friendship with this gentle child filled Laurel with timid happiness for a whole afternoon.

But when she told her mother about the conversation, Stella had exclaimed, "Heavens, we can't know those people, Laurel. They're foreigners! So is the family above us. I've discovered this place is riddled with them. Mr. Hinckly couldn't have known what he was talking about! We've simply got to get out sooner or later."

Until Stella moved to Boston, Laurel had preferred a tramp in the country, or a call on Jake, or Tony, or peg-legged Eddy, to the movies; or a stolen pilgrimage to the little house that used to be red, where the mysterious old man who she must never tell was her grandfather lived, to a vaudeville or play. But in her new solitude, where there was no place to go and nowhere to call, Laurel looked with interest upon the diverting interior of any amusement place.

She went to the movies with her mother three times a week regularly. They climbed to gallery seats at Keith's every time the bill was changed. On Saturday nights Stella and Laurel usually dressed up in their best clothes, and dined at a fashionable hotel, ordering the lowest-priced entrée on the bill, dawdling over their bread and butter, as they observed the gay parties about them, and watched the waiters bear in marvelous planked steaks and Peach Melbas.

It was a bleak and forlorn sort of an existence for both mother and child, and terribly shorn of human contacts. But it needn't have been quite so bleak and forlorn and shorn, Stella said, if Laurel hadn't taken such a dislike to Alfred Munn. Ed tried to be awfully kind. He called at the apartment before they had been in it a week. He tried to be awfully kind to Laurel especially. But the child wouldn't let him.

4

"I can't bear that man, mother," she had said as soon as the door had closed upon him after his first call. "Don't let him come again." There was a red spot in the center of each of her cheeks.

"Mercy, mercy, Lollie," laughed Stella. (Lately Lollie would flare up like a little firebrand every once in a while over the littlest things! Her age, probably, Stella concluded.) "Why, what's the matter with Ed?" she asked lightly, humoringly.

"He's horrid!"

"Horrid? How's he horrid?"

"He tickled me in the ribs and said I was pretty, and kissed me."

"Well, what of that? You're only a little girl. Why shouldn't he tell you you are pretty, and kiss you?"

"His lips were wet, and his breath smelled. Oh, mother!" shuddered Laurel. "Don't let him kiss me again. Don't let him come here again."

"Now don't be silly, Laurel. I can't tell Ed Munn not to come here again. It would be awfully rude and bad-mannered."

"But *he's* rude, *he's* bad-mannered."

"Why, Laurel, how can you talk so about a gentleman who's trying to do so much for us?"

"He isn't a gentleman."

"He's more of a gentleman, I guess, than that dirty old cobbler you like so, who spits and swears, and that Dago who sells fruit, and came over steerage."

"Jake isn't dirty—only on the outside, and Tony is not a Dago. He's a Greek and he comes from a place in Greece where the most beautiful things in the world came from! Besides, Jake and Tony don't kiss me, and Jake and Tony don't say horrid things to me about *you*."

"And what things did Ed say about *me?*"

"When you were out of the room he put his arm around me, and told me he thought *you* were pretty, too."

"Well?"

"He shouldn't have said that, should he? Not to me? The way he did?"

"Why not? I don't call that horrid."

"Don't you? Really?"

"Certainly not. Why shouldn't he say it, if he thought it?"

Laurel stared at her mother, confused, perplexed. She didn't know how to answer, how to explain. She had never liked Ed Munn, but her dislike of him had never swept over her like this. It was frightening. Her sudden hatred of the man was like a big dense cloud that had rolled upon her unawares and enveloped her completely. She had turned toward her mother for help, for comprehension. She had groped for a steadying

"Don't let him kiss me again. Don't let him come here again."

hand. But no hand had been held out.

Suddenly Laurel turned and buried her face in the pillow on the couch and burst into violent weeping. Of late many of her emotions were like enveloping clouds—love and worship, as well as hate and scorn. Her passion for Mrs. Morrison was big, dense, un-understandable. As she lay with her face buried in the dark of the pillow, she could see great masses of red and purple light-dust, shapeless and conglomerate, rolling and shifting senselessly in the dark behind her closed lids. Life was like that. Oh, if only somebody would show her a straight easy little path leading through the confusion.

"Oh, come, come, Lollie," exclaimed Stella. "Don't do that way. Of course if you feel so badly as all that about poor Ed, why—he needn't come, I suppose. But for the life of me, I don't see what he's done to you."

It was the first time for years Stella had seen Laurel cry like a little girl. It was the last time she ever saw her. After that one outburst, Laurel never again betrayed to her mother her fear of the shifting clouds of the twilight stratum of the dawning of her soul.

Stella was not mistaken in attributing Laurel's sudden aversion to Ed to her age, but she soon discovered it was no whim. In fact, Laurel seemed so terribly set against "poor Ed" that she almost was inclined to believe that Stephen must have "poisoned" her mind somehow. Why, when Ed invited Laurel and her mother to go to the theater with him, and choose their own show, the child refused absolutely to stir an inch. She wouldn't touch a piece of the generous box of candy he sent them. "Oh, how can you bear him?" she remarked quietly (for all the world like Stephen) when she found his name written on the card in the envelope tucked underneath the showy bow of ribbon.

Stella had to tell Ed the truth at last. She hated to give up all the good times he stood ready to shower upon them. She didn't mind giving up Ed himself. She always got sick of him after a little while, anyhow, and she must confess he had run downhill considerably even since last September. He had changed his business again. He was working in some sort of machine-shop now, and his finger-nails were terribly broken and greasy.

CHAPTER SEVENTEEN

1

Laurel sat on the end of the pier with her feet swinging over the edge. A girl about her own age sat on each side of her. Their arms were thrown lightly around her shoulders, and hers lightly around theirs. All three of the girls were in white, except for their Boutet de Monvel colored sweaters—pale pink, pale yellow, and faintest lavender. The three girls made as pretty a display against the gray-blue of the lake as a fragment of rainbow. Beneath their swinging feet floated a flotilla of canoes, their bright red and green sides flashing in the sun. On the pier behind the girls was a collection of boxes, leather-encased thermos-bottles and jars, and several tea-baskets.

The three girls were waiting for "the crowd" to assemble. "The crowd" was going on a picnic to Stag Island to-day. Laurel was one of "the crowd."

Laurel was seventeen years old now, and this was the first time in all her life she had ever been one of a crowd. The thrilling experience had lasted for ten days. It would be three weeks the day after to-morrow since Laurel and her mother had arrived at this unexpected Paradise.

Laurel was keenly conscious of the careless arms about her shoulders, but she didn't show it. Laurel could conceal joy and pride, she discovered, quite as successfully as disappointment and chagrin. She was keenly conscious, too, of the girl she had always been before on occasions of this sort, as she had strolled by just such intimate little groups as she now miraculously found herself one of, she and her mother taking in what details of exciting preparations as they could, in a glance or

two, or covert backward look. Laurel felt sorrier for that girl on this happy morning, she thought, than she ever had before.

Now, down the long pier that stretched out into the lake from the lawn in front of the hotel drifted other fragments of rainbow, other groups of two-and-three girls with arms linked; and among them occasionally a boy or two—tanned, lean, loose-knit, tough-muscled, dressed in light trousers and soft shirts—typical American college boys. There was a whole rollicking bunch of them behind the last trio of girls. By the time "the crowd" had all collected, the pier was as noisy as an ivy-covered wall full of sparrows on the first sunny day of spring.

Laurel and the two girls beside her jumped up and joined the general chatter. Mrs. Adams and Mrs. Grosvenor, the two chaperons for the day's festivities, leisurely approaching the bevy could catch bits and snatches of characteristic conversations.

"Gorgeous day! Good-looking sweater, my dear! One exactly like it in henna. Last one in the dining-room—perfectly stunning! Absolutely! Crazy about that color."

Laurel didn't contribute much to the staccatoed exclamations, but her eyes shone, and her cheeks were bright.

"Did you ever see any one quite as lovely as Laurel Dallas this morning?" remarked Mrs. Adams to Mrs. Grosvenor.

"She's perfectly exquisite."

"How is your mother, this morning. Laurel, my dear?" Mrs. Adams inquired a moment later.

"Oh, better, thank you, Mrs. Adams," Laurel replied, turning her flushed, pleased face toward the older woman. "The sweet-peas you sent up to her were lovely. She told me to thank you ever and ever so much."

"I left another book at the desk, to be sent up to her later," remarked Mrs. Grosvenor.

"Oh, mother will be so pleased!"

"I hope she likes Wells, and hasn't read his latest."

"I'm sure she hasn't. You're awfully kind, Mrs. Grosvenor."

"Not a bit. I've been ill in a hotel-room myself, Laurel, dear. I know what it is like."

• • •

"Oh, Miss Dallas!" suddenly somebody exclaimed, close beside Laurel's other shoulder.

Laurel turned and looked up into the eyes of Mrs. Grosvenor's son Richard—her older son. She had two. Richard was a senior in college. He was one of the oldest boys who played with the "crowd." All the girls were "simply crazy" about Richard Grosvenor.

"But he can't see anybody but *you,* Laurel Dallas," one of the girls who had been sitting on the edge of the pier with Laurel had just told her.

"You're going with me, in *my* canoe, aren't you?" he now said to Laurel, smiling.

Any of the other girls would have known how to respond in the bluff, hearty, good-comradeship style of the day. "Thanks, Dick," or, "Crazy to," or, "Sure I am," but Laurel hadn't acquired all the ways yet. "Am I?" she replied, in the same pleased surprised manner with which she met all attentions shown her.

"Yes, you are," he assured her quietly. He turned away.

"There! What did I *say,* Laurel Dallas?"

"I'll bet he picks a single canoe."

"He was here all last summer and never as much as looked at any of us younger girls."

All the boys were now busy among the canoes, loading them, rearranging the cushions and seat-backs, shoving the dainty little crafts up against the pier, ready for the girls to step into.

"All ready, Miss Dallas."

Laurel turned. Yes, Deborah was right! He had selected a single canoe! He stood up in it now as Laurel approached him. He reached up both hands toward her, the canoe drifting away a little from the wharf as he did so. Laurel placed her hands in his, and he swung her across the widening gap between them into the center of the luxurious nest of cushions he had arranged for her in the bottom of the canoe. She alighted in the frail little boat like a bird on a tender twig. There was something of the same birdlike adroitness in every motion that Laurel made.

Laurel had lost none of the peculiar woodsy quality of her charm in the last four years. Her freckles had disappeared, however. (Stella always maintained it was white vinegar and salt.) Her long curls had disappeared, too. Laurel did her hair up now. Rolled it into a simple knot behind. But the gray eyes with their changing moods from dark to light—like a lake beneath varying skies—were still the same. So was her grave listening manner—like trees on a windless night. She was still slight and sleek in body, too—as un-undulating as a low bas-relief when you draw your hand across its surface, but as possessed of lovely curves, too, and as suggestive of softness and warmth.

"Won't you sit down?" Richard Grosvenor asked her, still holding her hands, though he knew she did not require steadying now. Richard had arranged the pillows so that Laurel would be facing him all the way up to Stag Island.

"Couldn't I paddle, too?"

"Do you want to?"

"I'd like to."

"Oh, all right."

2

They were off ten minutes before the others. Mrs. Adams and Mrs. Grosvenor watched the pretty skiff, with Laurel in the bow and Richard in the stern, disappear like a lazy bird around a clump of trees.

"Richard seems quite taken by her," remarked Mrs. Adams.

Mrs. Grosvenor smiled indulgently. "I can't deny it."

"Well, he certainly shows excellent taste. I think she is a lovely girl."

"Yes, Richard has always been very discerning. I've often told him he's really almost too particular—*too* fastidious about girls. This is his first serious affair since he has been in college as far as I know."

"It really is, then, serious?"

"Oh, I couldn't say that. It is obvious, that's all. Laurel is only seventeen, you know—a mere child, though Richard, absurd boy, says she's more like twenty in many ways than most girls he knows of twenty-two. It's serious enough, you see, for him to want to talk about her to me. He confided to me yesterday he intends inviting her to the game in November and to Class Day next June. She was motoring with us yesterday afternoon and we discovered some mutual friends. It seems she visits at Mrs. Cornelius Morrison's, you know, of New York and Long Island. I am on two charitable boards with Mrs. Morrison. She is a charming woman. Bob, my other son, is at St. Lee's, with Mrs. Morrison's oldest boy, Cornelius. They're delightful people.''

3

It was about an hour's paddle to Stag Island, as the bird flies, but Richard guided the canoe along the irregular coastline, gliding through the dappled shadows of the beech and birch, of dogwood, and wild hydrangea, and occasional denser stretches of close-growing spruce and hemlock.

For the first ten or fifteen minutes Laurel didn't say a word. Not a single word! She sat in her perch in the bow, and steadily, rhythmically dipped her paddle into the water, drew it back, raised it, reached forward, dipped it into the water again. Richard, a few feet behind her, followed her slow revolutions. The effect upon him was almost hypnotic. It was awkward to be silent with most girls. He seldom was. Most girls avoided any such lapses as this. But Laurel Dallas would drift into silence as naturally, as unconsciously, as a canary, whose song is interrupted by some simple cause, and out of it in the same unexpected spontaneous fashion.

The crowd had been left far behind—they couldn't even be heard—when Laurel and Richard slipped into a little sequestered cove, almost a cave, with a leaf-covered roof—a lovely spot. Instinctively both the paddles dug deep into the water and held the canoe stationary. Laurel lifted her paddle very gently, and laid it noiselessly across her knees. The only sound in the sylvan sanctuary was the drip—drip—drip of a few drops of water from her paddle's broad end.

Finally Richard said softly from his seat behind Laurel, "Are you there?"

She broke into a low pleased laugh at that. "Every bit of me is here!"

"I wondered. You've been so noisy."

She leaned her head back and gazed up at the blue sky through the low-hanging branches. She drew in her breath deep. "Oh, isn't it too beautiful to be true!"

Richard, gazing only at her, thought it was! He didn't say so, simply smiled and remarked, "You like the woods, don't you?"

"I love them!" Laurel exclaimed.

But it wasn't the woods she was loving so much just then. It was life. Life had never seemed so kind and generous, so good and beautiful to her as now! She sighed, then suddenly lifted her paddle, plunged it into the dark water at her side, and slipped out of the little cave-spot, into the sunshine again. Slipped out into silence again, too.

"You aren't talking to me very much this morning," later Richard informed her.

She made no reply.

"You're a funny girl. I never knew a girl in my life who had silence for a line."

"Do you want me to talk?"

"No."

"When I'm in a canoe, near the shore, like this, I love sneaking around the corners on the birds and animals when they're not expecting you, and see what they're up to."

Some five, ten, fifteen minutes later, the canoe, pushing its nose around a bit of wooded peninsula, came abruptly upon a deer standing upon the shore. Laurel made no exclamation at sight of him, nor did she stop paddling or vary her stroke. She simply gazed in silent admiration for a second or two, then abruptly turned and looked back over her shoulder, to find out if her companion saw the beautiful creature too. Richard thought he had never seen anything so lovely, so blinding as Laurel's eyes as they met his! He smiled, nodded. She turned back satisfied. Not a word was spoken, but sharing the deer that way was— well—"Look here," said Richard a moment later, "haven't you paddled enough? Come, won't you please sit down here on the cushions and talk?''

She did finally.

"You're different from any girl I ever knew."

Most girls liked being told they were different. It seemed to distress Laurel.

"I try hard not to be."

"Don't try."

Laurel had never been talked to by any boy like this before. She was at a loss to know how to banter back.

"Are you already booked for the game in November?" asked Richard.

"The game?"

"The big game, I mean. It's in Cambridge this year."

"Oh, no, no, I'm not," Laurel's heart fluttered. He meant the big Harvard-Yale game! Oh, how happy her mother would be!

"I want you to go with me."

"Why, but I—do you think your mother—I mean—we—"

"I know," he interrupted, "that we've known each other only a week, and all the rest of that silly conventional stuff. But I'm not a perfect stranger to you. You can tell your mother that my kid brother knows Con Morrison. He visited him once. Con has been at our house. Anyhow, when your mother is able to come downstairs, she'll know us herself. It will be all right *then*. I simply had to get my word in now for fear you might get booked with somebody else. I want you to go to the game with *me*, if you go with anybody. Will you?"

"Yes, I will," said Laurel, looking off toward the shore, her eyes again suddenly dark and luminous.

Richard looked toward the shore, too. Had she seen another deer?

When they landed at Stag Island half an hour later, "Don't forget you're going to paddle back with me, too," Richard whispered.

175

All day long one happy moment followed another as uninterruptedly as one telegraph-pole after another flashing by the window of a railroad train. It had been like that ever since the morning Mrs. Adams had fallen into conversation with Laurel on the hotel veranda. That was ten days ago, yet Laurel was only just beginning to become sufficiently used to the steady succession of kindnesses as to take them for granted, as to forget for an hour or so, occasionally, the phenomenon of their unfailing repetition.

Mrs. Adams had noticed Laurel the first morning she had appeared alone in the hotel dining-room. So too, had others noticed her. The head-waiter had shown Laurel to a table by a far window. After she had sat there alone during breakfast, lunch, and dinner, Mrs. Adams made inquiries of the clerk. It seemed the new girl's mother was ill upstairs. Tonsillitis. The hotel doctor was taking care of her. Mrs. Adams spoke to Laurel that morning, asked her if there was anything she could do to help, and introduced her to two girls standing, near by, with tennis racquets.

"Do you play?" asked one of the girls.

"*Will* you play?" asked the other.

It was as easy as that. That very morning Laurel played tennis with three girls of "the crowd"; that very afternoon played golf with three others; that very evening met the boys and danced until the music stopped, running upstairs between numbers to see if her mother was comfortable, and to let her share what she knew would make her happier than anything else in the world.

"Well, I guess we've struck the right place at last, Lollie," Stella exclaimed from her pillow, with a glint of triumph in her eyes. "Don't think of me. Don't come up again, dearie. I'm all right. I'm bound to be. I just knew we'd happen on to gold some day."

It had all been pure luck. Stella had chosen this particular hotel from a circular, on the strength of the fact of its high rates. The start had been anything but propitious. Either she or Laurel had been ill from the first moment of their arrival. Laurel was confined to the bedroom the first twenty-four hours, and Stella had been obliged to wander about the unexplored regions downstairs companionless. Then the moment the fever left Laurel, didn't it go and settle itself upon Stella—settle and stay, too! At the end of two weeks Stella was only just beginning to sit up in a chair by her bed.

5

After lunch under the tall pines on Stag Island the boys went off to explore the coast; and the girls (after the tea-baskets were repacked and the pine-needle bank made as neat and clean as the inside of a pine chest) grouped themselves in colorful bunches on the soft brown background, and producing gay work-bags, began plying various tools—knitting-needles, crochet-hooks, and tatting-bobbins; conversing the while lazily, meanderingly, breaking into shrill peals of laughter, now and then, or fragment of popular song.

Laurel lay back, flat on the ground, idle, her hands folded under her head, and gazed up at the murmuring tops of the trees. She wished her mother might be hiding up there among the needles, gazing down at her through the gaps, seeing, hearing.

Deborah, seated beside Laurel, was tickling her nose with a spear of field grass, Laurel attempting to catch it in her mouth by occasional puppy-like snaps. Frances on the other side was amusing herself by weaving pine needles through the meshes of Laurel's sweater. "I'll pay you back, somehow," purred Laurel contentedly.

Now they were telling her about the theatricals they gave every year in August, discussing what sort of a rôle would be best suited to her; now describing the delights of the night she would spend on the top of Spear Mountain before the season was over; now commanding her to make herself useful and sit up and help wind some yarn.

Oh, was it all true? Did they like her a little? Were they her friends? It seemed to Laurel that afternoon, as the shadows grew longer on the western margin of the lake and the hour for the homeward paddle with

Richard Grosvenor through those shadows, approached, that her cup of happiness was full to the brim.

6

At the end of the homeward paddle it seemed to her that that cup was overflowing. Richard had asked her to be his partner in the tennis tournament on Saturday; he had asked her to go to lunch at a neighboring hotel with his mother and himself to-morrow noon; he had asked her to come out alone with him, in the canoe, to-night after dinner, when the moon rose; he had asked if he might write to her after he returned to town. He was going back in four days. He had taken a job in his father's office for the rest of the summer.

As they had drawn near to the pier in front of the hotel, he had said to Laurel, interrupting his paddling as he did so, leaning forward, "It doesn't seem possible that I met you only a week ago" (Oh, it was the beginning of the old, old story). "You seem to me like somebody I've known a long while" (told in the old, old way).

Laurel closed her eyes a moment—he didn't see her—then opened them wide. She had a feeling she might wake any moment and find it all a dream.

As she jumped out of the canoe on to the pier beside him, a look passed between them that was like the look when they had shared the deer silently together. For the third or fourth time that day Laurel's heart fluttered and seemed almost to turn over.

Several of "the crowd" were on the pier when Laurel and Richard arrived. Deborah called out brightly to them. "Come along, walk up with us."

She linked a free arm familiarly through Laurel's as she approached, and Richard fell into step on Laurel's other side. Frances and two boys were also with the group. They all moved up the pier together. The girls began singing a popular song. Then suddenly in the midst of the chorus, Deborah stopped singing, stopped walking, too. So did the others.

"Oh girls! Look!" she exclaimed. "There is that woman!"

Laurel glanced up. Coming down across the lawn in front of the hotel approaching the pier, she saw her mother.

7

Stella was several hundred yards away, but Laurel was familiar with the black-and-white striped foulard which she now wore. Stella had remodeled her foulard this spring. She had given it a lot of fresh "pep," with generous dashes of Kelly green. Deborah seemed familiar with the foulard, too.

"What woman?" Frances inquired.

"Why, my dear, look, look for yourself, and see. Don't you remember that dreadful dress? Of course you do! You were with us. You saw her about two weeks ago. She was around the hotel all one day."

"Good gracious! Of course I do! We wondered how such a person ever got in here, and then decided she must have come, just for the day, from the unspeakable place on the other side of the lake."

"Notice her, Laurel," laughed Deborah, giving Laurel a little squeeze. "I believe she is coming down toward the pier. Take her in. She's a perfect scream. Paint about an inch thick, and plucked eyebrows, and dyed hair, and not a day under forty. Oh, she's a mess. You remember her, Richard, don't you?"

"Yes, I remember her. Awful dame! Horrible creature!"

Behind Laurel lay only water. On either side of her lay only water. She could not turn and run. She watched her mother choose the gravel path that led to the pier. ("She is! She's coming this way, girls!" delightedly ejaculated Deborah.) Then suddenly Laurel exclaimed, "I've lost something."

"Lost something?"

"My watch!" She held up an empty wrist. "It must have dropped off in the canoe."

She turned back immediately. Richard turned back, too.

"Shan't we all come and look?" Deborah offered.

"No, please," Laurel called back.

"You all go along," Richard ordered. "We'll find it."

"I think it must be among the cushions somewhere," said Laurel. All during the torturing ten or fifteen minutes when she and Richard shook the cushions and pillows, each separate one, and then ran their hands into every possible corner and crevice of the canoe where a watch might lodge, and even searched between the loosely fitted boards of the pier, Laurel kept a constant watch of the shore. She saw her mother walk slowly down the path toward the lake, arrive at the water's edge, hesitate, and then sit down on one of the rustic seats built on either side of the pier, where it joined the bank. She saw the group which she had just left approach the rustic seats, draw nearer to her mother, pass her mother! Thank kind heaven above, they didn't stop! Her mother didn't introduce herself to them after all! Laurel breathed freer. But only for a short time. It soon became evident that her mother was going to wait for her at the rustic seats until her errand at the end of the pier, whatever it was, was finished.

Laurel couldn't keep up the silly search among a half-dozen sofa-pillows and one canoe indefinitely. She must go back along the pier and pass between the rustic seats with Richard Grosvenor beside her, in minute or two. Would she tell him now—immediately, that the "awful dame" was her mother?

"Well, I guess my watch isn't here, after all," she said with a catch in her voice, with almost a sob. It was over—all over. And so unbeautifully, so hideously.

"If the watch isn't here, it's probably up at Stag Island. If we both paddle hard, we can be there before dark. Jump in, we'll find it."

Laurel gave Richard a look that was like that of a dog to the god who releases his foot from the jaws of a steel trap. "Oh, you are good!" And she jumped into her place in the front of the canoe, he jumped in behind, and they were off, out of sight, out of sound, in three minutes.

They didn't find the watch. They hunted until it was dark on Stag Island and paddled back by the light of a slowly rising July moon. They hardly talked at all. Richard was aware of a high current of feeling that seemed to be coursing through this mysterious girl ever since the first moment that she had noticed that her wrist was bare. It awed and silenced him.

It wasn't until they were returning from Stag Island that he remarked, "You must think a lot of that watch."

She replied, "I'll never forget you're coming to help me find it."

"But we haven't been successful."

"That doesn't matter. I'll never forget it. Never, never, never, never."

A similar high current of feeling coursed through Richard, too, at the sound of her low voice, earnestly repeating the single word to him.

8

It was after nine o'clock when Laurel and Richard reached the pier for the second time that evening. It was deserted. So, too, Laurel observed, with a fresh wave of gratitude for the boy who had saved her, and her mother also, were the rustic seats.

"I'm going in by a side door," Laurel said to Richard, as they walked toward the lighted hotel. "You go in the other way. You see the crowd. I want to go right up to my mother as quickly as I can."

"But you'll be down again?"

"Not to-night."

"You haven't had any dinner."

"I'll have some sent up."

"But—"

"Please."

"Shan't I see you again to-night?"

"Not to-night."

"When shall I see you again?"

(In ten—in five minutes, when "the crowd" told him, he wouldn't want to see her *ever* again.)

"To-morrow," she managed to smile.

"Yes. Don't forget. We're going to have lunch together to-morrow."

"I won't."

"I've only four days left," he went on eagerly, "give me the morning before lunch, too, will you? Please. We've so much to talk about, and I've only four days left. We'll go somewhere alone."

They had reached the rear door now. Laurel had one hand on the knob.

"Will you? Please answer. Will you?"

Laurel turned and looked up at him, and nodded.

"Right after breakfast?"

She nodded again.

"Promise?"

For the third time she nodded, then suddenly reached out her free hand and touched Richard Grosvenor on his arm, drew her hand back quickly, and whispered, "Good-night."

Her eyes were as black as the lake beneath the moon.

"Laurel!" Richard moved toward her, but she had turned, she had gone. The big door with its heavy spring closed softly upon him.

CHAPTER EIGHTEEN

1

Laurel found her mother propped up in bed.

"Well, of all things! Where have you been?" she exclaimed as Laurel came into the room.

"Didn't any one tell you?"

"Not till just about half an hour ago; then that Mrs. Grosvenor sent a bellboy up with a note, saying not to worry, you had lost something and had gone back to the island with her boy to hunt for it. What did you lose, Laurel?"

"My watch."

"Your watch! Why, don't you remember you said this morning you wouldn't wear it because it might get wet? There it is on the bureau!"

"Why, that is so."

"Gracious! What's the matter with you?"

"I must be losing my memory, I guess," smiled Laurel wanly. She crossed the room and slipped the watch onto her wrist.

"Had a good time to-day?" Stella inquired.

"Wonderful."

"You must tell me about it. Every word! I'm crazy to hear."

"I will. How have you been, mother?"

"*Where* have I been, you better ask."

"Well, where have you been?"

"Downstairs!" she announced with a triumphant nod of her head.

"Downstairs!"

"It's a wonder you didn't see me. I saw *you*. The doctor was here

183

this morning, and said it would do me good to get up and around as soon as possible now. At first I thought I better not till tomorrow morning. Then I said to myself it would be fun to surprise you. So I dressed about four o'clock, and sat around on the veranda for a while. I felt just fine, and when I saw all your party coming down the lake in the canoes, I walked down to the pier to meet you. I saw you when you went off with that young man, heaven knew where. I supposed you would be right back. I waited for over an hour in that little summer-house at the end of the pier. I thought it would be so nice to meet him like that, offhand, and I was looking rather well.''

Laurel, occupied before the mirror—pulling off the lavender sweater over her head, removing the soft felt tam-o'-shanter that matched it, giving her hair gentle little presses and pokes—inquired casually, "Did you stay downstairs to dinner?"

"No, I didn't. Though I felt all right. But I thought *this* way—it would be nicer to meet all your friends when you were around to introduce me. I'll go down to breakfast with you to-morrow morning. I feel just great.''

"Then you didn't meet anybody?''

"Not yet.''

"Mother,'' said Laurel, turning toward her from the mirror, "I'm going downstairs just a moment if you're all right. I won't be long.''

"Mercy! Don't think about me. Stay as long as you want, and have a good time. Gracious, you deserve it. I'm as contented as a clam, so long as you are happy, Lollie. But you can't go like that, in that wrinkled waist and your hair all mussy.''

"Oh, it doesn't matter.''

Laurel did not take the elevator downstairs. She walked. The elevator would leave her the whole length of the foyer away from the hotel office. The stairs came down just behind it. Laurel felt fairly sure that none of "the crowd'' would be near the office at this time in the evening. She was right. Nobody was near the office. The clerk was alone.

"We're leaving to-morrow'' she told him.

"Leaving! I thought your mother—''

"My mother is much better, and something has happened that makes it necessary for us to go home immediately."

"Why, but—"

"Oh, I know we've engaged the room for the season. You'll have to charge us for it, if that is the way you do. We've got to go, anyway." There was something very convincing about Laurel. "We're going on the early train," she said.

"Oh, but the early train isn't necessary. The train that connects with the Boston Pullman at the Junction, sixty miles below here, doesn't leave until evening."

That didn't matter to Laurel. If she and her mother preferred leaving on the early train, they could do so, couldn't they, and pick up the Pullman, when it came through the Junction at night?

"Why, of course—but it would be very foolish—nobody ever does it."

"We're going to," Laurel announced.

2

"Mother," she remarked ten minutes later, "you must lie there in bed and watch me pack the trunks."

"Pack the trunks!"

"We're leaving this place to-morrow morning, at half-past seven."

"What are you talking about?"

"We're leaving. We're going."

"What do you mean?"

"What I say. I've just been downstairs and told the clerk."

"Have you lost your mind, Laurel?"

A faint smile drifted across Laurel's features, softened for a moment her firmly set jaw and chin.

"Oh, I'm sorry, mother! I'm ever so sorry."

"What's happened? What's the meaning of this?"

"Oh, I just don't like it here any more," shrugged Laurel. "I just can't stand it here any more."

Stella's eyes narrowed. She nodded her head, slowly up and down.

"Humph! Sounds mighty like a quarrel with your young man to *me*."

"Oh, don't say 'my young man,' mother."

"There you go! Just like your father again! Criticizing my language every other minute! Well, then, Richard Grosvenor. Sounds mighty like a quarrel with Richard Grosvenor, to *me*."

"Mother," said Laurel, "I never want to see Richard Grosvenor again as long as I live!"

"I knew it! I knew it! Come, Laurel, don't be a little goose. Mercy, I never saw such a pepper-box! You can't fly out of a hotel like this, on a moment's notice, just because of a little lover's quarrel. Heavens alive! You come to bed and sleep on it. You'll feel entirely different in the morning. So will he. Gracious! I know how those things work. Quarrels make the heart grow fonder. There's a saying something like that. You come to bed, Laurel."

"Not till the packing is finished," said Laurel.

She turned her back upon Stella, crossed the room to the bureau, pulled out a lower drawer, and removed a pile of underclothes.

"You don't mean to say you're going to pack up and clear out of the only place we ever even had a 'look-in' at?"

"Yes, mother."

"Where do you think we're going to at this late date?"

"Why, back to the apartment."

"Back to the apartment in July!"

"Yes, mother."

"Do you mean to say, Laurel, you're thinking of putting me in a train in the condition I'm in?"

"I stopped and asked the doctor. He said it wouldn't hurt you to travel, he thought."

"And what about the expense of this room?"

"The clerk said we wouldn't have to pay for it. But even if we did, it wouldn't make any difference. Oh, mother, don't talk. Don't argue. We're going, anyway."

Laurel was emptying all the bureau drawers now. Stella, from the bed, stared at her speechless, as helpless, as powerless as if *she* were the child. She recognized that look in Laurel's eyes.

"I've brought you up all wrong," she sighed.

Laurel made no reply to that. Swiftly, effectively, she sorted and piled. Swiftly, effectively began filling the trunks.

"Laurel, you're doing a crazy thing," Stella broke out afresh, "and for the life of me, I don't know how to stop you."

"Don't let's go all over it again."

"You're throwing away the best chance you've ever had. Listen to me. Most of these people here come from Philadelphia. I had it all worked out in my mind that if we got the right sort of a start with them this summer, here, we might take an apartment down around Philadelphia somewheres next fall. Then you'd have some of the right kind of friends to play around with, and when the time comes for you to come out, why—"

"Where's the tissue-paper, mother? I think I'll do the dresses next."

Five minutes later Stella became tearful. Laurel brought her a handkerchief.

"I should think," she wailed, after she had vigorously blown her nose and mopped her eyes, "you'd want me to have a little of the good times you've been enjoying these three weeks while I've been cooped up here in bed. *I* like nice people, and things going on myself. You know I do. But just the minute I am able to get out of bed and take in a little of the gayety and excitement, *you* let a silly quarrel with a young fellow you never saw three weeks ago cheat me of it all."

"Where are the trees for your satin slippers? Do you know?" called Laurel from the closet.

3

Laurel and her mother spent all the next day, from ten in the morning, until eight at night in the waiting-room at the Junction. The waiting-room at the Junction was hot and dusty. It swarmed with flies, attracted by discarded lunch-boxes and paper bags. It smelled of cinders and hot steel. There were settees built around the edge of the waiting-room. They were painted mop-colored gray, divided by iron arms into spaces, so that no one could lie down upon them. Laurel arranged the suitcases as best she could, for her mother's feet, and rolled up a traveling-coat into a pillow for her head. All day Laurel hovered solicitously about her mother, offering her frequent drinks of water, which she brought in a paper cup; trying to tempt her with crackers and cheese and sweet chocolate, which she procured from a general store, half a mile up the road; asking her from time to time how she felt; showing concern, anxiety, but not the slightest sign of yielding or regret. Stella, resigned now, and stoically submissive, sat silent and unresponsive all day long. At measured intervals she sighed deeply, eloquently.

At eight o'clock in the evening a Pullman car was backed up to the Junction and side-tracked there for an hour or so to await several incoming trains from various points of the compass. Laurel and her mother crawled in between the sheets of a lower berth in the Pullman car a little after nine.

Laurel was on the inside of the berth. Stella's obdurate back was turned toward her. As Laurel stretched her long slim body down beside her mother, she slipped her hand under her mother's arm—around her waist, as she always did when she went to sleep—though she hadn't last night.

"Mother," she whispered, "aren't you going to forgive me pretty soon?"

Stella pressed the precious hand, drew it closely around her.

"Of course I am, you crazy kid," she whispered back. "I don't care what you do, just so I've *got* you to do it. Gosh, I can't stay mad with you any longer!"

Laurel's arm tightened. That was all right then. Oh, if only Richard— if only he—her arm loosened, grew limp. Laurel fell to sleep almost immediately. So did Stella. They both had been asleep for an hour or more when the hotel train whistled into the Junction at about half-past ten.

Laurel was drifting off into unconsciousness for the second time when she became aware of her name being spoken, just outside the heavy curtain of the berth. She had been dimly aware of voices conversing in low tones for five or ten minutes before the sound of her own name prodded her wide awake. The section opposite had not been made up when she and her mother went to bed. Probably, Laurel concluded, some of the people who had come down on the evening train were sitting there and chatting.

"Yes, that very pretty dark girl, who was so popular with the younger set—lovely eyes. Laurel Dallas. Such an odd name."

"But how is it possible? She seemed so very refined, so distinctly nice in every way."

"Well, I asked the clerk. He told me—"

"You mean the woman in the striped dress?"

"Certainly, certainly. She is that lovely child's mother."

"What a handicap to the poor girl."

"I should say so. All those people she's been playing around with had no idea what her mother was like, I suppose. She's been ill ever since she came. I wish I could have stayed a few days longer and seen just what would have happened when that woman appeared on the scene."

"What's the woman's story?"

"I don't know. I never heard of her before. Dallas is her name, from Boston."

"Poor girl. It's like having a ball and chain around her ankle to be obliged to drag a woman like that after her wherever she goes."

"Yes, but those things happen. Once I knew of a young man— charming—such aristocratic manners, and he came from the commonest family—vulgar people. Of course, being a man, he could escape his family, but a girl—a young girl like that"—the train began to move— "perfectly helpless—branded"—it moved faster—"a shame. Such a pity—Richard Grosvenor—" It moved still faster. The voices were drowned in the rumble of flying steel.

"Poor girl. It's like having a ball and chain around her ankle."

Oh, had her mother heard? Was her mother awake? No, Laurel thought not. Her breathing was heavy and slightly audible. The hand that had grasped hers so tightly a little while ago was limp and lifeless now. Her whole body was limp and lifeless. It moved slightly with the motion of the train, as unresisting as the curtains.

Oh, had Lollie heard? Was she awake? No, Stella thought not. Her soft breathing was as regular as the swinging of a pendulum. The arm that encircled her waist was as unconscious as a sleeping baby's.

So that was the story! Oh, what a fool she had been! A handicap to Laurel! And not because of unfair stories, of whispered scandals (these women didn't know who she was, didn't even know she wasn't living with her husband), but just because of *herself*. Was she so awful—so God-awful, then?

Stella had been listening to the voices for ten minutes before Laurel had become aware of them. She had heard herself described in detail, in cruel detail. She didn't suppose anybody knew that she "touched" her hair a little now and then. Why, even Lollie didn't know it. Up to two years ago it hadn't been necessary, but she did so hate the soft-boiled-egg look when yellow hair begins to turn white. Other women kept themselves young and attractive without being criticized. She had tried not to become a perfect sight for Laurel's sake, to keep in the running, as far as appearances went, so the child need never be ashamed of her, as she had been of her mother and the mouse-colored wrappers. But she had failed. Why, it was the same story right over again. Laurel was ashamed of her mother, too. It was as plain as the nose on your face. That was the reason Laurel was leaving the hotel. She would die rather than confess it, of course. That was the way Laurel was—as considerate, as gentle, as delicate with her common, ordinary, vulgar mother (weren't those some of the words the voices had used?) as with the charming Mrs. Grosvenor or the flawless Mrs. Morrison.

Well, what was to be done about it? Now that Stella knew the truth, knew that just her own personality, just her own five senses and the old hulk of a shell they lived in, was like an iron ball tied to Laurel's ankle (pleasant to learn *that* about yourself in the middle of the night, when you so wanted to be wings for your child), well—now that she *had* learned it, what was the next number on the programme? Laurel being a girl, the voices had said, couldn't escape, couldn't break the chain to the ball. Well, then (Stella's fingers very gently closed over Laurel's. She still slept—and she really did sleep now)—well, then— It would be pretty awful without her, wouldn't it? Dear little Lollie!— Let's see, let's see. No. No other way.

8

A narrow ribbon of sunlight was shining into the berth through a crack by the tightly pulled window-shade by Laurel's feet when she stirred and woke. Stella was waiting for her, had been waiting all night.

"Well, honey!" she said lightly. "Had a good night?"

Their eyes met.

"Splendid. Have you?"

"Great. Feel lots better."

"No, she didn't hear," thought Laurel.

"No, she didn't hear," thought Stella.

CHAPTER NINETEEN

1

Helen Morrison sat in the big library-sort of room where Laurel had first watched her serve tea. She sat by one of the long windows that looked out upon the willow-shaded avenue that wound up to the front door; by the same window, it chanced, out of which she had run to meet Laurel the first time she had come to visit her four years ago. She was dressed very much as she had been then (it was morning and July), in white skirt and waist and low shoes. She sat in front of a desk, writing, in a dilatory fashion. Every little while she glanced back over her shoulder at the clock upon the mantel, then out the window down the willow-shaded drive, then back again to her pen.

Looking at Helen from the clock as she bent over her writing, she seemed not to have changed at all in the last four years, or in the last fourteen years; the same young-girl slenderness (not the slightest thickening of neck and shoulders, hip or ankle), the same young-girl lightness, as she sat poised on the edge of her chair, which was tilted forward on its two delicate front legs. But, when she raised her head, and looked back at the clock, then one saw without a shadow of doubt that she was no longer a girl. It wasn't only her hair (for in the last four years the few white threads Laurel had discovered had become a definite streak of silver cloud that drifted about the left side of her brow and reached backward to the still dark coil in her neck)—it was something more convincing, something less obvious but deeper-rooted. There was on Helen's face a look of settled calm (or was it settled hopelessness?) that hadn't been there four years ago when she had rushed out of the long window down the lawn to meet Stephen and Laurel. There had been laughter and anticipation in her eyes then. Now there were only quiet smiles and submission.

To-day, again, Helen was awaiting the arrival of an automobile. She had sent the car down to the station to meet the train due at ten-forty. It was now after eleven. It was only five minutes to the station. The train must be late. She finished her letter, then rose, crossed the room, and stood looking out of another long window that opened out upon the terrace. Helen was awaiting the arrival of Laurel's mother, of Stephen's wife. She had telephoned last night from New York.

"I'm Mrs. Stephen Dallas," the strange voice had announced. "I want to talk with you. Will you be home to-morrow morning if I come out?"

Helen had replied, with no surprise in her voice, that she would be glad to come in town and meet her there if she preferred.

"No. I'd rather come out."

They had arranged the trains. Helen had told her she would have her met.

When finally the bell rang, and the maid announced Mrs. Dallas, Helen crossed the hall to the reception-room with a sensation as near dread as she had ever felt in her life when about to meet a guest.

Stella was standing up. She had on a dark-blue tricolette suit, and wore a summer fur—white fox, fastened behind. The dead animal's head hung halfway down her back. Stella's coat was tightly buttoned, and fitted her generous bust and hips without a ripple. Her hat was large and broad-brimmed, and didn't take a veil well. Therefore she had adjusted her veil over her bare head before putting her hat on. The veil was drawn tightly over her generous cheeks and chin, and it also fitted without a ripple.

2

Helen looked at nothing but Stella's eyes, as she came toward her smiling, with her hand outstretched.

"Good-morning, Mrs. Dallas," she said. "I hope the chauffeur found you."

"No, he didn't. There was quite a crowd. I walked."

"Oh, I'm sorry. It is such a warm morning. Let me send for some water." She made a movement toward the bell.

"I don't want any water." Why, her hair was snow-white on one side! She couldn't be a day under forty!

"Well, do take off your coat and unfasten your fur."

"No, thanks."

"And sit down. Let us come into the other room. It's pleasanter there."

Helen led the way across the hall, shoved a cool, linen-covered armchair in front of one of the terrace windows. "I always like it here better on a warm morning, looking out on the shadows rather than on sunshine. And there's usually a breeze."

Opposite the armchair Helen placed one of the Sheratons for herself. She made a little waving motion toward the armchair. "Sit down, please," she said; "take that chair."

Stella complied—at least partially. She took the extreme edge of the chair. It was one of those low deep affairs. She'd have a frightful time getting out of it if she sat back. Helen sat down, too. There was a pause—a pause that threatened to become awkward.

"Is it very warm in town this morning?" Helen inquired.

Stella ignored the question. Might as well take the bull by the horns.

"I suppose you think it's funny my coming here."

"No, I don't," earnestly Helen assured her, leaning forward, clasping her hands upon her knees. "You and I have a great deal in common. I don't think it's funny at all."

"Well, funny or not, I had to come. I thought of writing at first, but, gracious, if a thing is important enough to you, you'll do it the right way—at least, the way that seems right to you—whatever any one thinks. There are some things I had to know that nobody but you could tell me, so I decided to come right down here myself and ask them."

"That was the right way."

"I've heard a lot about you."

"And so have I—heard a lot about you."

"From Laurel, I mean."

"Yes, I mean from Laurel, too."

"I suppose you know it, but Laurel thinks a lot of you."

Helen smiled. "And I suppose you know it, but Laurel thinks a lot of you."

"Well, I'm her mother. She has to. But she's got what they call a sort of 'crush'—'mash' we called it when I was a girl—on you. She hates to have me call it that. She won't talk about you very much, now. Thinks I might be jealous or something, I guess. Perhaps I was a little at first, though I hardly knew it. Laurel did, though. Trust her. She's the sort of child knows what you feel before you do yourself almost."

"I know. Sensitive, isn't she—oh, *so* sensitive! I think a great deal of Laurel, Mrs. Dallas. You have a beautiful child, I think."

"She *is* a nice kiddie," said Stella.

For an instant the two women's eyes met. Was that bright look tears, they both wondered.

3

Stella was the first to look away. She cleared her throat, coughed, made another attempt.

"How's Stephen now?"

"I think he's well."

"I suppose you see him now and then?"

"No. The last few times Laurel has visited me, Miss Simpson has brought her, and taken her away. Stephen and I haven't met for two years."

"Oh, that so?" Stella looked back at Mrs. Morrison. Gracious! What had happened? The shining look had all gone from her eyes and the light from her expression. She looked gray, ashen, and old, terribly old.

"Look here, Mrs. Morrison," Stella went on, "I'm not going to beat about the bush any longer. I've been thinking a good deal lately of the advantages to me if I got things fixed up between Stephen and myself, the way he wanted them fixed up a while ago. But before I do any more thinking I want to find out how things are now between Stephen and you."

Helen's clasped hands tightened upon her knee, but she showed no feeling when she spoke.

"Mrs. Dallas," she said, "I don't want to be unkind, but self-denial, our duty to others, the toll that must be paid for mistakes, separation from each other—nothing will ever destroy that which exists, even though without form or expression, between Stephen and me."

Stella looked puzzled.

"But what I want to know is, if Stephen was free, if I stepped aside, the way he suggested, would you two get married?" Might as well come right out with the nub. After all, it didn't make her jump.

"We would," Helen replied.

"Are you sure?"

"I'm sure."

"But you haven't seen Stephen for two years."

"I know, I know. Oh, I'm sorry, Mrs. Dallas. But the truth is best. I think you want it."

"It's what I came for."

"It's what I shall give you, even though it costs me Stephen himself."

"Well, the next thing I want to get clear is, if you two did marry, what about Laurel?"

"If we did—" Helen drew in her breath quickly, "why, if we did—if we did—"

"Yes, if you did, what about Laurel?"

Helen let her breath out ever so carefully, ever so carefully drew in another.

"Oh, Laurel. Laurel is yours, Mrs. Dallas. A child is always her mother's, I think."

"You mean, Laurel would keep right on making her headquarters with me, the same as she does now?"

"Why, of course. I am a mother, Mrs. Dallas. Once I was the mother of a little girl. My little girl would be just Laurel's age now. As long as I live I shall never be guilty of robbing any woman of her only little daughter."

Stella glanced down at her shoe, out upon the terrace, back to her shoe again, cleared her throat, then boldly raised her eyes to Helen's.

"But if the woman didn't want her daughter. I mean if she couldn't have her very well, if it was inconvenient—"

"Don't you want Laurel, Mrs. Dallas?" Helen exclaimed.

"Oh, of course, I *want* her, but you see she's a great expense now, and I haven't many maids—no one to leave her with. I'm quite tied down by her, and—"

"Oh," broke out Helen, and again her eyes were shining, "I'd love to have Laurel! I'd love to have Laurel, even if I had her without Stephen."

"No, that wouldn't do," said Stella, hard and practical, her eyes shining, too, but not with tears—with triumph. "If you were married to Stephen your name would be Dallas then, and Laurel's name would be Dallas, too. Don't you see? And everybody would think, who didn't stop to ask, that Laurel was yours. Gracious, she's enough like you—dark and slim as a smokestack, and you've been her model for years, as far as ways and manners go, and when you begin to do things for her—like giving her, well—a coming-out party, or something—you know she's seventeen now—why, then the invitation cards, 'Mr. and Mrs. Dallas, and Miss Dallas,' would read right, don't you see? I've thought it out. And later, if one of the nice young men in your circle fell in love with Laurel, and married her, why, then again, it would read right in the papers and society columns, where those things are printed. And the same way," Stella pursued, warming to her subject, "at hotels and places when you have to register—that is, if you should travel with Laurel in Europe or California. Laurel really ought to travel. It is so expensive, I couldn't manage it myself, what with all the private lessons in riding and skating, and dancing and music, and heaven knows what-not. You'll find she's quite up in those things. Oh, really," earnestly, eagerly she hastened on, unaware of the increasing wonder and surprise in Helen Morrison's wide-open eyes, "really, if you *do* want a daughter of your own to take the place of that baby you spoke of that died, I'll say this, I don't think you'll ever be *ashamed* of Laurel. She takes after her father, and if you're crazy about her father, why, it popped into my mind that—honestly I can't see a trace of me in Laurel. Nobody can. She's so refined, and sort of elegant in her ways. You know that yourself. Oh, you needn't have a minute's doubt about what sort of a success Laurel will make if you should bring her out in New York society sometime. She makes a wonderful impression upon strangers. Why, if that girl didn't have *me* shackled round one foot everywhere she goes, she'd just *soar*. And another thing I want to make clear to you, don't be afraid I'll be appearing at embarrassing moments. I won't—*ever*. I've got some common sense, thank heaven. I know what sort of an impression *I* make, too."

There was no mistake about the tears in Helen's eyes now. She rose, went quickly over to Stella, sat down on the arm of her chair, and put her arm about her shoulders.

"I see! I understand!" she exclaimed, softly.

4

Stella stiffened. No woman had ever understood before. She had never understood herself. The undercurrent of her life had been flowing beneath the surface waters, unnoticed, unobserved for years, wearing a deeper and deeper channel, gathering strength and power in its hidden course. But not until Mrs. Morrison put her arm around Stella had any one looked down through the flotsam and discovered the crystal waters underneath.

"Everything shall be as you wish," said Helen. "Everything. Travel and parties and friends—everything, that to you means happiness for your child. I'll treat her as my very own, but she will always *be* yours. You will not lose her. You shall see her often. We'll arrange that. Oh, I wonder if I could have done so big a thing for my little girl."

Stella dabbed her eyes with her handkerchief through her veil, struggled to her feet, dabbed her eyes again, bit her lip hard—Good gracious, she mustn't break down and bawl like a baby.

"I'm an awful old fool sometimes lately," she murmured.

"Don't go. Sit down again. Please. We've so much to talk about. I've got so much to learn."

"No, I can't. Laurel thinks I'm in Milhampton, and I must hustle along back to Boston to-night or she'll get suspicious. You've got my idea. There's no need of staying any longer. You tell Stephen I'm ready to get the divorce any day now, and the quicker the better. Only tell him, for goodness' sake, don't put that man Morley Smith on it. I don't believe I could meet that excrescence and be decent to him. Every time I think—but never mind. That's all over. Oh, by the way, one thing more—when Laurel is down here this September visiting you, don't tell her what's up. I can't stand long-drawn-out good-byes. I may mention I'm getting a divorce, but I shan't tell her what for. Don't let on a word till we're ready to shoot. You and Stephen get married, have Laurel down for a Sunday. I'll send her clothes on afterwards. Something like that. I've thought it out. No soft-music sob-stuff for me, thank you. Is this the living-room?"

"Yes, this is the living-room."

Stella gazed at the high, dignified walls silently a moment. "I can just see her in it, entertaining her young friends; walking around on that terrace with Richard Grosvenor—he's somebody your sons know, a young man that is just crazy about Lollie—walking along in her slow grand way under those big aristocratic-looking trees down there; yes, it will suit her fine. That's why I wanted to come out—to see what it was like. I walked by your city house last night. It was closed, but I could get an idea. I suppose you think that's funny, but I've picked out Laurel's clothes so much—" she stopped. "I couldn't see some of the other rooms, could I? I'll never be here again, and, well—you know, it's sort of nice to be able to think of a person in a house or a room you've seen yourself, when they write. I thought Laurel and I might write.''

''Of course you'll write. Oh, it will only be as if she were away at school or college, having all the things you want her to have. Come out into the dining-room. Come out into the garden. Laurel loves the garden. And then come upstairs. The violet guest-room is Laurel's now. Come and see her pretty valanced bed.''

CHAPTER TWENTY

1

Stephen sat in his office, fifteen floors above the sidewalk and street thermometer that registered ninety-five. He sat in the gentle breeze of two silently revolving electric fans, in front of his desk, in a big chair with his elbows on its arm, and his hands folded. He was dictating, gazing out of the high window toward the northeast with a look in his eyes as if he saw a hundred miles away.

To-day, as Stephen sat and gazed, searched, and selected, he was aware of the heat, aware of the rumble of the city outside, aware of the loud insistent pound—pound—pound of a riveter at work near by, aware of his own fatigue, too. He sighed deeply now and then. When Stephen was tired, and gazed out of the high windows in the direction of the green lawns and white beaches of Long Island, there was a Helen between every careful phrase that he spoke.

At a quarter of one that day, or thereabouts, Stephen raised his wrist and glanced at it.

"Time for one more, I think, Miss Mills. Pretty hot, isn't it? Can you stand it? All right. Ready."

He was attacking a difficult second paragraph—twice already had murmured, "No, start again"—when there was a repressed burr at his side. He frowned, turned away from his engrossed contemplation of the illimitable space outside his window, and reached for the telephone, supporting it upon his chest as he leaned back again and spoke into it.

"Who is it?" he asked.

"Long distance. Green Hills, New York, Mrs. Cornelius Morrison," the operator in the outer office announced.

It was as if a current of electricity passed through Stephen. Though he didn't move a hand or foot, Miss Mills observed his sudden alertness, the sudden tightening of the muscles around his jaw and cheek-bones. Discreetly she turned away.

"Connect me," she heard him say. Then he turned to her. His eyes were like spots of phosphorescence. "We'll finish that later. I'll call you." He nodded toward the outer office. She rose. "Please close the door."

Alone, Stephen leaned forward, placed the telephone on the solid foundation of his desk, drew his chair close to it, jerked himself to the edge of the chair, crouched over the telephone eagerly, cupping his hand over the transmitter.

Helen's voice sounded clear and sweet, as if she were in the very room beside him. He hadn't heard her voice for two years.

"Hello."

"Hello, Helen."

"Is it you, Stephen?"

"It's I. Yes. What is it? Are you all right?"

He caught her little laugh.

"Oh, yes, yes. I'm all right. I called you up to find out if you had an engagement for to-night."

"What do you mean?"

"Well, *have* you an engagement?"

"No. Of course I haven't. But—"

"Then could you come down this evening?"

"Helen, what has happened?"

"Nothing awful. Could you?"

"Yes. I could. But—"

"About eight o'clock?"

"Yes, eight o'clock. All right. But, Helen, please—"

"Eight o'clock to-night, then. Good-bye."

She had sent for him! Helen had sent for him to come to her! At one o'clock, at half-past one, at two, Stephen was still sitting in his big chair before his desk, looking far out over the roofs. Miss Mills was still sitting outside the door, waiting to finish the dictation.

2

"I'm sorry to have called you at your office, Stephen," were Helen's first words when she saw him that night, standing ten feet away from him, just inside the threshold of the big room. "I suppose you were having a consultation or doing something important"—she tried to make her voice sound light and careless—"but I wanted to get you, right *straight* off, so that you wouldn't fall down an elevator-shaft, or get killed in an explosion, or something"—she laughed tremulously—"the way they do in novels, sometimes, before I had a chance to tell you that after all our years of waiting, that—that—after—Oh, Stephen—"

3

Stella arrived at the apartment on Commonwealth Avenue at eleven o'clock that night. She telephoned to Laurel from the Back Bay station that she would be out in half an hour, and when she puffed up the last flight of stairs—it grew hotter and hotter as she approached the roof— Laurel, in her thin sleeveless nightgown, with her hair pulled tightly back and braided, was in the hall to meet her.

"I've made some lemonade, mother. It's on the ice. And there's some cold watermelon. Come in and get those horrid hot things off. I've pulled the bed out where it will get the breeze, if there is any, in the early morning. How is Mrs. McDavitt and the children?"

Ten minutes later, Stella, nightgowned and hair pulled back and braided, too, sat on the back porch under the clothes-reel and drank lemonade, and ate cold watermelon, and gazed at Lollie, seated on top of the coal-box with her bare arms locked about her knees, not talking much, looking up at the lop-sided moon that had been full three nights ago on Stag Island.

Funny place, thought Stella, for the lovely Miss Laurel Dallas, who would be staggering New York society one of these days, to be perched in midsummer. Oh, if she could only tell the poor suffering little kiddie (for she was suffering—she had been pretty crazy about that Grosvenor boy, Stella guessed)—if she could only tell her it was only for a short time now; that everything would come out all right in the end. But of course she couldn't. Mum was the word.

"It's simply horrid for you here, honey."

Laurel gave a start, as if she had been a thousand miles away.

"Oh, no, it isn't," she assured Stella lightly. "Really, I like it. Oh, we'll have a good time. See if we don't. There's Revere, and Nantasket, and Norumbega."

"Was it awful lonesome without me?"

"No more awful for me than for you when I'm away, I guess."

"What did you do?"

"Oh, I sat out here."

"Gracious! Seventeen, summer, a moon, and alone, out here."

"About nine o'clock the bell rang. It was that Mr. Munn."

"Oh, Ed! Really?"

"He said he saw the light and thought it was probably *you* who were here, alone, while I was off visiting somewhere. When he discovered it was I, he said please to excuse him, and went away."

"That sounds real polite of Ed."

"No, it wasn't. He didn't have any right to ring the bell for *you*— a man like that. He knows we don't want him. We've shown him. Oh, I hate that man, mother."

"I know you do. You've told me so enough times. Funny. You're your father right over again, Lollie."

"Did father ever see Ed Munn?"

"Mercy, yes!"

"Did father ever hate Ed Munn?"

"Like fury," laughed Stella; "and there was never any sense in it either—no more than with you—just a whim."

Laurel still gazing at the moon and the few far dim stars that seemed to lie beyond was silent. Was Alfred Munn one of the pieces of the puzzle, too?

4

Helen and Stephen were quietly married one afternoon the following spring. The same day Laurel received a note from Mrs. Morrison inviting her to spend a week-end with her, a fortnight later. The invitation did not come as a surprise to Laurel. Mrs. Morrison had told her last September that she hoped to have Laurel stay with her for a few days in the spring. Laurel had told her mother of the possibility. Stella had been working on Laurel's wardrobe, in preparation, for weeks before Mrs. Morrison's note arrived.

Helen was at the station to meet Laurel. She and Mrs. Morrison (she was still Mrs. Morrison to Laurel) were quite alone in the back of the limousine as it threaded its way out of the congestion of Forty-Second Street, and turned north on Fifth Avenue. Laurel sat forward on the edge of the seat beside Helen, cheeks flushed, chin raised, breathing in deep breaths of the intoxicating, Mrs. Morrison-charged air, not saying anything at all.

"Glad to be here?" finally Helen interrupted from her deep corner.

Laurel simply nodded, keeping her starry eyes steadfastly turned away. Her worshipful regard for Mrs. Morrison had not changed in quality in the last four years. The only difference was that she was able to adapt herself a little sooner now than formerly to the dazzling presence of her goddess. Give Laurel an hour and she would find her tongue. Give her several hours and the same emotion which choked, confined— later unloosened, unlocked, threw the gates wide.

"Your father is going to be with us for dinner to-night," briefly Helen announced before the car had left them at the door.

"Oh, I wondered when I'd see father."

Helen and Stephen had decided to tell Laurel together. They waited until after dinner. Con and Dane were away at school, and little Rick, who had been cautioned not to mention the great news, had finally been torn away from Laurel's side (little Rick was devoted to Laurel) and had gone upstairs. Helen and Stephen were alone with Laurel in Helen's lovely ivory-tinted room, seated, all three, before the fire, on the long Sheraton sofa, with Laurel in the middle.

Helen slipped an arm through Laurel's and, smiling across at Stephen, said, "Shall I tell Laurel a story now?"

The story that Helen told was the story of her own life. She told it exquisitely. "And then—and then—and then—" step by step, from the first time when she knew that she loved Stephen when only a little older than Laurel, down through all the years, when their paths diverged, met, diverged, again. It was a simple, straightforward statement of facts, with no excuses nor explanations. It sounded to Stephen like some beautiful epic poem. He had to close his eyes frequently to shut out tears. When she reached the end, "And so here we are, Laurel—Stephen and I, together at last."

Laurel whispered softly, "Married?"

"Yes."

"I wondered when you would be," was Laurel's unsurprised reply.

"How long have you wondered that, Laurel?" eagerly Stephen inquired.

"Oh, ever since I saw you together in the big room at Green Hills, when I came down from upstairs that first time, I felt then that you were meant to be married, only—"

"Yes, only?"

"Only you must have taken a wrong turn way back somewhere—you know how it is—a wrong turn or a detour makes all the journey different sometimes."

Stephen slipped his arm through Laurel's too. "Are you glad?" he asked her.

"Oh, *ever* so glad!" promptly she assured him. "It's like a book, or a play, coming out the way you hoped it would; or a journey ending where it should, even though there was a wrong turn. What shall I call you, Mrs. Morrison?" she broke off. "I've wondered and wondered. Isn't it funny?" she laughed. "You aren't Mrs. Morrison any more!"

What a little girl she was, after all, thought Stephen, and how merciful. It had been easier than he feared to tell her that he had become to another woman what he had one day been to her mother. How simply, how serenely, she accepted that which had been so painfully won.

"Let's call each other by our first names," lightly Helen suggested.

"Oh, I wonder if I ever could! Your name is so—so *special*. Mrs. Morrison is like the word 'America' to me. It *means* things. I couldn't possibly call America anything else."

"You could call it home, couldn't you?" said Helen.

5

Later, placing her hand over Laurel's, and Laurel turning hers palm upwards, and interlacing her fingers with Helen's in impulsive response, Helen said, "There's more to my story, Laurel."

With infinite gentleness she explained to Laurel that she was a part of *this* home now—was a member of *this* family; they were hers and she was theirs. She must have been talking five minutes before Laurel caught the import of her words.

"You mean," suddenly she interrupted, "I'm to live here?"

"Yes, here, and at the place at Green Hills. With us—with your father, with Con and Dane and Rick—they're so happy about it—wherever we are—as one of us, Laurel."

"I never thought of that." Laurel gazed wonderingly around the lovely room. This her home? This beautiful place? A family like other girls? A mother and father who lived together? Mrs. Morrison? "Yes, yes," she gasped, "but what about—what about—"

"What about your mother?" Helen asked for her. "I know, I understand. You shall see your mother often, Laurel."

"You mean"—she still had a manner as if gasping for air—as if groping for light, for comprehension. "You mean mother would still live in Boston?"

"That would seem wisest, wouldn't it?"

"Yes, yes, of course," Laurel nodded. "Yes, that would seem wisest." For a long quarter-minute she was silent, staring straight in front of her, then unlocking her fingers from Helen's, withdrawing her arm linked through her father's, "No," she said quietly, "it wouldn't do."

"You may visit your mother in Boston, Laurel."

Again for a moment Laurel was silent. "No, it wouldn't do," she repeated. The little girl in her had disappeared. The spontaneity, the soft tender impulsiveness had faded, gone. "I'd like to be a member of your family, father," she said, turning toward Stephen, "of yours, too, Mrs. Morrison," turning toward Helen. "Thank you ever and ever so much, but I'm sorry, I couldn't."

"But, Lollie, my dear child—"

"But, Laurel, listen—"

For twenty minutes, for half an hour, both Stephen and Helen labored with Laurel; but to no purpose, to no avail. "I'm sorry. I couldn't," was her unvaried reply.

Finally Stephen exclaimed, "But, Laurel, my dear child, this isn't a matter we are consulting you on. It is a matter that has already been arranged. We are simply telling you about it."

"That makes no difference. I'm sorry. I couldn't," she persisted.

"Why, of course you can, my dear. You don't understand. You are not of age to make your own decisions yet, Laurel."

"Oh, yes, I am, father."

"But you're not. Not on a matter of this sort. Your mother and I have decided this for you."

"Does mother know of it?"

"Certainly, and approves. She is sending your trunks to-morrow."

Two little bright spots appeared in the center of Laurel's cheeks.

"The trunks will have to be sent back then," she announced. "How silly to have tried to force me like that!"

"We didn't think it would be forcing. We believed it would be a plan that would make you very happy. It was your mother's idea, to say nothing about it beforehand, to avoid, I believe, good-byes."

Laurel replied calmly, "I came down here for four days and I am going home in four days, father."

"This is home now," he told her.

"Oh, no, it isn't," she flashed back, "and it never will be home either, as long as my mother is alive." Laurel stood up. "Of course you can lock me up if you want to," she went on, "but I shan't stay any other way. Please understand that."

The bright spots on her cheeks had not disappeared. There were unfamiliar lines and shadows, too, about her chin and jaw. Helen and Stephen stared at her. They had never felt the steel in Laurel before.

"But, Laurel—"

"Oh, don't let's argue about it, father. It won't do the least bit of good."

"Why, this is absurd, impossible. I cannot allow—"

"Just a minute, Stephen," Helen interrupted. There were bright spots in the center of Stephen's cheeks, too. "Laurel, dear," she said, reaching for Laurel's hand, drawing her down on the sofa again. "Listen. Let me explain. It is your mother's wish. It's all your mother's planning. This—all this"—with a wave of her hand she included the whole house and all it stood for in way of happiness for Laurel—"is her gift to you." (The truth was best, Helen concluded.) "She came and saw me about it last summer. We talked it all over in detail, together."

"When last summer?" Laurel exclaimed.

"Last July."

(Oh, then, it flashed across Laurel, her mother had heard! She hadn't been asleep that night on the train! She hadn't been to Milhampton the next day to see Effie McDavitt. She had been to New York to give her Mrs. Morrison!)

"Well, I shan't take her gift," said Laurel. (Her mother! Her wonderful mother! And they had called her "That woman!" "That awful creature!" "That dame!")

CHAPTER TWENTY-ONE

1

"How foolish of you, mother," four days later Laurel scolded Stella, as they stood side by side in front of the sink in the kitchen of the Boston apartment and washed and dried the three-days' collection of dishes Stella had allowed to accumulate. "How foolish to think you could work up any such scheme as that on *me*. You'd think I didn't have any such thing as a will of my own."

"Oh, I know," sighed Stella. "I suppose we did it the wrong way. I ought to have told you, I guess."

"Telling me wouldn't have made any difference. I wouldn't have listened."

"But I don't see *why*. He's your own father, and you've always been crazy about him, and she—"

"I know, I know," Laurel interrupted. "Oh, look here, mother," impatiently she broke off. "Listen to me. I'm never going to leave you as long as you live. Do get that through your head. Do try; and don't talk about it any more." Then, suddenly gentle, "Why, mother," she caressed, "don't you remember you said to me once, way back, when I was a mite of a child, 'I'll never leave you, and you'll never leave me, will you, Lollie?' I've never forgotten that."

"Oh," groaned Stella, "what a fool I was to have talked that way to a little kid!"

"No," Laurel retorted. "Rather, what a fool you were to have worked and slaved for that little kid for seventeen years, and skimped and saved for her all that time, and given her everything under the sun you thought

"'I'll never leave you, and you'll never leave me, will you, Lollie?'"

would make her happy—oh, that was an awfully foolish way to treat a child you hoped would trot off and leave you the first chance she got.''

"What nonsense," Stella scorned. "Why, I didn't even want you before you were born. I didn't like babies.''

"Yes, so you've told me before," laughed Laurel, "and you don't want me now, do you? Poor thing! But you've *got to have me,* just as before I was born. You've *got to have me.* You see we happen to belong to each other, mother.''

"But you belong to your father, too.''

Laurel puckered up her brow, thoughtfully, mopping the plate which she held half in the water, half out, round and round slowly with her dishcloth.

"Yes," she acknowledged, "I suppose I do belong to father, too, but it's different. I'm fond of father. I love to be with him. We always have wonderful times, but father and I have never been through anything long and hard and disagreeable. We've always had just fun together. Somehow, having fun together doesn't make two people feel as if they belonged the way suffering together does. Besides, father doesn't need me the way you do.''

"Pshaw! I don't need you! I get along all right alone.''

"So did I last summer, those two days when you left me. I got along all right alone, too. Nobody to wash dishes with, nobody to talk with, nor to eat with, nor to sleep with, nor to do anything with. I know what it is like. No, mother, you can't live like that. It isn't decent.''

"Decent! What do you mean?''

"Why, look at the way the apartment looks, for one thing. Not only the kitchen, but all the other rooms, too. I never saw them in such a mess.''

"Well, but I didn't know you were coming. If you'd written—''

"Exactly. Without some human being to clean up for, and have a little pride for, this place would look the way grandpa's used to before he died, in a little while. No, mother. You can never live alone. Come, let's change the subject. What show shall we see to-night?''

Stella threw down her dish-towel and sat down at the kitchen table, her hands dropping limp into her lap. "But I've gone and given your father his divorce now," she lamented. "I didn't want a divorce! It will be all for nothing, if you won't go and live with him for a while."

"Mother, I've told you, and *told* you, I'm glad you've given father the divorce. It was exactly the right thing to do. Father and Mrs. Morrison cared about each other before you and I ever saw either of them. You've fixed something right that was wrong."

"Yes," sneered Stella, "especially *you*. I've fixed you fine and right! Oh," she sighed, her eyes resting mournfully on Laurel's back as she stood before the sink, "it just almost kills me to see you doing work like that, Lollie."

Laurel was wiping out the large tin dishpan, now, with her dishcloth, which she had just wrung out with several vigorous little twists. Afterwards she hung up the dishpan on a hook underneath the sink and spread out the dishcloth to dry on top of it. Then proceeded to clean the soapstone sink. She used a small rubber-edged shovel for the purpose, scooping up small bits of refuse with it, and emptying it now and then into her free hand.

"I like making things bright and clean," she called out above the loud scraping noise she was making with her shovel, "but if you prefer," she went on cheerfully, "we'll have a servant. You've often said, since the divorce, we could afford several servants if we wanted them."

"Oh, but, Lollie, *I* don't know how to run a lot of servants. Besides, what's the use of servants when there's nobody to serve? *I* can't give you a coming-out party. I used to think I could, but I know now I can't. No. It's no use. It's not in me. I've done all I can for you." She lifted her upturned hands, lying idle in her lap, and then let them drop, dead and lifeless. "*She* was going to bring you out in New York society, Lollie," she droned on, "she said she was. You'd be going to dinners, and dances, and balls. You'd be having lovely clothes. You'd be having lovely friends—young ladies in limousines calling mornings for you to go shopping with them; young men in limousines calling evenings for you to go—"

"Mother! Please stop. You've told me all that before."

"I haven't told you *one* thing. I haven't said one word about one *special* thing. Laurel, listen, if you go to New York for a season you'll be almost sure to run across Richard Grosvenor! He knew Mrs. Morrison, and—"

"Oh, don't drag in Richard Grosvenor."

"And if you did—you can't tell. He was crazy about you—"

"Now, mother."

"Well, he was."

"I'm all over Richard Grosvenor, now, mother."

"You're not. No such thing."

"But I am! I am! I never even answered his letters last fall."

"His letters!"

"Yes. He wrote me—twice. Mrs. Morrison forwarded them. I never told you because you were so silly about him."

Stella shoved her chair back from the table with a fierce jerk and stood up.

"I know why you didn't answer his letters. I know mighty well! Of course you couldn't answer his letters! Of course you couldn't, with him in college right across the river, here, likely—no, sure, to look you up in this hole, and find out we didn't know any of his Back Bay friends, not a single one of the young ladies whose dances he's been ushering at! Oh, I've seen his name in the lists in the papers, too. I've got eyes, and I've just suffered for you, Lollie. Of course you couldn't write to him and have him come here, and find out how we live, and what sort of a freak *I* am—"

"Mother!"

"That's all right. *I* know—I'm no fool, Laurel. Oh, Lollie, please— *please*, go to your father just for a little while—just for a year or so, just long enough—"

"No, mother. I'm not going."

Stella sank down in her chair. It was useless, futile to beat herself against this soft child's will once she had set it up. Experience had taught Stella that a big buzzing fly is as ineffective in breaking through a plate-glass barrier.

"Well," gloomily, "what are you going to do with yourself, then? You can't hang around a five-roomed apartment all your life, can you, reading two library books a week, and practicing on a piano two hours a day?" (Laurel had not taken any "Courses" this winter.) "What are you going to do to amuse yourself, I'd like to know?"

"I've got a plan," nodded Laurel, smiling.

"Humph."

"I must have something to do, of course. Busy people are always the happiest. I'm going to be very busy. I'm going to be a stenographer, mother."

"A what?" gasped Stella.

"A stenographer. I've thought it all out."

"A stenographer! A stenographer!" Stella repeated, and a third time, "A stenographer!"

If Laurel had said that she was going to be a German spy, Stella couldn't have been more shocked.

"Yes, mother, dear, a stenographer. Don't you see it's the one thing I *can* be, and live along here with you, and keep up our nice times together evenings, at the theater and the movies? And have Sundays with you, and holidays, and nights? I'm going to start right in, next week—this week, if I can—at the very best business college there is in this city, and work *hard*. It's going to be lots of fun!"

"Oh, no, Laurel," Stella broke out. "Not that! Not *that!* Please. Please." Her voice pleaded, her eyes beseeched, implored. "You wouldn't do that. Say you wouldn't. Not *you*. It would break my heart. Say you wouldn't, dearie. Please—please." She grasped hold of Laurel's hand. "Lollie, for my sake! It would kill me, Lollie!"

Laurel drew her hand away. "Oh, come, mother. Don't be silly. Don't be a goose."

A stenographer! Laurel, her beautiful Laurel, shut up all day long in an office, reeking with tobacco smoke? Laurel the servant of a lot of men, taking dictation, taking orders? Laurel wearing paper cuffs and elastic bands and pencils in her hair; eating lunch out of a box with a lot of other girls, also wearing paper cuffs and elastic bands and pencils in their hair? No. No. It mustn't be. It simply mustn't be. Why, even she herself wouldn't have been a stenographer.

Stella lay wide awake in the bed beside Laurel. It was nearly two o'clock. Laurel had slept like a baby—sweetly, steadily, all night long so far. She hadn't changed her position. Twice Stella had risen and lit the light to see what time it was, had stopped a moment by the side of the bed, and gazed down upon Laurel.

"Like a lovely Sleeping Beauty, she is. Oh, my God, she can't be a stenographer!" It would be like planting an orchid between the cobblestones at the corner of Washington and Winter Streets to stick Laurel in front of a typewriter, inside of one of the big grimy office-buildings downtown. She'd get all dust and dirt and trampled and spoiled in no time. She mustn't be sacrificed like that! Why, New York would go simply crazy about Lollie. It would exclaim over her, oh-and-ah over her, like the people at the Horticultural Shows over some new amazing flower. "Oh, gracious, what can I do? What can I do to save the kid?"

She must do something, and quick—now. Laurel was all ready to show *now*. Next year, the year after—too late. She'd be touched, handled, brown on the edges. There'd be a story about her—a tale. "She was once a stenographer, you know." People would whisper, "Really! You don't say!" And eyebrows would be raised. That must not occur. Whatever it cost, by whatever means, *that must be avoided*.

About three o'clock in the morning Stella crawled out of bed and, wrapping herself up in a blanket, sat down on the window-seat by the open window. She could always think clearer in a vertical position. "If it wasn't for me, Laurel would go. I'm the reason she's tossing aside her opportunity, dumping her happiness overboard, as if it was so much rubbish, and then scrapping herself—her lovely self, all ready to sail (yes, that's what she's like, too—a ship, beautifully made—beautifully fitted out). Oh, gracious, what can I do? She's ruining her life for *me*—for a big old water-logged hulk like *me*. (The Lord knows how I happen to be her mother. Talk about miracles!) Oh, why couldn't I have whiffed out last summer at that hotel when I was so sick? She'd have gone to New York then, just as a matter of course. She'd be there, now, today. She'd be under steam this minute, admired, desired, flags flying, sun shining. 'As long as you're alive.' Those were her words. Oh, why couldn't I whiff out *now?* Say, why couldn't I feel a little dizzy and topple over out of the window, down there on the concrete—it's four stories—and clear the job up quick—right now, and no more talk?

"No, I can't. I'm afraid. I haven't the nerve. I haven't the guts. It might only smash me up. Poison would be better, or gas, or a revolver. Poison—what kind? Gas—how long would it take? A revolver—where were they bought? How did you load them? Oh, it would be horrid—horrid! I wonder if I dare."

Stella got down from the window-seat and went over to the bed. The early light of dawn was in the room now, like gray smoke. She stood looking down at Laurel through the thick intangible haze for a long time—for a minute, for two minutes, for three minutes, perhaps.

"Ought I? Oh, gracious, ought I?" she whispered.

The memory of a certain other early morning, when she had stood thus and gazed down upon the sweetly sleeping, defenseless child, recurred to Stella. Then, also, as now, she had whispered, "Ought I? Oh, gracious, ought I?" It was when the doctors were due to arrive in a few hours to perform an operation upon Lollie—years ago, a slight operation, only tonsils—but they were going to make her limp and lifeless, and cut her with a knife.

"Ought I again cut her with a knife?"

It would hurt her, of course—poor kid—at first. Her face would get all white with horror and dismay. "But she'd be rid of me—free, and after a while she'd forget it. She's young, she'd get over it. Or would it also be a story—a tale, to whisper about behind Laurel's back. 'Her mother committed suicide!' 'You don't mean it!' 'And her father's father, too, so I've heard.' 'Really.' 'Runs in the blood on both sides.'

'How shocking!' " Years ago Stella had read in a magazine somewhere that suicidal tendencies were inherited. She recalled it now. Heavens! What if Laurel should grow up and read that, too? Good Lord, it might make her afraid for herself if it was on both sides! She must be saved that horror. A wave of relief swept over Stella.

"I must think of some other way." She went back to the window-seat again. "Oh, how scared I was! What a snivelling coward I am!"

All the next day she submitted compromise after compromise to Laurel. She would keep a servant if only Laurel would go to New York. She would keep two servants, a companion; two companions, return to an apartment hotel, if only—if only—But Laurel simply shrugged her shoulders.

Again and again that day Stella was forced to face the unwelcome consideration of discovering some method of whiffing out that might not arouse suspicion. Slipping down in front of an automobile, making a mistake about sleeping-powders. It might be done. But, oh, she didn't want to die that way. Not that she was much on religion, but she didn't want to take any such chances with immortality. There must be some other way.

It was sometime during the course of the second night, when she was wearied and exhausted almost to the breaking point, that the "some other way" flashed across Stella's mental field of vision. The first consciousness of it made her feel queer and hollow inside for a moment. It was like having a messenger suddenly run onto the scene with your pardon, just when you were settling yourself in the electric chair.

Tremblingly, anxiously, she groped her way across the hall to her desk in the front room. If only she could find the address. It was on a card. She had never thrown the card away. It must be *somewhere*. Oh, what if Laurel in one of her raids upon the cluttered desk had torn it up, tossed it aside? What if it was ashes now? She had no other clue. If the card was lost, *she* was lost. "Help me find it. Help me find it."

It was about the size of a calling-card, a little larger, very grimy, because she had carried it about in her shopping-bag for a long while. Here! This looked like it! Yes, this was it! No, it wasn't! Yes, it was. Yes! Yes! She had found it. She held it up close to the electric light.

ALFRED MUNN,

172 North Blank Street,

Boston, Mass.

She'd go to bed now. She'd go to sleep. "Thanks, oh, thanks," she said on her knees three minutes later. "Do please help me bring this business out all right."

Stella as well as Laurel was sleeping soundly and sweetly at dawn on the second morning.

CHAPTER TWENTY-TWO

1

Stella set forth in quest of 172 North Blank Street the next afternoon. She might have written, of course. If it had been a matter of less importance she would have written. When Ed had given her this address he had meant that she should write.

"Uncle Sam will find me here," he had told her. "Drop me a line sometime when the offspring's away and you're feeling lonesome."

That was over a year ago, when she had chanced to run across Ed one afternoon in the lobby of a moving-picture theater. She hadn't seen him since. She hadn't heard from him since. He might feel entirely different about her now. A year was an awfully long time. Perhaps he wouldn't want to marry her now. Perhaps he'd never really wanted to marry her. He had always laughed when he had suggested it, and she had always laughed back, when she had refused his crazy offers. For years it had been sort of a huge joke on both sides. She guessed Ed would be surprised to be taken seriously all of a sudden. She did hope he hadn't married anybody else. Not that she could imagine such a thing. Ed wasn't a bit the marrying kind, but just hoping so hard made her think of all sorts of catastrophes. Perhaps he'd moved away from Boston entirely. Perhaps he was dead, or perhaps—what if she wasn't attractive to him any more? She was a whole year older, and a whole year after you're forty—well!

He'd find her alimony attractive, anyway, she guessed. Ed hadn't been very successful in his various business ventures. But say—look here, there wouldn't be any alimony, would there, if she married again?

Hadn't there been some such clause? She had never given it much thought because she had been so dead sure she never was going to marry again. Gracious, she hadn't thought of that. Well, never mind, she could contribute *something* in the way of funds. She had a savings-bank account amounting to over a thousand dollars. That wasn't to be sneezed at. Last time she had seen Ed, it looked to her as if *he* hadn't a bank-account amounting to anything.

"I'm sort of out of luck this year," he'd told her apologetically. (The lining of his overcoat had been frayed and ragged round the cuffs. He had caught her looking at it.) "But I can still give you a good time, little girl, just the same. See?" He had opened his overcoat. She had caught a glimpse of a bottle shining. He had patted it tenderly. "More where this comes from, too," he had winked, "but say, it's awful expensive stuff now. Awful! Dearer'n a woman! Prohibition has played the devil and all with my capital, Stella." No. Ed might not scorn her little nest-egg.

She became more and more convinced he might not as she approached the vicinity of the address on the card. She had never been down this way before. Why, it was slums—regular slums! North Blank Street was a narrow, roughly-cobbled sort of alley. There was a row of low brick houses on each side, dilapidated and out of repair. There was a dark damp look to the alley and a dark damp smell, too, that reminded Stella of underground cellar stairs. Unlike most of the other doorways in North Blank Street, 172 still had all three of its digits clinging to the battered brown paint. Stella, standing on the narrow sidewalk, reached up over the two front steps and knocked loudly just below the number. She knocked three times, then receiving no answer, turned the loose knob and walked in.

"Anybody here?" she called up the rickety stairway.

"What yer want?" A young woman of about twenty, with a mop of black bushy hair, cut short, stuck her head out of a door at the rear of the hall.

Stella told her.

"What do you want of *him?*" the young woman demanded eyeing Stella with interest.

"I want to see him on business."

"Ma," called the woman in a powerful voice. "Here's a lady wants to see Munn on business."

"Ma" came to have a look at Stella, too. Both mother and daughter stared at Stella with hard suspicious eyes. It didn't make Stella flush. She didn't blame them. It did look funny.

"He ain't here any more," crisply "Ma" told Stella.

"Oh, ain't he?" groaned Stella.

"No, he ain't. This is a respectable place. This ain't no dope-den."

"Do you know where he has gone?"

"Nope."

"I do, Ma. He's over at Liz Halloran's. She was tellin' me 'bout him."

Eagerly Stella turned toward the younger woman. "Say, take me there. Take me there *now*. I *got* to see him."

But she didn't see him. Not that day. Liz Halloran, a thin haggard old woman with no front teeth had told Stella, standing in her miserable black hole of a doorway (like the opening into the cavity of a decayed tooth, it was), that he wa'n't fit to be seen to-day. "He's just layin' there like dead to-day."

"How often does he get this way?" Stella inquired.

"Oh, off and on, I don't know! I don't keep track. Couldn't get no hooch. That's what done it."

"When do you think I could see him?"

"Oh, he'll be rousin' up to-morrow or the day after. He'll be real bright for a spell, too."

"I'll come day after to-morrow," said Stella.

2

An hour later, as Stella sat gazing out of the window of an electric car that was bearing her back to the apartment and Laurel, she kept saying to herself, grimly, doggedly, "I can stand it. I wasn't brought up in a pink-and-white nursery, thank God! I shan't mind it after a

"He's just laying there like dead today."

while. I'm tough as tripe. Anyhow, it's better than jumping off the Harvard Bridge.''

3

Ten days later, nonchalantly to Laurel, Stella remarked one morning, ''I shan't be here, most likely, when you get back this afternoon, Laurel.'' Laurel was attending business college daily now. ''I've got an invitation for luncheon and the matinee.''

''An invitation? From whom, mother?''

Stella smiled. ''I haven't got so many admirers. I guess you can guess.''

The color flooded to Laurel's cheeks. ''Mother, not Mr. Munn! You haven't accepted an invitation from Mr. Munn!''

''I'd like to know why I haven't!''

''Knowing how I feel about him—how I dislike him.''

''Gracious, Lollie! Honestly, it's funny! You act as if *you* were the mother, and I the child.''

''Mother, you haven't been seeing that creature again, have you?''

''That creature! How you talk! Why, Laurel, Ed's a real nice man.''

''I don't want to discuss him, mother. I don't want to hear you stand up for him. I don't see why you're bringing him up again. I thought we'd decided we'd drop him long ago.''

''You mean *you* decided it. I never did. Mercy, I've got to have a little independence. With you away so much every day, Laurel, and nothing for me to do, I'd be a very foolish woman indeed, to allow a notion of yours to cheat me out of a little harmless entertainment.''

Thus did Stella proceed. She mustn't marry Ed immediately, out of a clear sky, on top of the discussion with Laurel following her return from New York. Laurel might smell a rat. There must be no blundering this time. Ed must be slipped onto the field of action naturally, inadvertently. Funny how things worked around. That which Ed had been years ago between herself and her husband, through carelessness and indifference, *now, to-day,* through diligence and effort, she must make him become again, between herself and her child—an issue, a sore point, a bone of contention. Not until then would the time be ripe to marry Ed. Steadily, unswervingly, Stella set herself to her task.

It was easier than she had supposed. Laurel's hostility to Ed was so white-hot that even a reference to him kindled a controversy. Therefore Stella referred to him frequently in a light and inconsequential vein, laughing at Laurel's opposition. Not only did she refer to Ed, but she saw him; she made engagements with him; she kept engagements with him; she stayed out with him until after one o'clock on one occasion; failed to appear for supper, or to telephone, on another. One afternoon, defiantly, she established Ed in an armchair in the living-room of the apartment, and arranged that Laurel, due home from downtown, should find him when she came in. She repeated this a week later. Oh, it was too bad. She hated to watch the slow torture her procedure was to the child. But it couldn't be avoided. Somehow she must make her marriage to Ed seem logical.

Laurel's light laughter faded, disappeared; the soft light in her eyes hardened like a disillusioned lover's. Night after night she lay, on the extreme edge of the bed, beside her mother, silent and unrelenting, and drifted into an unrefreshing sleep. She grew years older.

One afternoon in early June, after a particularly difficult morning of argument with her mother about Alfred Munn (afterwards Stella had called good-bye to Lollie out of the front window, but she wouldn't answer), she returned to the apartment to find it empty. There was a note fastened to the handle of the oven-door on the gas-stove in the kitchen. Laurel discovered it when she went out to get some supper.

> DEAR LOLLIE [the note said]
>
> I guess you won't be much surprised. I guess you've sort of seen the way the wind was blowing. Ed has wanted me to marry him for years, and as I hadn't any good reason not to now, I'll be Mrs. Alfred Munn when you read this. I would of told you all about it, but I knew how you felt about poor Ed, and it would only of meant more fuss.
>
> Ed's got a grand job down in South America, and he's crazy

*to have me go down there with him. You know I never had much
of a chance to travel, and it seems a big chance for me. So I'm
jumping at it. We may be gone a year or two. I'll send you an
address when we get one.*

*I've had this up my sleeve quite a long while, marrying Ed, I
mean. You can't explain everything to a child. That was why I
hoped you'd stay with your father. But when you didn't, of course
I had to keep my promise to Ed just the same. It wouldn't of been
fair if I didn't, and he wouldn't listen to anything else. He's been
waiting for me all the time you've been growing up, and I won't
say I haven't been waiting, too. I've tried my best to make you
see Ed the way I do, these last weeks, but you just won't, so I've
given up trying, and gone ahead and done what I think is right.*

*Ed and I will be back and close up the apartment, sometime
before we sail. I guess we all three can fit in somehow. I expect
you to be nice to him though, now he's your sort of father.*

*When you're out, leave the key under the mat, same as usual.
Ed and I may be back anytime.*

*Love from
Your MOTHER*

*P.S. It was too bad you wouldn't turn round this morning and
wave good-bye.*

4

Stephen and Helen, returning late from town the next evening to their
summer home on Long Island (they had just moved down), were surprised upon entering the hall to hear a sound in the living-room—a
chair suddenly shoved back, soft swift foot-steps. They stepped to the
door of the room.

It was Laurel! She still wore her hat. Her suitcase still stood by the
chair where she had been sitting.

"Why, Laurel! Why, my dear!" exclaimed Stephen, exclaimed
Helen, both hastening toward her.

They met her in the middle of the room. They kissed her—both of them. She returned neither caress.

"What is it, Laurel?"

She was very white. Her eyes had a startled, frightened expression. "I've come back," she said quietly. "I'll stay now, if you want me—if you'll take me." She made no gesture, her expression did not change. There was fixed calmness about her as hard as adamant.

"What has happened, Laurel?"

"I've been put out. I've no other place to go but here. If you don't want me—if—"

"You know we want you!" exclaimed Helen. "Dear child! Come. Sit down. You're tired. You've had a long journey. Why, you haven't even taken off your hat."

Laurel remarked, not moving, making no sign of response, "Mother has married," and after a pause, "Mother has married." It was like the wailing of a tolling bell.

Stephen said, "Oh!"

Helen said, "I shall take off your hat myself." And quickly, deftly, she removed the small toque and laid it aside on a table, Laurel standing listless and indifferent beneath her administrating hands. "There! That's better. Why, you must have been waiting a long time," lightly she went on. "You ought to have telephoned when you reached New York."

"She's married Alfred Munn, father," said Laurel to Stephen, and after a pause again, "She's married Alfred Munn," as if the tolling bell had changed its note.

Helen touched Laurel gently on her shoulder. "Come upstairs to your room now," she said. "We'll talk about it in the morning. I'm going to give you some food and put you to bed now."

"Father, you knew him. You couldn't stand him either. I understand now. I see. Of course you couldn't live with her. I couldn't live with her myself."

"Don't take it so hard, Lollie," said Stephen.

"Don't call me Lollie!"

"Don't suffer so, dear."

"I'm not suffering. I'm not suffering at all."

"Will you bring up Laurel's suitcase, Stephen?" asked Helen. "Come, Laurel." She slipped a steadying arm through Laurel's. "You must go to bed now."

5

They mounted together to the lavender-tinted room, which Helen had told Stella last summer would be Laurel's. ("She'll be sleeping in that, I suppose," Stella had remarked, from the threshold of the room, as she had gazed upon the bed, fresh and crisp with muslin valance and canopy. "I'll be thinking of her in that," and she had wiped her eyes.) Helen recalled the scene, the voice, the tears, as now she set about preparing with her own hands the waiting bed for that absent woman's child.

Behind her Laurel was standing, here, as downstairs, impassive and indifferent, just where Helen had left her when she withdrew her arm that had guided her hither.

"Come. We'll undress now."

"Mother has married a man I hate." Laurel took up the interrupted motif again. "She's married a man she knew I hated. She has chosen him instead of me. She has married Ed Munn. He's awful. He's horrible. An animal is clean beside him. And she likes him. My mother! She's fond of him. She's been waiting for years to marry him."

"Oh, no, Laurel."

"Yes, she has. I know. Read that. Read that."

She drew her mother's letter from the front of her dress, and passed it to Helen.

"Do you want me to?"

Laurel nodded.

Helen sat down on the foot of the bed and opened the folded sheets. The letter had been written by Stella in pencil, carelessly, in haste apparently. It was read by Helen slowly, painstakingly, as if it had been written in blood. She read it twice. Afterwards she looked up at Laurel.

Laurel gave a little shrug. "You see."

230

"Yes, I think I see," said Helen slowly.

"I thought it was for me she gave father the divorce, so I could come and be with you. And it made me glad. It made me proud. But I was mistaken. It was for *him*. It was to marry him, that creature. He's her kind, down underneath. She is his kind. She chose him. Father's right. The others are right. I'm the one who's been wrong about her all this time. Oh, Mrs. Morrison, she's killed my respect for her, and she knew she would—we have been quarreling about that man for weeks—she knew she would! But she didn't care. She didn't care." Thus pitilessly Laurel sunk her sharp young teeth into the hand that hurt.

Helen murmured, "Greater love hath no woman than this."

Laurel didn't hear her. "I'm very unhappy, Mrs. Morrison," she stated dully.

Helen replied, "You are very tired. You need sleep. Does it fasten behind?"

Very tenderly, as if she were handling a precious body from which life had departed, Helen unfastened Laurel's dress. She slipped it off her shoulders. It fell to the floor. Bare-armed, bare-shouldered, a shiver ran through Laurel—like a breeze rippling a docile sail. Helen put both arms about her shelteringly.

"Oh, Mrs. Morrison! Mrs. Morrison!" Laurel cried out at the touch, and suddenly the storm broke, the long withheld flood burst, the boat tossed, the sail strained and pulled. But Helen's hand was firm and steady on the tiller. She held Laurel close.

"That's right. Cry. You'll feel better. Cry. Cry."

Later in the morning, she would show Laurel the rainbow.

6

When Helen went downstairs half an hour later she found Stephen in the big room waiting for her. He had been smoking ever since she left him—the ash-tray bore witness to that—and walking up and down the room. The two Sheraton armchairs had been carelessly shoved out of their usual places to clear a straight path from the fireplace to the window. As Helen entered the room she replaced one of the chairs, apparently unaware of Stephen's agitation.

"Well?" said Stephen at sight of her.

Helen looked up at him and smiled.

"She's asleep," she said, and started to replace the other chair.

"Poor child. Poor child!" Stephen broke out in a tone that was almost a groan. "It's torture to me to think my own child should have to bear the burden of my mistake like this."

Immediately Helen crossed the room to Stephen. He was standing by the fireplace staring down upon the unlighted logs.

"Why, Stephen," she said gently, reassuringly, "she'll be better in the morning. It's hard to see her suffer, I know, but it's mostly from shock. In a day or two she'll see clearer."

"See clearer!" Stephen exclaimed bitterly. "Why, Helen, don't you know who the man is whom Stella has married?" he inquired.

"Yes, I know."

"Well!" he shrugged. "Don't you see it justifies our suspicions? For Laurel's sake I hoped they might never be justified. I didn't want the evidence which Morley Smith brought to my attention several years ago forced before me for consideration again. For Laurel's sake I've hoped there was that spark of controlling decency in her mother that wouldn't accept intimate relations with a man like Munn, even though she could endure his society. That hope has gone. This act of hers has destroyed it."

Helen gazed at Stephen and shook her head slowly, wonderingly. "You, too?" she murmured.

He didn't hear her.

"To think," he went on, still bitterly, still despairingly—"to think she chose, of her free will, existence with a man like Munn after Laurel had given up everything to be with her! To think she was willing to allow her child's wonderful love for her, her child's wonderful loyalty to her, to become shame and scorn! To think of it!"

"Yes, to think of it!" repeated Helen, softly, starry-eyed.

"What do you mean?" demanded Stephen, looking at her sharply. Why did she speak like that?

"Everybody saw Stella 'through a glass, darkly,' even her own child."

Helen replied slowly, distinctly, looking at Stephen. "Laurel is here. She is here to stay. Who has accomplished it?"

He didn't answer her—just looked at her a moment, then shook his head, and gazed down again into the dead logs in the fireplace.

Helen placed her hand very lightly on one of his folded arms.

"She has always been judged just by appearances," she said in a low earnest tone, "valued just by impressions. Some people go through life with nobody seeing the good in them because of the blurred, unbeautiful reflection they give back. 'Now we see through a glass, darkly.' I think it means in a mirror indistinctly—a dim, dull, imperfect mirror. It seems as if everybody saw Stella 'through a glass, darkly,' Stephen, even her own child to-night."

She withdrew her hand. Stephen replied, still staring into the lifeless fireplace, "I lived with her. I knew her."

"Oh, but, Stephen—"

"My dear, my dear," he interrupted tenderly, fondly. How strange that Helen should be the one to try to show him the good in Stella! "You see with the eyes of an angel."

"No, I don't," said Helen prosaically. "Simply with the eyes of a mother, Stephen."

CHAPTER TWENTY-THREE

1

The proof that Helen's rainbow was real—no illusion, no mirage—
came in the form of a shadow the following fall. It is dark by five
o'clock in the afternoon in New York in November. Returning one late
afternoon with Laurel from a tea, where with a dozen other girls of her
own age she had been assisting (nominally assisting, but really, like
the others, simply submitting herself to the demands of a crowd of
young men blocking the entrance to the room cleared for dancing),
Helen observed, as she left the car and crossed the sidewalk to her own
door a shadow, a stationary shadow cast upon the sidewalk.

There was an alley ran down to a rear entrance at the spot where the
shadow fell. There was a light a few feet down the alley. The light was
dim. But in spite of the unrecognizable shape of the blurred outline of
the shadow, it had startled Helen into a sudden suspicion.

Once inside the house she had mounted to an upper room, where
there was no light, where she would attract no attention, and raising
the drawn shade in a bay-window, gazed down into the alley, just back
of the spot where the shadow had lain.

There was no one there now.

Quickly she turned and raised the shade of the window opposite.
This window looked toward the rear of the house and commanded a
view of the narrow, illy-lighted tunnel, along which towered the high,
spiked walls of several scores of rear entrances. Proceeding along this
tunnel, closely skirting the high spiked walls, Helen could make out

the outline of a woman —a short stocky woman. Twice she stopped and looked back at Helen's roof.

Helen's first impulse was to raise the window—to call. She hesitated. It might not be she. The alley lights were dim and far away. And if it proved to be, was it wise to establish communication with her when she was taking such pains to avoid it? No. Laurel's mother knew best. The minute she became even a recognized shadow in her child's life she ran the risk of defeating the object of her sacrifice.

Laurel believed her mother was somewhere in South America and submitted without protest to the futility of locating her, submitted, too, without protest to the futility of breaking her determined silence. If she even suspected that her mother was near by in hiding somewhere, watching, looking on in the old eager anxious way, she would not be content till she had found her; and if she found her, and if it proved, indeed, that it was as Helen had persuaded her to hope, that her mother had married Alfred Munn for *her* sake, as likely as not—no, more likely than not—Laurel would insist upon returning to her mother under whatever circumstances. She was capable of it.

Laurel was almost her old self now. She smiled again, laughed again, shone and glowed again over old delights and joys, over new delights and joys. Occasionally the troubled, hurt look would steal across her features. And at such times Helen knew that Laurel was doubting again, suffering again, longing to be brought face to face with actual proof of her mother's high motive. But it was better that the doubts should remain than that her mother's act of self-abnegation should be robbed of its fruit. Helen pulled down the window-shade and went downstairs.

It was not until she was in her own room with her door closed, with the window draperies drawn close, seated before her dressing-table brushing her shining hair, that she thought about the alimony. Stephen had felt just as she had when she first broached the subject to him, that of course Laurel's mother must live as she was accustomed to live whatever had been the terms of the divorce. So far, however, Stephen had failed to establish communication of any sort with Stella. She had left her Boston apartment as a bird a nest, and the route she had taken was as trackless, as scentless as the bird's through the air.

She had left no trace of any kind, anywhere—not even with her lawyer, not even with her bank from which she had withdrawn her account. Since her marriage to Alfred Munn not a single check of Stephen's had been cashed by her. Not a single check had even been received by her. They were returned to Stephen unopened, with the recurring announcement "Not known" in the corner of the envelope. Helen looked into eyes that were troubled as she gazed into the mirror before her. "It might have been she! She might need money! Should I have called, after all?" Usually Helen could depend upon her first instinct in regard to such matters. Her first instinct had said, "No." By the time Helen's hair was rolled again in its soft knot at the back of her head, her eyes had lost their troubled look. Of what importance was money to a woman who was willing to pay for her child's happiness with the child's love if it menaced that happiness? And communication, even secret communication, *would* menace it. It was far safer that she, Helen herself, should remain in doubt as to Stella's hiding-place. It was necessary to be so very honest with Laurel. Helen, too, must not know but that Stella was beyond call in some far country. She mustn't allow herself even to look for the shadow again. She mustn't tell any one about it. Oh, Stella should not be defeated, if Helen could help it.

2

But others were not as protective of the shadow. That same evening, a few hundred miles away, in a dainty and exquisite drawing-room in Milhampton, Massachusetts, four women in dainty and exquisite gowns stood before an open fire, stirring black coffee with tiny gold spoons in tiny porcelain cups. Their motions were as dainty and exquisite as the room, as their gowns. So, too, were their voices and their accents.

They chatted lightly, inconsequently, touching now one subject, now another, like humming-birds passing from one flower to another, whiling the time away in as amusing a manner as possible till the men should join them for bridge.

"Oh, yes," sighed Phyllis, "one sees the name of Laurel Dallas in the New York society columns frequently now. The new Mrs. Dallas is doing her best for the child. I call it awfully decent."

"Oh, it shouldn't be difficult," said Myrtle, "with her social position."

"And the child is really very pretty," Mrs. Kay Bird contributed. "That helps. There isn't a suggestion of her mother in her."

"How fortunate! What has become of that dreadful woman, anyhow?" asked Rosamond.

"Oh! Haven't you heard, my dear?" Mrs. Kay Bird raised slim bare shoulders in surprise. "Myrtle, haven't you told Rosamond you saw the poor thing in New York last time you were down?"

"I haven't seen Rosamond. I returned only night before last."

"Oh, well, tell her. Do. Prepare yourself for a choice bit, Rosamond."

Rosamond placed her empty coffee-cup on the mantel and curled up cozily in a corner of the cushioned divan.

"Tell me first, please, about the divorce. You know I was in Europe all last year. I didn't get a bit of the gossip, and there was no account of it in the papers sent me."

"There was no account of it in any of the papers," Mrs. Kay Bird informed her. "Stephen Dallas obtained his divorce without even a flutter of a struggle, which does not surprise any of us who know the facts. We agree with the former Mrs. Dallas, it would have been very unwise for her to contest her husband's charges."

"Oh, did he make charges?"

"That's the usual proceeding, my dear."

"And what were they?"

"Well, he lives in New York. You know the New York laws, I suppose."

Shrugs. Soft laughter.

"And the child," Phyllis added, "was put immediately into the custody of her father."

"Oh, dear! You never can tell what a woman is at the core, can you?" deplored Rosamond. "Why, when we first knew Stella Dallas she didn't seem really *bad*, though she always was awfully ordinary, of course. Even after that time you saw her at Belcher's Beach, Myrtle, I couldn't believe she'd really fallen as low as that. I thought you must be mistaken."

"Tell Rosamond about New York, Myrtle," said Mrs. Kay Bird. Myrtle placed her coffee-cup on the mantel, too, and extending a slender hand to a silver box near by, selected a cigarette.

"I saw Stella Dallas in New York, Rosamond," she announced impressively. "I saw her down near Washington Square. I was down that way seeing a friend of mine who has the most fascinating studio in an old stable. I saw Stella Dallas with the Munn man again! They seemed to be on quite familiar terms."

"Did you, really?"

"It was not a pretty sight, I assure you. The Munn man was intoxicated, I think. Anyway, she had to help him walk. I won't say *she* was intoxicated, too, because I don't *know* that she was, but she didn't look *right*. And she has coarsened—oh, terribly, girls! A woman of that sort always does. And has lost her self-respect as to appearances, as is also usual, I believe. Her clothes were really shabby and *his* were in actual rags. City's dregs—that's all I could think of as I looked at them—city's dregs."

"How unpleasant," shuddered Rosamond.

"Disgusting, was my word," said Phyllis.

"Revolting, was mine," laughed Mrs. Kay Bird. Myrtle extended a languid arm. "Please pass me the matches, Phyllis. Thank you, dear. She's a depraved woman, girls," she announced. "Always was, and always will be. Oh, here come the men." She flipped her match into the open fire. "Let's cut for partners."

3

Miss Laurel Dallas was to be formally presented to New York Society at a tea given at the home of her parents, Mr. and Mrs. Stephen Dallas, on the afternoon of November the twenty-first, from four until seven-thirty o'clock. Several luncheons in her honor were scheduled for the week following the tea; also several dinners. The names of Miss Dallas's various hostesses were mentioned. So was the fact that Brightswood, her parents' summer home at Green Hills, Long Island, was to be opened over the Thanksgiving holiday, and filled with a house-party, including a number of this season's débutantes. One of the most anticipated affairs of the season was the ball to be given for Miss Dallas in early January. So the papers said; so the various society columns repeated and repeated again. "Miss Dallas is one of the most popular débutantes of the season, etc., etc." ("oh, she'll like that," thought Helen to herself), "whose picture is printed below" ("she'll cut that out," she smiled).

Helen avoided newspaper notoriety usually. Stephen wondered at her willingness to allow Laurel's name to appear frequently in print, and in conspicuous print.

He wondered at another sudden oddity of Helen's. The servants wondered at it, too. In fact it was one of the servants who brought it to his attention. Twice, lately, upon arriving home in the late afternoon, he had noticed that the shades in the house were not all drawn. He had been able to look into Helen's room on the second floor, and see Laurel seated under the light, at the piano, playing. He spoke to the parlor-maid.

"I know, sir. It hardly seems safe, sir. But it's Mrs. Dallas's orders, sir."

Later to Stephen Helen explained, "But it looks so pretty from the street. Why shut in all our loveliness? I'll run the risk of burglars."

Even on the afternoon of Laurel's tea, Helen ordered the shades raised. She went even further. With her own hands she pulled back the lace curtains in the bay-window where she and Laurel were going to stand to receive their guests.

"It looks out only on the alley," she shrugged.

4

It rained on the morning of Laurel's tea. It rained in torrents.

"Gracious, don't it pour!" exclaimed Stella for the dozenth time to the woman next to her, and for the dozenth time to herself, " 'Twon't make any difference, though. They've all got limousines." Then out loud again, "Gracious, don't it pour!"

Every few minutes she looked up from the machine which she had been feeding with coarse white cambric all the morning, and gazed anxiously out of the streaked window beside her toward the building opposite, against the dark background of which she could see the rain sweeping.

About noon she exclaimed, "Say, it looks lighter! Say, don't it look lighter to you?" Then, "It is letting up. It looks to me as though it was letting up a little." And finally, "Gosh, it's going to clear off!" And it did!

At five o'clock that afternoon, when Stella, with a hundred or so other women, emerged from the big black building through the little opening at the bottom (like the opening cut at the bottom of a big black hogshead; every little while a thin dark stream of humanity would pour out of the building; it housed over a hundred small factories), the air was clear and crisp and cold. Stella stepped out of the little stream, once on the sidewalk, stood still, and gazed straight up. Yes! It was all right! The stars were shining like mad, up there, at the top of the canyon, beyond the dizzy precipices.

CHAPTER TWENTY-FOUR

1

This was Stella's fifth week in the shirt-waist factory. She must be getting used to it, she guessed. She didn't feel a bit tired to-night. If it wasn't so late, she wouldn't have minded walking the whole way. Laurel would be all dressed now. People would be just beginning to arrive. Gracious, she must hustle. But she'd simply got to go over to the room a jiffy first. It wouldn't take long. She had locked the door on Ed, but she always got feeling nervous after a whole day's absence during the times he was bad.

Stella was pretty sure that this landlady guessed what was the matter with Ed, but she could never feel certain how many of the roomers were "on." There are roomers who find it helps to pass away the time to make a fuss over a thing in the house like Ed. Stella didn't want to have to move again. This landlady had been awfully decent about the rent since she had got a job. Gracious, but it hadn't taken that thousand dollars long to fade away. It cost something to keep yourself and a sick man—who has to have a "particular kind of medicine"—going these days, though you didn't buy yourself a single rag, nor spend a cent on theaters, or the movies, or desserts.

Everything was all right at the room, thank heaven! Stella stopped only long enough to light the candle placed upon a chair by the door, hold it aloft a moment, and gaze down upon the double bed. Ed was still there, still harmless, breathing heavily, inert and unconscious.

There wasn't much furniture in the room besides the bed—a commode, a table, and three chairs. One of the chairs was an old Morris chair. It was worth all the rest of the furniture put together to Stella. It was Stella's bed. The back of it was let down so that it extended on the same level as the seat. There was a blanket folded over one arm, and Laurel's old worn-out, outgrown coon coat over the other. There was Ed's cheap suitcase and a pillow piled up on one of the remaining chairs, and this was shoved up close to the end of the makeshift bed to lengthen it. Surprising how well you can sleep on an old Morris chair if you work hard daytimes, or even on the floor if you get cramped. It's all a matter of getting used to it.

The candle spit and sputtered as if it objected to the scene it lighted. Stella didn't blame it. It wasn't especially beautiful. Stella would be busy in the room till midnight "redding it up," when she got back. She did like a neat room to sleep in. It looked like somebody's back yard just at present, with all Ed's clothes and a few of her own hanging up to dry on a cord she'd stretched back and forth from wall to wall. Ed's unwashed breakfast dishes were on the floor beside the bed. He'd roused enough to take the nourishment she'd left for him apparently.

She blew the candle out, put it back upon the chair, closed the door and locked it, descended four flights of bare stairway, and went out again beneath the stars.

2

Stella could have spoken to Laurel if the window had been open. She was as near to her as that! She could see her as clearly as if she had been inside. How lucky the curtains had been forgotten again. How lucky this particular window had been selected in which to stand to meet the guests! Gracious, but the flowers were lovely. Stella had never seen so many in one room in her life. They must smell like a funeral. Those flowers had been sent to Laurel by her friends and admirers. She certainly had a few! The papers hadn't exaggerated any, Stella guessed. Laurel, standing in the midst of her garden, was like a great big flower herself.

Stella had never seen her look more beautiful. Her dress was white, chiffon, she thought, made over something silvery, that made her shine as if there was dew all over her. No dress Stella had ever provided for Laurel could *touch* this. One of those artists, whose address only the few and fortunate possess, had made this fairy gown for Laurel, Stella guessed. My, how she became it! Gosh! She looked like a regular queen to-night!

She carried a sheaf of white orchids on her left arm. Through the chiffon ribbon that tied the flowers Stella caught a glimpse of something that looked like diamonds sparkling on Laurel's wrist! A moment later, as Laurel turned a little, she caught a glimpse of what was clasped about her throat. Pearls! A string of pearls! "Oh, Lollie! Oh, dear, *dear* Lollie!" She had come into her own! She was being crowned in her rightful kingdom at last!

Stella left the window for a moment and stole to the front corner of the house. Yes. There was an awning running from the front door to the street; there was a man in livery at the curbing, shouting numbers; there was a long row of automobiles on both sides of the street, reaching far away in both directions. All for Lollie!

Stella glanced up. Every window was faintly aglow. Through one of them that must have been open she could hear music, dance music—piano, violins, saxophone, and drum. All for Lollie! She went back again to her window in the alley.

Everything was as it ought to be. Even Lollie's mother was as *she* ought to be—also wearing a gown made by an artist, also wearing pearls, also beautiful, also queenly. My! Mrs. Morrison was made for the part. As the guests approached her, Stella observed that there was that look of high approval and homage in their eyes that *should* be in the eyes of everybody who shook hands with Laurel's mother. Stella observed, too, that when the guests shook hands with Laurel—with the little queen herself—there was more than high approval in their eyes. There was sudden and spontaneous pleasure, and afterwards murmured words of praise.

For more than an hour Stella stood in the shadow of an electric pole, and feasted and feasted. A policeman finally discovered her and told her to move along.

"All right," she replied cheerfully, "I will. I'm ready now. I've seen enough." For the instant before she had seen straight into Laurel's heart for a fleeting ten seconds!

Laurel didn't know it. Laurel had no idea that her mother's eyes were in the depth of the mirror she had gazed into, at her own reflection. It had happened like this. Stella had seen it all. She had observed the first faint flush of color creep down the back of Laurel's neck as a young man had rushed up to her, and eagerly taken her hand in his, in greeting. Apparently the young man had asked Laurel to dance with him. As yet she hadn't left her post in the bay-window. She hesitated, glanced around the room—the guests were beginning to thin out—then accepted the invitation.

Still flushed, her neck was still pink beneath her pearls, she looked about her for a place to lay her flowers, spied the window-sill, took three steps toward Stella, and laid her flowers down, almost as if in Stella's lap; paused, raised her eyes. The window was just in front of her. The clear plate-glass with the light behind it was a perfect mirror. Laurel gave herself a long look. Six feet away Stella caught that look, hugged it to her close. She had never seen anything so dazzling, so luminous, in all her life before! It wasn't meant for her. It wasn't meant for any one on earth. It was like catching a bit of shooting star—of shooting heaven.

The young man to whom Laurel gave her hand a moment later—the young god who had made Laurel look at herself like that—was none other than Richard Grosvenor. Stella would have known him anywhere.

"That's all right, then, too," she murmured.

3

"Didn't I tell you to get along there?"

"Yes, sir. I'm going. I was only seeing how pretty the young lady was."

THE END